1985

WELFARE
BUREAUCRACIES

Their design and change in response to social problems

David Billis

 Heinemann

Heineman Educational Books Ltd
22 Bedford Square, London WC1B 3HH
LONDON   EDINBURGH   MELBOURNE   AUCKLAND
HONG KONG   SINAGPORE   KUALA LUMPUR   NEW DELHI
IBADAN   NAIROBI   JOHANNESBURG
EXETER (NH)   KINGSTON   PORT OF SPAIN

British Library Cataloguing in Publication Data

Billis, David
  Welfare bureaucracies.
  1. Public welfare administration
  I. Title
  361'.0068   HV40

  ISBN 0-435-82058-3
  ISBN 0-435-82059-1 Pbk

To Jacquie, Neeve and Tal

Typeset by Inforum Ltd, Portsmouth
Printed in Great Britain by Biddles Ltd, Guildford, Surrey

Contents

Acknowledgements   *iv*
Introduction   1

PART I   THE CONTEXT   7

1   Social Policy and a Philosophy of Organizations   9
2   The Generation of Usable Theory   24
3   The Bureaucratic Middle-Ground and Social
    Administration   43

**PART II   USABLE THEORY FOR THE DESIGN
            AND CHANGE OF WELFARE
            BUREAUCRACIES**   59

4   The Categorization of Welfare: the Case of Social
    Services Departments (SSDs)   63
5   The Bureaucratic Grassroots   81
6   The Higher Reaches of Bureaucracy   96
7   Alternative Bureaucratic Responses to Social
    Problems   108
8   Authority, Delegation and Control: Towards an
    Alternative Approach   132
9   Individual Initiative Meets Bureaucratic Structure   154

**PART III   THE GENERATION AND
             UTILIZATION OF USABLE THEORY**   167

10 The Generation of Usable Theory: a Historical
    Note   169
11 Day Care: the Case of the (Almost) Disappearing
    Category   177
12 Levels of Decision-Making and 'Entry into
    Residential Care'   189
13 The Intermediate Treatment Officer   199
14 Differential Administrative Capacity: the Kibbutz
    Experience   208

PART IV   CONCLUSIONS   222

15 Recollections and Implications   223
    Bibliography   238
    Index   249

Acknowledgements

In this book I have attempted to draw together research projects which now stretch back over a period of 16 years. Inevitably, I have accumulated substantial debts to numerous individuals and groups.

Most of the material has been developed and tested in collaboration with many hundreds of staff from the governmental and voluntary sectors who have joined in the research projects and workshops. To all these I owe a general and profound debt. Whilst I have worked with many Social Services Departments and voluntary agencies, I recall with particular fondness the help afforded by Harry Whalley and his staff in Brent. We worked together for 12 years, and I hope it was to our mutual benefit.

A number of other people have also commented on aspects of several of the earlier notes and papers which went towards the completed study. Amongst these are the many experienced students who have taken the MA in Public and Social Administration at Brunel University. Part II of this book now serves as the basis for a course of lectures for those specializing in the personal social service option.

As a member of a research institute, my colleagues, past and present, have naturally played an important role. In particular I acknowledge the assistance given by Ralph Rowbottom with whom I have collaborated for many years. Together we developed the theory of levels of work which underpins several of the chapters in Part II. I also received helpful comments on an earlier draft from Helen Bolderson. More recently, Margaret Harris, who has joined me in the work with voluntary agencies, gave generously of her time in providing detailed comments on the final draft.

I doubt that I can adequately do justice to the deep and longstanding debt owed to Elliott Jaques, the Director of the Brunel Institute of Organisation and Social Studies. For many years he has provided support and guidance, and has given both general and detailed comments at various stages of this study.

For most of this peiod the research was funded by the Department of Health and Social Security, without whose sponsorship this book would not have been possible. I would also like to pay tribute to David Gerard, one of the first people to recognize that organization and management are important aspects of voluntary sector studies, and who has assisted me generously over the past few years.

Zena Pereira has seen this book through its various drafts with patience and great efficiency. I am constantly amazed by her ability to transform my unintelligible manuscript into superb type.

Introduction

The studies on which this book is based were mostly completed after I joined Brunel University's Institute of Organisation and Social Studies (BIOSS) in 1970, following 14 post-graduation years working in a youth organization, farming, the army, accountancy, politics, and doctoral studies. In some of these settings I had been a member of the rank and file; in others I had been given considerable 'administrative' duties. For a large part of this time I was a member of a co-operative settlement which was part of a larger federation with a highly developed sense of the role of 'theory' in social life. What I found striking – and the reason for this biographical aside – was the void that existed in many settings between the grand statements of general intent (ideologies, theories, and the like) and life at the institutional grassroots.

In my personal and research experience with organizations over the past 25 years it has seemed that organizational 'theories' have borne little relevance to real life; whereas real life has been content to pursue activities which have been based on vague and sometimes damaging slogans. Thus, for example, the brilliant but potentially dangerous declaration 'small is beautiful' (Schumacher 1974). Small is certainly different from large, but the claim that it is beautiful can be manifestly absurd. What was, or is, beautiful about the small sweat shop, or the small coal mine, or the heavily exploited piece-workers struggling in the smallness of their own homes? What is beautiful about the petty rivalries and jealousies which can abound in the tiniest of organizations? Small can be awful.

This problem – the gap between theory and practice – has led me to employ the phrase 'usable theory' to describe ideas that can actually be utilized in organizational design and change, and which can perhaps play a part in closing that gap.

However, in the preparation of this book it seemed that merely to *present* theories and claim that they are 'usable' would be unsatisfactory. For, if I claim for them a status beyond rhetoric and description, there is an immediate and prior need to indicate their broader *context*. Just as important, then, would appear to be a third need to demonstrate *where* and *how* these specific ideas have been *generated and utilized*. These three interdependent needs give rise to the main parts of the study. But more of this a little later. I am acutely aware that as yet I have said nothing about 'welfare bureaucracies' which is, after all, my main title.

Welfare bureaucracies: part of social policy's middle ground

At first glance 'welfare' and 'bureaucracy' seem strange bedfellows. The former conjures up images of goodness, happiness and prosperity; whereas the latter (Carlyle's 'continental nuisance') more readily brings to mind the negative attributes of inflexibility, insensitivity, and red tape. And we shall indeed find, in a later chapter, tension between these two concepts which, one way or another, occupy a central place in the study of social policy and administration. However, my intent is not to take up cudgels for or against 'welfare' or 'bureaucracy'. I suspect that too much is expected of both, and I have consequently attempted to eschew polemic in the search for analysis.

Perhaps the 'welfare bureaucracies' of my title are most usefully regarded as part of what might be called 'the middle ground' of social policy and administration. That is to say the territory that lies between political statements of policy and the citizen receiving services. Other authors have referred to those occupying this ground as 'policy mediators', pointing out that:

policy is rarely applied directly to the external world. Characteristically, it is mediated through other institutions or actors.[1] (Young 1981: 35).

Described in this fashion, the middle ground is vast. Its institutions include governmental, voluntary, and private agencies, in addition to self-help, community, neighbourhood and other groups. Within this vast territory I shall focus on an area which is sufficiently substantial and complex to warrant detailed attention in its own right. I refer to those numerous mediating agencies *that employ staff* – the 'bureaucracies' of the title. Whilst, as we have already noted, the words 'bureaucracy and bureaucratization are now usually intended as pejorative terms' (Friedrich 1976: 49), I shall restrict the use of 'bureaucracy' to describe those agencies that have paid staff. Used this way, bureaucracy is both longstanding and pervasive (Pinker 1971: 63).

It appears to be the case that, although not essential, the employment of paid workers is a widespread phenomenon even in what is usually called the 'voluntary' sector (Gerard 1983). Therefore, this study assumes that paid staff will continue to be a major feature of the provision of welfare, and the employment of such staff will continue to be an important policy option, in particular when it is intended to make what might be described as a 'systematic' response to social problems.

Had I been writing about these bureaucratic mediating agencies five or six years ago it might have been difficult to justify a title that went beyond 'social services departments'; for it was there that much of the fundamental research was undertaken. And it is still true that these statutory agencies in England and Wales provide most of my case studies and many of the illustrations. However, during this period I have been able steadily to enlarge that inner core of experience. For example, the typology of organizational responses to social problems has been utilized in several workshops with managers of European social welfare agencies. Furthermore, for the past five years I have been directing a programme of research and training in the voluntary sector. More than one hundred agencies have participated in workshops and seminars, and these have been followed by eight collaborative research projects. In this work much of the material seems to have been found useful. Several housing associations are amongst those who claim to have found the 'four-dimensional' approach to organizations (in Part II) illuminating. The theory of levels of work, developed together with my colleague Ralph Rowbottom, has been utilized in other parts of the statutory sector, in particular the health services. Education and housing departments have also used the concepts. In the same period many students on the Masters Course in Public and Social Administration at Brunel University, most of whom hold responsible positions in various parts of the welfare system, have found the ideas relevant in their practice-based research.

These and other opportunities have steadily enlarged my research experience to the point where the title 'welfare bureaucracies' seems justified. At minimum, the term may be construed as referring to those agencies that employ staff and provide personal and allied social services. More ambitiously, 'welfare bureaucracies' may be stretched to encompass a rather wider range of organizations that would regard themselves as responding to 'social' problems.

To sum up therefore, I hope that the ideas about the bureaucratic middle-ground contained in this study will be of interest to agencies that consider themselves somehow or other in the welfare arena. More importantly, I hope also that the theories will be *usable*; that is to say, *that the book will provide students, policy-makers and practitioners in the field of social policy and administration with ideas for the design and change of welfare bureaucracies.*

Structure of the book and issues
The structure of this study reflects that constant concern about the relationship between theory and practice voiced in the opening section.

In Part I I shall attempt to provide what might be called the 'context' of the usable theory. By context I refer to several of the main topics that are judged both to underpin, and to be influenced by,

the core material that appears in Part II. A constant temptation has
been to chase, like my disobedient Jack Russell terrier, a large number of fascinating scents and trails. I hope that most (I doubt if all) of
the minor contextual trails have been eliminated in earlier drafts. The
major contextual paths that remain might very broadly be regarded as
'philosophical' (chapter 1); 'methodological' (chapter 2); and 'disciplinary' (chapter 3).

The philosophical path will lead us into a consideration of the links
between social 'policy' and 'bureaucratic structures'. Indeed, it is the
problem of making an organized (policy) response to social problems
which may be regarded as the central task of the book. The methodological trail grapples with issues of concern to all policy-orientated
researchers. What sort of approach might close the theory-practice
gap? How might we develop 'better' theory? What do we mean by
'collaborative-research'? Is it 'science'?

The last contextual trail raises questions about the relationship of
studies of the bureaucratic middle-ground and the discipline of social
administration which, despite its title, contains only a few studies that
focus on administration and organization. This lack of enthusiasm, or
what we might call the 'bureauphobic tendency', may perhaps be a
consequence of what has been called a 'lack of morale' of social
administrators who 'have to face, at least in the short run, the prospect
of living in a type of society for which they have very little enthusiasm'
(Pinker 1979a: 42).

Part II addresses the central task. How can we make a systematic
response to social problems? A four-dimensional analysis for the
design and change of welfare bureaucracies is presented. We shall
examine, and question the utility of, several themes such as 'social
distress', 'prevention', 'reception', 'delegation', 'authority', and 'control', which link the bureaucratic middle to its two neighbours, political intent and service delivery to those in need. For example, I
question whether 'preventive' social services work, or current formulations of the boundaries of governmental welfare bureaucracies,
or the level of service offered to clients, stand up to critical enquiry. In
an effort to lessen this confusion, new concepts and models are
introduced, and illustrated by examples drawn from the statutory and
voluntary sectors. These concepts form the basis of the typology of ten
alternative organizational responses to social problems – a central
feature of this part. The concluding chapters question the ability of
the idea of 'delegation' to provide an answer to the chronic and
sensitive question: who 'carries the can' for what in our welfare
bureaucracies?

The book moves on in Part III to consider the approach: how the
usable theory of Part II has been generated, and to demonstrate in

more detail than was necessary for the exposition earlier, how theory has been used in practice to illuminate problems. The case studies of this part are included in order to illustrate the approach and, within the constraints of the overall balance of the book, to expose to public gaze part of the process of theory development. I have not provided a blow-by-blow account of the projects which formed the basis of most of these chapters. On balance it was felt that this would result in an infuriatingly slow journey.

Humanitarian intent and effective results

The period in which this book was researched and written has witnessed dramatic changes in the context within which mediating agencies function. The place of governmental intervention has been severely challenged. Voluntary agencies have become more acceptable as potential deliverers of welfare services. And we may yet see the private sector playing a significant role in the welfare scene.

In the main, I have attempted to avoid taking detailed issue with the major social policy statements of the period. If 'Seebohm' receives greater attention than 'Wolfenden' or 'Barclay', it reflects the historic impact of that document. It also reflects my belief in the intimate relationship between social policy and organizational arrangements. Indeed, it is intriguing to note the way in which the 'grand debate' about the role of the various sectors in the provision of welfare often rests on organizational premises, and even more specifically on judgements about the pros and cons of 'bureaucratic' provision.

To those who have become deeply involved in working with, and researching, the governmental and voluntary sectors, the current stereotypes – of the disadvantages of the former and the virtues of the latter – must seem wildly unrealistic (Billis 1984). Welfare bureaucracies, of whatever size, are complex social arrangements. Simplistic stereotypes do not do justice to the nature of that complexity. They certainly are of doubtful value for the client, the receiver of services, for whom after all, we claim to have set up all these organizations.

I doubt, therefore, whether social administration, as a subject of study or discipline, can avoid coming more adequately to grips with the nature of the organizational response to social problems. For as Miringoff succinctly declares:

it is at the organizational level that humanitarian intent can be translated into effective results and it is there that programs ultimately succeed or fail. (Miringoff 1980).

I hope that this book might make some small contribution to narrowing that gap between humanitarian intent and effective results.

Note

1. At a 'non-institutional' or informal level we must also include those situations where private troubles are responded to in an individual and more fleeting fashion by family, friends and neighbours. Although the very nature of this 'unorganized' sector precludes easy measurement of size or contribution, personal experience is probably adequate to persuade us of its significant role in the overall provision of welfare.

PART I

The Context

The main purpose of this book is to present usable theory for the design and change of welfare bureaucracies. Nevertheless, the researcher in this area must also continually peer and probe into more extensive pastures of a less immediately usable nature. Since these adjacent *contextual* territories are vast, and embrace many academic disciplines, such peering will naturally be selective and limited. Nonetheless, for all its limitations, it is invaluable. Without this continual probing, usable theory can become fossilized into packages of eternal verities.

In chapter 1 we explore several of the broader organizational assumptions of usable theory. After this discussion of a *philosophy* of organization, we proceed in chapter 2 to examine issues which might be described as setting the *methodological* context. Chapter 3 attempts to analyse the way in which usable theory of the bureaucratic middle-ground fit within the *disciplinary* context of social administration.

1 Social Policy and a Philosophy of Organizations

In this opening discussion, I would like to outline what I consider to be a major social policy task, an analysis of which will occupy much of this book. *The task is to make a response to social problems which moves beyond the isolated and ephemeral — that is systematic.*

After outlining this task I shall move on to consider several assumptions which lie beneath that outline. These assumptions, which concern the links between social policy and the philosophy or organizations, are:

- that organizations are set up in order to respond to problems;
- that a systematic response probably entails a hierarchic, bureaucratic, structure;
- that there is a link between setting up our organizations in response to problems, and the words and explanations that we utilize or produce;
- that organizational structure is at least as important as individual behaviour.

Finally, I shall look briefly and selectively at how or why we might have come together to undertake our task in the first place. This might be described as the struggle for an institutional response, and is another area of study in its own right.

The task: beyond the pinching shoe

Let us assume that we are the members or representatives of a group faced with the task of responding to some 'social' problem. We might begin by admitting that 'social' is an adjective open to wide interpretation. Titmuss, in comments preceding the development of three models of social policy, questions the exaggerated use of the word by a motley group of disciplines, professions and groups. He warns that attachment of the adjective to a noun, as in 'social policy', does not automatically invest it 'with a halo of altruism' (1974: 27). There are those who feel more strongly. For example, Hayek who declares that 'social':

has become an adjective which robs of its clear meaning every phrase it qualifies and transforms it into a phrase of unlimited elasticity, the implications of which can always be distorted if they are unacceptable (1967: 238).

Nevertheless, for the sake of this exercise, let us assume that we have not come together in order to establish an industrial enterprise. We are concerned with 'human services'. The task before us is to respond to problems which we, or those whom we represent, have decided are social and are 'real enough to be argued about'.

. . most definitions of social problems have a factual basis. The definitions may be mistaken; they may leave out important elements; they may be open to argument. But they refer to a situation or condition in society that is real enough to be argued about. (Becker 1966: 6)

Let us further assume that our response is to be 'systematic ', that it is not casual or sporadic. The task proposed is neither unusual nor unreal. In one form or another *it is one which lies at the centre of social policy considerations*. Indeed it might be claimed, that the very phrase 'social policy and planning' must imply a systematic response to social problems, a point tellingly made by Ford writing of the period 1815–30:

Unless efforts were to be limited to easing the pinching shoe a bit here and there, if there were to be any 'design' or 'planning', some general notions were needed which show the process as a whole, and review the relations of the separate problems to one another. (1968: 13)

We might be members of a national, regional or local government; we might be the representatives or members of a myriad of groupings prepared to respond in a more than private and isolated fashion to social problems. As such, we are part of the organized middle-ground of social policy. We might wish to tackle the problem of 'alcoholism', or 'the single homeless', or 'the elderly', or 'the mentally handicapped', or 'battered wives' – the list is vast. In coming together to consider a systematic organized response we are not necessarily of course, the only people acting in response to these problems. (For a more precise definition of the systematic response to social problems, see chapter 6). It is highly likely that many, perhaps most, of the issues are being confronted by relatives, friends, and neighbours. These more personal and discrete responses to individual problems are the 'unorganized' middle-ground.

Continuing with our task and making it somewhat more manageable, let us further assume that we would not have gathered together without a fair chance of securing resources. What then can we do?

It may be that we ourselves, as the group responsible for their resolution, have the resources to meet the social probelms. To take one example, a group of young people who have decided to provide support to a local society of parents of mentally-handicapped children by providing (themselves) baby-sitting and other services. We may also be able to recruit other volunteers. Or, we as the organizing group might decide to respond by raising money and resources.

There does, however, appear to be a stage, especially if the issues are many and complex, when it may be necessary to employ *paid* members of staff to deal with our social problems.[2] These staff will be expected to perform certain work. We shall have begun to enter the *bureaucratic* middle-ground. The fact that a decision has been made to employ just one or even several staff does not mean that we have created a 'fully-fledged' bureaucracy, but we have, it is suggested, entered bureaucratic territory where the concepts of staff, employment, and payment have replaced the less formal world of unpaid voluntary contribution of labour.[3]

I do not contend that the organized middle-ground must be highly bureaucratized. There may be only one, or a handful of paid workers, as in the neighbourhood care and Home Start projects (Abrams 1978; Van der Eyken 1982; see also Richardson and Goodman 1983). The degree of *governmental* bureaucratization, for example, is a matter of political choice. Central governments may decide, as in Holland, to leave organized service delivery largely in the hands of private and voluntary agencies and retain for themselves a primarily planning role. Or, they may decide to run the welfare service delivery bureaucracy itself, as in Cyprus. Or, service delivery might be mainly left to the local level of government, as in the UK. Even if they decide to wash their hands of actual service delivery, governments will need some sort of machinery to control, negotiate with or, at the very least, be aware of, what is happening. No modern government, of whatever political regime, has been prepared to abandon all responsibility for social welfare. As Thursz and Vigilante point out in their study of 22 countries:

It is not accidental that all industrialized and emerging countries are committed to the establishment and development of social services . . . the problems of policy, organisation, manpower, general strategies, and specific methodologies are shared by all. (1975:14).[4]

However, whether our response is private, governmental or non-governmental – if large-scale work is required – we may find ourselves, irrespective of political or other stances, willy-nilly in the bureaucratic middle-ground. If we intend to move beyond 'easing the pinching shoe' of our chosen area of intervention it will almost certainly be necessary to set up some form of *structure* consisting of organizational roles, which may be regarded as the basic building blocks of such structures.

This notion of structure has received increased attention as a topic of enquiry and it is undoubtedly used in many different ways. Most usages do however share the implications of *inter-dependence, perma-*

nence, and primacy (see, for example, Bouden 1971 and Piaget, 1971). In fact, these general descriptive attributes of 'structure' are close, if not identical, to those associated with 'social policy', which is also concerned with issues that are regarded as interdependent, ongoing, and of prime significance. Both sets of terms are thus intimately connected, and it is difficult to envisage quite what 'social policy' might mean or contain without its organizational structures. Hospitals, clinics, schools, education departments, numerous voluntary agencies, day centres, hostels, residential homes, SSDs, 'patch' and area teams, housing departments and associations, job centres, the Department of Health and Social Security – these are but a few of the organizational and mainly bureaucratic structures of social policy interventions.

So, in order to fulfil the task set at the beginning of this chapter, it is highly likely that we will need to set up an organizational – possibly bureaucratic – role structure. But before proceeding we need to examine in somewhat more depth several of the 'assumptions' that I have made in outlining this central task. The first, briefly, is the argument for considering organizations as problem-solving.

The problem-solving organization

The dominant view of the essential nature of organizations to be found in most of the literature emphasizes their 'goal-seeking' and 'purposeful' nature. In the main, the literature emphasizes 'aims' rather than problems. The organizational literature is now so vast that it is possible to provide only a few scattered examples.

The general overviews include numerous references to the dominant standpoint. Mouzelis suggests that 'purposiveness and goal specificity seems to be the two crucial criteria differentiating organizations from other types of social units' (1967: 4). More recently, Jacques van Doorn defines organizations as 'social constructs deliberately developed and maintained to seek after and attain specific goals' (1979: 62). Sofer's excellent history and analysis of the organizational literature opens with an equally emphatic declaration that 'organizations are associations of people grouped together around the pursuit of specific goals' (1973: 3).

My contention that organizations might fruitfully be regarded as problem-solving as an alternative to the dominant goal-seeking view relies both on a personal sense of organizational reality and on the Popperian premise that man is essentially a problem-solving organism. In his essay 'Of Clouds and Clocks' he elaborates twelve theses, the first of which is that: 'All *organisms* are constantly, day and night, *engaged in problem-solving*' (1974b:242). This is developed into a schema which I shall utilize in chapter 2. In his autobiography, Popper explains the intricate relationship between theories and problems, and defends the position that '. . . it is better to look upon organisms as problem-solving rather than as end-pursuing' (1976: 178; see also chapter 29 for the relationship with theory).

The notion of 'problem' is central to this approach, and in the search for a working definition I have turned to Berger and Luckman who suggest that:

As long as the routines of everyday life continue without interruption, they are apprehended as unproblematic. (1971: 33).

So, problems may therefore be defined as 'interruptions in the routines of everyday life'. How and why certain interruptions become regarded as suitable for an institutional response is the topic of the final section of this chapter. For the moment, I wish only to suggest that Popper's emphasis on problem-solving rather than 'end-pursuing' is an interesting philosophical approach which might shed new light on the study of organizations. It also has methodological implications which I shall pursue in chapter 2. Indeed, the analysis of *prevention* in chapter 4, whilst it draws heavily on departmental reality, also gains considerable strength from this problem-orientated philosophical position.

Bureaucracy and hierarchy

A second assumption in the opening section was that not only were we establishing an organization in response to problems, we were probably going to enter 'bureaucratic territory'. I chose this broad phrase in order to suggest that although we might need to employ staff, we might not find it necessary to establish a fully-fledged bureaucracy with its hierarchy of roles. There are a large number of small agencies with one, or a handful of staff, all of whom report directly to their governing body, and which do not have an internal managerial hierarchy (see chapter 8). *Neither* is it being argued that *all* organizational structures are in bureaucratic territory. For example, welfare bureaucracies, however small, are not the only or necessary organized response to social problems. Alternative, non-bureaucratic forms of organized response to social problems might be, for example, co-operatives, partnerships, or independent practice.

However, the limiting factor in these and other alternatives appears to be their inability to cope with large-scale issues. Thus Herbst (1981), in the search for 'non-hierarchical' organization, identifies three types.

(1) The *composite autonomous group*, where 'all members are capable of carrying out all or at least most tasks'. This group 'has no specific structure' but can adopt any temporary structure which is judged

by the members to be appropriate at any given time.

(2) The *matrix group*, where each member has a specialist function but each has an overlapping competence with some other group members.

(3) The *network group*, where members 'are normally dispersed individually or in small subjects. . . . The basic characteristic is the maintenance of long-term directive correlations, mutually facilitating the achievement of a jointly recognized aim.'

But as Herbst himself points out, 'the problem at present is that of investigating the relevance and feasibility of the design principles for larger social units'. *Autonomous* groups are limited in size by the requirement that everyone should be capable of doing (more or less) everything. As far as *matrix* groups are concerned, these I suggest are a normal part of any complex bureaucracy and readily comprehended within the context of pluralist authority presented in chapter 8. *Network* groups, it seems from Herbst's account, are 'temporary systems . . . members normally retain their role in more conventional settings' (p.251).

Another leading commentator (Bennis) went rather further when he wrote in 1966:

In the next twenty-five to fifty years we should witness, and participate in, the end of bureaucracy as we know it and the rise of new social systems better suited to twentieth-century demands of industrialisation . . . Adaptive, problem-solving, temporary systems of diverse specialists, linked together by coordinating and task-evaluating specialists in an organic flux . . . will gradually replace bureaucracy . . . I call this an organic-adaptive structure. (1972: 211–26).

Well, time is running out for Bennis. Bureaucracy as an organizational form still remains – as at the time of his forecast – 'the dominant form of human organization employed throughout the industrial world' (p.213).

The difficulty of avoiding the construction of authority-backed hierarchical roles is evident from the early history of the kibbutz movement, which provided an invaluable insight into the way in which such roles emerged from the need to solve problems on a more than *ad hoc* basis. And this took place *even* in a situation where the very thought of 'manager' or 'management' had been bitterly opposed, and an anathema to the members of the *kvutza* (which was the early name for the kibbutz). Furthermore, there did not exist any system of financial reward for work, so that role differentiation and its link with authority could be seen as unambiguously related to the need to resolve an increasing number of complex problems. In the words of one of the founders of the first kvutza, Degania Alef:

During the three years, 1911–1913, we refrained from electing a management or committee because we were apprehensive of a managerial regime. It was better for all of us to meet every evening in the dining-room, crowded around the large table, and discuss the work arrangements for the next day or for that week; to talk about the affairs of the kvutza, its fate and future. If nobody was vested with official authority, they had moral authority, which we all needed. . . . But as the membership increased, we recognized (saw) the vital need of introducing reforms in the democratic procedure in the assignment of work, including community (public) work. (Viteles 1967:40).

So in 1914, one of the basic kibbutz institutions was created. It was decided 'to elect one person who would have the decisive say about our work' (Viteles 1967:40). In other words, the move was made from Herbst's 'composite autonomous group' to a hierarchy.

The resolution of problems on any substantial scale, then, appears to entail a close acquaintanceship with the ubiquitous hierarchy. To ignore its existence, or to bewail its necessity, is, I suggest, a rather 'precious' and unhelpful social policy strategy – a case I shall argue more forceably in later chapters.

Problems, explanations and organizations

In setting up our (probably bureaucratic) organization in response to social problems we are also making assumptions about the resolution of those problems. We are utilizing and formulating explanations. The relationship between problems, explanations, and organization might be illustrated as in Figure 1.1.

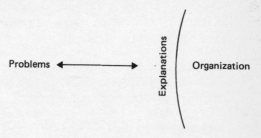

Figure 1.1

Explanations may vary in the range or extent of the cluster of problems encompassed. The major philosophies and religions represent ambitious attempts at explanation, ranging across centuries and subsuming the secondary national organizations whose problem-solving explanations are regarded as less comprehensive than the particular philosophy or religion advocated. The appeal of these major theories lies in their construction of worlds with seemingly stable boundaries.

Explanations may be explicit, perhaps expressed in the law of the land or a body of writing; or unwritten customs and norms. They may differ in their degree of impermanence. Some weaker specimens may shake and collapse at the first onslaught from a new urgent problem. They can also be 'absurd' – although absurdity by itself will not necessarily provide sufficient impetus for change either in the explanation or in the dependent social organization.

For example, in attempting to answer the question, who is a British Citizen?, two explanations have been offered as reasons behind the drive for the reform of the British Nationality Laws.

Such reform is necessary partly because it is absurd that there should be no satisfactory definition of who is a British Citizen, and also because the lack of such definition has complicated the problem of immigration control. (Leader, *The Times*, 31 July 1980).

According to this view the definition of who is, and who is not, to be considered a citizen needs reform – because it is 'absurd' – *and* because it has 'complicated the problem' of immigration control. But of the two reasons advanced by *The Times* for the move for change in the citizenship laws, the absurdity of current definitions would not by itself give rise to enough pressure. Absurd definitions and explanations can be tolerated as long as they provide a tolerable basis for organizational action. As *The Times* leader continues: 'The White Paper also proposed changes . . . because of the Government's fear of creating a pool of British citizenship abroad who would have the right to come and live in this country.'

So, it seems that changes in organization will require both a 'less absurd' explanation *and* a crisis in the real world of problems.

Labour members of Parliament could tolerate decades of competing explanations. But it required the threat of drastic changes in their power, in addition to the publication of several explanations (a lecture by Roy Jenkins and books by David Owen and Shirley Williams), to change 'social democracy' from an explanation to an organization. Or, as Wolin puts it when analysing the political theories of Plato, Machiavelli, Hobbes, Locke and Marx:

The intimate relation between crisis and theory is the result not only of the theorist's belief that the world is deeply flawed but of his strategic sense that crisis, and its usual accompaniments of institutional collapse and the breakdown of authority, affords an opportunity for a theory to reorder the world. (1968:148).

On the same issue, but nearer at hand, Donnison (1974) suggests that 'Innovation starts from the collision between theory and reality within an irreverent mind.'

Explanations require adjustment, abandonment, or development, in the light of their problem-solving ability. But organizations, built even in a distant past on these explanations, must attempt to retain at least partial stability. Without the ability systematically to resolve problems over time, the organization disintegrates and may be replaced by isolated, private problem-solving outside the organization. *Maintenance mechanisms* to preserve stability are therefore essential for organizations. A variety of such mechanisms have been developed; from the legal system with its imprisonment and other sanctions, to the bureaucratic system with its career appraisals and dismissals; to other subtler maintenance mechanisms, represented by such words as 'commitment', 'motivation', 'responsibility' – all designed to prescribe the individual response to the organization.

Those who have become voluntarily encompassed by the persuasive explanations and powerful maintenance mechanisms of some religious groups and parties, face daunting sanctions. The strength of the sanctions are often difficult for outsiders to comprehend. Excommunication is rivalled by expulsion from the Communist Party for intensity and power of impact.[5]. And voluntary departure from church or party appears to be marginally less traumatic in its effect. As far as voluntary self-exclusion is concerned, there are numerous accounts of the difficulties of 're-entry' and the regaining of a critical approach. A matter-of-fact and moving account is supplied by the late A.H. Hanson. He describes the six years which were needed before he 'even attempted a reappraisal' after leaving the Communist Party where he had been devoted to a 'series of dogmas . . . which put my intelligence in a straitjacket' (Hanson 1969).

Whilst explanations maintain their full strength only as long as they are considered to be adequate in their problem-solving ability, they nevertheless retain a residual potential strength. Once having been successful, how can we be sure that new problems will not emerge and the discredited explanation again be useful? ' . . . new and pressing problems may rekindle interest in solutions previously rejected or placed in cold storage' (Parker in Hall *et al.* 1975: 490). Explanations without problems may be barren, but the hope of a new problem-based fertility drug is ever present.

In the end, the explanation constructors may have the last laugh. Whilst they can formulate nothing truly permanent, we must continually glance over our shoulders and peer into improbable quarters, and give due cognizance to any explanation that holds out the hope of better problem-solving ability. For the only thing at all certain is that better explanations can be constructed, and, who knows, may have already been constructed.

In this section we have considered the assumption that there is a possible relationship between the problems we wish to resolve, the explanations for their resolution and the organizational response.

According to the view presented here, organizational change is dependent on the existence of both a crisis in the real world of problems and the availability of a suitable explanation. We concluded with a few comments on the necessity and power of maintenance mechanisms, and the persistent potential strength of explanations.

The importance of structure

My fourth assumption concerned the importance of something called organizational *structure*. The implications of interdependence, permanence and primacy were seen as central to both structure and social policy. I did not, however, discuss why the assumption was made that structural features are at least as important as behavioural factors in the study of organizations.

Our attempt to understand the relationship between structure and behaviour can be aided by Popper's philosophical thesis of the Three Worlds:

the world consists of at least three ontologically distinct sub-worlds; . . . the first is the physical world, . . . the second is the mental world, . . . the third is the world of intelligibles, or of *ideas in the objective sense*; it is the world of possible objects of thought: the world of theories in themselves, and their logical relations; of arguments in themselves; and of problem situations in themselves. (1974b: 154).

According to this 'pluralistic' philosophy, World One and World Three cannot interact. It is the second (subjective) World which acts as the mediator and interacts with each of the other Worlds.

It can be seen that 'organizations' can be regarded as occupying all three Worlds. Of particular interest for the present discussion will be their occupation of Worlds Two and Three. The study of organizations cannot avoid taking into account both the separate and interacting nature of Worlds Two and Three. The (World Two) individual *in* the organization acts within the context of the same organization seen as (World Three) theoretical construct. Thus, for example, the theory of a 'social services department' existed before the first director of social services was appointed. Once established, the (World Two) subjective experiences of staff interact with the 'department' – a World Three product of the human mind (Popper 1976:chapter 38). In the World Three sense, the 'individual' becomes a 'role' and the organization can then be defined in terms of sets of roles. 'Organizations' can therefore be regarded both as subjective occupants of World Two and as major inhabitants of Popper's World Three.

The study of organizations in their World Three sense gives rise to two main categories of difficulties.[6] *The first category* consists of problems concerned with the *methods* used by workers or the way they *behave*. It consists of problems concerned with the acts of production; with the behavioural disposition of workers; and with the relationship between the worker and the product. *The second category* consists of problems of the structure itself; of problems of the objective role structure (the World Three organization).

My claim is that problems of role structure (category 2) are at least as 'fundamental' as problems of behaviour (category 1), *since both categories of problems are dependent upon the fact that such objective structures exist*. The existence of the structures themselves may be said to create *both* categories of problems.[7] But Popper has argued that the subjective (World Two) acts as a mediator between the physical world and the world of theories. Therefore, in order to understand organizations and their impact, it will be necessary also to possess theories of the subjective world of individual work – of capacity – and this too will be discussed.[8] The proposition outlined here may be used to underpin the earlier discussions.

In arguing for the importance of structural considerations I am not dismissing theories of behaviour in the study of organization. The main purpose, at least as far as subjective problems are concerned, has been to focus attention on *the pivotal areas for design and change*. This emphasis on structure, rather than behaviour, excludes therefore any consideration of what is often called 'informal organization' (Blau and Scott 1963:chapter 1). We have, in other words, concentrated on the 'enacted' rather than the 'crescive' (Sumner 1907). And as John Child points out, the use of terms 'formal' and 'informal' has generally been:

misleading because it fails to distinguish between the degree of formality in a structure and the separate dimension of whether it is officially sanctioned or not . . . . Unofficial practices . . . often point to a deficiency in the official structure. But organizational designers do not implement unofficial structures. (1977:9).

So, if we link the discussion in this and previous sections, it might be argued that organizations in their Third World sense can be regarded as based on *explanations* or theories for the resolution of problems. The power of explanations for good and evil arises from their utilization in the construction of (World Three) organizations which attempt (World Two) to translate these explanations into action.[9]

The struggle for an organizational response

We have suggested that organizations are constructed in order to formulate and translate explanations into action. Both explanations and their organizations were regarded as (temporary) attempts to control instability. According to this presentation, organizations might be understood and analysed in relation to their explanations for problem resolution. New problems and new explanations will threaten existing institutional arrangements.

In defining organizations in relationship to problems, I am not claiming that all problems, and in particular those generally regarded as 'social', inevitably lead to the construction or realignment of organizations. How and why then do interruptions in the routines of everyday life become 'clusters' of social problems? Why are new institutions set up, or existing ones adjusted, in response to some rather than other explanations? This intervening ground – between interruptions and clusters of social problems on the one hand, and institutions or constructed organizations on the other – is a major field of study attracting attention from a number of disciplines whose foci are the forces and pressures underlying the process. (For an important essay in this field see van Meter and van Hom 1975.) Since my own focus is the construction of organizations, all I can do is to draw attention to the main battle lines, note a few major studies, and indicate my own preferences.

In the field of social policy an important book of case studies takes as its main starting point the question: 'Why do certain issues gain precedence over others? Why do particular kinds of changes occur in social policies?' (Hall *et al.*, 1975:23).[10]. The authors develop a set of 'emerging propositions' in order to understand what determines the priority that an issue attains in the competition for government attention. They identify three criteria against which the claims of an issue are assessed: its 'legitimacy' (whether or not it is a legitimate sphere of government); 'feasibility' (a complex notion which includes the general state of knowledge, understanding and technology, the views of actors in the policy-making process, resource availability, commitment, and administrative practicality); and 'support' (the stock or credit of the government). However, the authors are not satisfied with these general influences and continue by indentifying additional factors which more specifically affect the fortunes of an issue. Amongst these factors are the scope and association of a problem, that is to say, how issues are separated or brought together.

Whilst I cannot do justice to their full analysis, it is possible to register in passing several points made by the authors which are relevant to my problem-based model of explanations and organizations. We would expect, as these case studies indeed indicate, that severe problems (issues) and the development of new explanations for problem resolution are an important factor in changing institutional responses. Thus, in their case study of the 1956 Clean Air Act, it is claimed that it was the catastrophic fog of 1952, which was responsible for at least 4000 deaths, which was crucial in the challenge to current explanations. 'A phenomenon which had been regarded as an inevitable feature of the winter months began to be seen as an unnatural and unacceptable hazard. . . . ' (Hall *et al.* 1975:407). But a significant part was also played by the National Smoke Abatement Society which was 'the only body adequately prepared with ideas and information. It was the Society which was able to submit the kind of general evidence and recommendations for feasible action which the Beaver Committee could incorporate into its report.' (p.389).

From our earlier discussion we shall also not be surprised to discover that the availability and attractiveness of remedies 'may advance the priority of certain problems' (p.49), or that 'even when the facts which identify certain problems cannot be disputed their impact would generally be slight unless remedial action is possible' (p.504), and that 'the most influential facts appear to be simple descriptions of unresolved problems' (p.505).

We can sum up their arguments by stating that problem resolution depends on the presence of explanations (legitimacy and aspects of feasibility), and the social institution with the resources and sanctioned authority (aspects of feasibility and support) to act.

In passing, we might note that the authors' prime interest in the political process probably leads them to undervalue the significant role of organizational structures in their historical reconstructions. For example, it could be argued that the statement in the Clean Air case study – that 'one explanation for the delay and resistance to [take action] . . . may be found in the divided ministerial responsibility for air pollution (p.38) – is too important to be subsumed within other general categories and that the 'administrative dimension' ought to have received greater prominence. We have here an example of the difficulties encountered in the categorization of problems that will be discussed in Part II. Was 'pollution' to be seen as a problem of 'housing and local government', or of 'fuel and power', or 'health'? (A problem-dominated rather than a goal-orientated approach might also have resulted in the case study being titled 'Coping with Air Pollution' rather than the 'Struggle for Clean Air'.)

There is a strong link between this work of Hall and her colleagues and the only other substantial work in the British context which attempts to explore social policy changes – that of Donnison and Chapman (1965). [11]. Donnison and Chapman, however, concentrated on the local level of the social services. Many of their conclusions are interesting and relevant for current studies. They point out that although local administrative studies 'lack the radical and dramatic character of a change in national social policies, they frequently provide the experimental groundwork that is later consolidated and codified by legislation, and they determine the manner in which Parliament's intentions are eventually interpreted and applied' (p.231). This earlier study emphasizes time and again the role of agency staff in initiating and developing new services. For example:

. . . our studies suggest that the providers of the service usually take this initiative . . . in an attempt to meet in an appropriate or satisfying way the actual or potential demand they perceive . . . their perceptions are crucial. (pp.237–8).

The development of these services . . . is begun and driven forward by *people within* the group providing the service. (author's emphasis, pp.253–4).

Donnison and Chapman give greater prominence to the role of bureaucrats in the development of service responses than does the later central government focused study. From both these collections of studies we can observe that the struggle for new and changing institutional responses appears complex and untidy.

Even these few examples demonstrate that this is a major political and sociological area. Probably it would be fair to say that the philosophical approach to organizations outlined here does not sit uncomfortably in the company of these collections of studies. Problems, explanations, and organizational responses form one interacting package.

Summary

We began this first of the context setting chapters by outlining the major social policy task of making a systematic response to social problems. In so doing, several assumptions were made which were the subject of discussion in the following sections.

The first assumption, drawing on the work of Popper, was that organizations might usefully be considered as *problem-solving* (an approach which has direct implications for the discussion in chapter 4). The second assumption was that the resolution of problems on any substantial scale seems to result in the need for *hierarchic* organization. Thirdly, we assumed that there is a relationship between *problems*, *explanations*, and the *organizational responses* – organizational change appears to require both a crises and an explanation. This discussion was not restricted to the 'substantive' field of welfare bureaucracies.[12] The fourth assumption was that in studying organisations we must pay due attention to *structure* as the pivotal area for the design and change of welfare bureaucracies.

The final section drew on the work of other authors to look briefly at the reasons for certain problems gaining precedence over others – what might be called the struggle for an *institutional response*. We suggested that these works indicate that the philosophy of organization presented in this chapter may be worth further exploration.

Notes

1. On social policy and 'planning', see Glennerster (1975) and (1981).
2. I am not attempting to analyse in any depth the growth of bureaucracies from voluntary associations. It may be, for example, that the employed staff are taken from the membership. The point here is merely to outline the major choices.
3. For the purpose of this exposition, a fully-fledged bureaucracy will be regarded as 'a hierarchically stratified managerial employment system in which people are employed to work for a wage or salary' (Jaques 1976: 49).
4. For a comparative study of France and America which incidentally makes a similar point see MacDonald (1981:6).
5. Etzioni (1968) presents a threefold classification of 'power' and relates this to the wider sociological debate. His classification is (i) utilitarian; (ii) coercive; and (iii) persuasive. Accordingly, excommunication is seen as an example of persuasive power, a category of power which is 'often perceived as either resting on personal attitudes and interpersonal relations', but in fact 'is structural and organized, allocated and applied, in much the same way as other kinds of power' (p.358).
6. This argument is an adaptation of one used by Popper in *Objective Knowledge* (1974b: 112).
7. Up to this point I have attempted to adapt Popper's propositions to the study of organizations. There are other interesting possibilities that – for Three. The detailed argument can be seen in Popper (1974b: 162–8).
8. There is an obvious difficulty concerning relationships of theories about the subjective World Two, since theories themselves belong to World Three. The detailed argument can be seen in Popper (1974b:162–8). The assumption here is that theories of role structure take precedence over theories of the subjective world.
9. This definition of 'explanation' comes close to one of Kuhn's uses of 'paradigms' which 'gain their status because they are more successful than their competitors in solving a few problems that the group of practitioners have come to recognise as acute' (Kuhn 1970a:23). See also the discussion in Lakatos and Musgrave (1974).
10. Later the authors explain that the use of the word 'issue' is used 'in describing the variety of claims, bids, proposals, demands, suggestions or exhortations that "something must be done" '; see also p.476.
11. Roy Parker was a colleague of Donnison's at the LSE, and commented on the discussion of the draft of Donnison and Chapman's book. In turn, about 20 years later, Donnison served as Chairman of the Advisory Committee for the work of Parker and his colleagues.
12. The discussion may also be seen as a move from 'substantive' (developed for an empirical area) to 'formal' (not related to any one substantive area). See Glaser and Strauss (1973: 32–3).

2 The Generation of Usable Theory

Many of the ideas presented in this book have been generated by a research 'activity' known as *social analysis*.[1] I hesitate, for reasons which will shortly become clear, to use the word 'methodology'.[2] At one level, this activity is part of the broad 'action-research' or organizational-development movement, where the point of impact is the organization. 'Change' is the dominant objective.[3] From another vantage point, social analysis might be seen as a way of generating usable theories, in particular as a way of developing patterns or models that avoid 'prententiousness' and 'quackery' (see final section for a discussion of 'pretentiousness' and 'quackery'). It can be used to convert inexplicit problems of social institutions into tentative theory. I shall suggest that social analysis comprises three components: (i) strategy; (ii) concept utilization and development; and (iii) situational analysis.[4]

In keeping with the other essays in Part I, this chapter discusses an aspect of the context of usable theory. It contains a limited perusal of one way in which such theory may be generated, and its relationship to social science. This is not therefore intended to be a comprehensive methodological essay but context-setting and speculative.[5]

Social analysis – 'bottom-up', 'grounded' and 'middle-ground'

Social analysis has been much concerned with the utilization and development of usable organizational concepts. Traditionally, it has been part of that social science which Shipman pertinently describes as 'bottom-up', rather than 'top-down' which is 'imposed by the researcher on to the respondents' (1981: 132). Top-down research

attempts to control the conditions under which responses have been observed or measured. It meant imposing the stimuli which produced these responses, and the terms in which they were summarised and interpreted. The interest in the respondents has been in their behaviour and its fit into established or anticipated models. (ibid.)

In contrast, bottom-up research accepts that it has to contend with humans who, amongst other things:

are capable of coming to their own conclusions about the meaning of events. The social scientist has therefore to find first the way those studied have ordered their world and then translate this into a scientific theory. The latter has to be organised out of the former. (p. 133).

Shipman desribes the many 'exotic labels' under which bottom-up approaches appear. I do not consider it feasible, or necessarily profitable, to attempt a more precise association with any of the various 'labels' or schools which have 'such wide variations in practice'. 'Bottom-up' will suffice as a useful, if inelegant, context-setting phrase.

Also by way of context-setting, the emphasis in this account on 'usable' theory accords with the view that theory 'must fit the situation being researched, and work when put into use' (Glaser and Strauss 1973:3). The authors' telling phrase, 'grounded-theory', strikes a sympathetic chord in the ears of an action-researcher, although (as with the other sociological schools) it is doubtful whether a detailed comparative analysis would be worthwhile. Thus, the four key interrelated properties of grounded-theory are, I suggest, broadly applicable to the 'conceptual' end-products of social analysis. That is to say that:

the theory must closely fit the substantive area . . . it must be readily *understandable* by laymen concerned with the area . . . it must be sufficiently *general* to be applicable to a multitude of diverse daily situations within the substantive area . . . it must allow the user partial *control* over the structure and process of daily situations . . . (p.237).[6]

However, whilst these four properties serve as useful shorthand markers for purposes of orientation, it is not necessary to accept the same authors' emphatic rejection of other methodological approaches. A 'tentative' attitude (see next section) may be wise. This applies not only to concepts and theories, but also when facing the passionate – sometimes wild – clutches of the methodology wielders. In like fashion, we might also agree that the concepts in this book are 'middle range' – another telling phrase – without feeling embarrassed that the advocates of 'grounded-theory' (a term which seems useful) found it necessary to engage in a fierce polemic with the author of this other helpful term.

Middle-range theory . . . is intermediate to general theories of social systems which are too remote from particular classes of social behaviour, organization and change to account for what is observed and to those detailed orderly descriptions of particulars that are not generalized at all. (Merton 1967: 39)[7]

Rather than take any particular side in those methodological wars and skirmishes, I have preferred to note a few useful orientating markers.

We will pursue in the following section an alternative possibility: that the Popperian schema $P_1 \rightarrow TT \rightarrow EE \rightarrow P_2$ illuminates, and indeed might be considered to underpin, the social analytic approach. In the course of this discussion another important underlying assumption of chapter I – *the tentative nature of explanations or theory* – will be examined.

The development of tentative theory

A basis for understanding the development of theory is provided by Popper's schema:

$$P_1 \longrightarrow TT \longrightarrow EE \longrightarrow P_2$$

Figure 2.1   The growth of theory

In Figure 2.1 it is suggested that P_1 represents the starting problem, and that we then proceed to a tentative solution or Tentative Theory (TT) which might be (partly or wholly) mistaken; in any case it will be subject to Error-Elimination (EE), which may consist of critical discussion or experimental tests; then new problems P_2 – generally unintentional consequences of our action – arise. Figure 2.1 represents the simplified version of the schema – what is described as the 'fundamental evolutionary sequence of events'. The final version has to take into account 'the multiplicity of the tentative solutions and multiplicity of the trials' (Popper 1974b:243).

In his autobiography Popper explains how he 'was always a little worried about this summary' since 'problems are soaked in theory'. [8] There follows a brief but complex argument concerning the problem, 'which comes first, the problem or the theory?' He argues that theoretical development often starts from *practical* problems; that these problems arise 'because something has gone wrong', which in turn means that a previous 'adjustment' has been made – and that 'adjustments' to the environment are a 'preconscious form of developing a theory'. He concludes by stating that:

. . . problems, even practical problems, are always theoretical. Theories, on the other hand, can only be understood as tentative solutions of problems, and in relation to problem solutions.

If this is accepted as a possible schema for the development of theory, we are still left with the need to find criteria for what might be considered to be 'better' theory. Popper suggests 'six types of cases in which we should be inclined to say of a theory t_1 that it is superseded by t_2 . . .

(1) t_2 makes more precise assertions than t_1 . . .
(2) t_2 takes account of and explains more facts than t_1 . . .
(3) t_2 describes, or explains, the facts in more detail than t_1
(4) t_2 has passed tests which t_1 has failed to pass
(5) t_2 has suggested new experimental tests, not considered before t_2 was designed . . .

(6) t_2 has unified or connected various hitherto unrelated problems. (Popper 1974a:232).[9]

But how will theories – and better theories – of organizational structure (our particular concern) be generated? It seems unlikely that we can look to organizations themselves to provide theories about general organizational structures, since the development of such theories implies that someone has been presented with 'the structure of *organizations*' as a problem. It will be the exceptional practitioner who will be able, and has the time, to develop theories of structure that extend beyond the explanations of a single unit. Structures, as the overall frameworks within which work takes place, will need to be the concern of those external to the individual organization and whose 'laboratory' can draw on the experiences of many individual units.

A problem-orientated approach (social analysis) to the generation of such theories of organizational structure is the topic of the following sections.

Social analysis: some definitions
Social analysis has been defined as:

> An activity devoted to (1) gaining scientific understanding of, and thereby (2) facilitating enacted change in (3) social institutions, through (4) collaborative exploration by those actors immediately concerned in their working, and an independent analyst.' (Rowbottom 1977:21).

This 'activity' or 'method' (social analysis) was pioneered by Elliott Jaques in his work with Glacier Metal which began in 1948. Rowbottom recalls that the phrase was explicitly used in the early 1960s by Jaques in the paper 'Social Analysis and the Glacier Project' (Brown and Jaques 1965). In the last decade a number of major projects, in particular health, social services, and education, have utilized this approach to varying degrees.[10]

This definition of social analysis sees as its objective the facilitation of 'enacted change', with the gaining of scientific knowledge a necessary precondition.[11] Collaborative exploration is regarded as the method by which these objectives are obtained. But we must take care before including even this change-dominated perspective as 'action-research', since the term is sometimes used in a very narrow sense in which gaining scientific knowledge does *not* appear as an objective. For example:

> action research can be described as a process whereby, in a given problem area, research is undertaken to specify the dimensions of the problem in its particular context; on the basis of this evidence a possible solution is formulated and is translated into action with a view to solving the problem; research

is then used to evaluate the effectiveness of the action taken. (Town 1978:161).

An alternative view of social analysis is to place it within the Popperian schema for the development of theory. Thus, it can be seen as an 'activity' which can be utilized to convert subjective 'troubles' of World Two into World Three theories (see chapter 1). It can be regarded as consisting of a number of distinct components (strategy, situational analysis and concepts) which require disentanglement.

Before moving on shortly to a discussion of the component parts we might note that, according to this alternative view, insider and outsider, whose paths are usually, in the longer run, quite distinct, join together for a temporary struggle with problems. ('Insider' is used to refer to employed staff of organizations at all levels; 'outsider' refers to the external analysts, researchers, and so on.) The insider is searching for explanations to solve specific issues so that action can be taken. The total problem path of the external researcher is different. If he is working in the field of social policy and administration, the ambition is also to construct better patterns or models which encompass a systematic and comprehensive response to social problems. One strength of social analysis lies in its attempt to bind tentative theory to genuine problems; to close, in other words, the theory-practice divide.

The following presentation is not exhaustive. It provides an outline only to several issues that remain to be explored more fully.

The first component of social analysis – strategy
Strategy is concerned with tackling the problems of genuine *access*; that is to say, of establishing and maintaining the best framework within which insiders and outsiders can collaborate.

Under what conditions will organizations permit outsider access to their problems? A rapid introduction to the topic leads to a number of initial observations about the basic preconditions for genuine access.

(1) Problems have to be painful before external advice is sought. Many interruptions in everyday life in organizations are tolerated as normal, borne with bad humour, but not tackled.

(2) The organization must have the desire, the willingness, to permit access. There must exist a pervading culture of openness; of what Alan Fox calls 'high-trust' relationships, which are characterized by, amongst other things, a readiness to 'communicate feelings freely and honestly' (1974:362).

(5) Genuine access (if organizational change is one of the stated objectives) necessitates that those who have the problems (and invite outside help) can if necessary resolve the problems. They must

have the sanctioned authority to implement, or at least be capable of strongly influencing, possible solutions.

(4) Insiders will expect credibility; that the potential collaborator has demonstrated his effectiveness, and is recognized. Together with credibility will be the expectation that helpers are 'professional', that they adhere to accepted codes of confidentiality.

A short personal example from kibbutz experience will perhaps illustrate the above points. As a kibbutz member for ten years I had no problems of access. I was there, the 'insider', involved in the problem situations. It was the advisers, consultants, researchers, and the like, who had difficulties of access. No doubt the kibbutz as a total community is particularly difficult to penetrate. From the inside it was possible only to be amused by, or in a more generous mood to feel sorry for, the aspirations of distinguished academics arriving to study 'the natives'. The inspectors and advisers sent by outside bodies to find out what was *really* going on fared little better. What sterling performances were laid on for these unwanted guests! Who had the time or inclination to reveal the really painful problems – of which there were many? To help with these we turned to veteran and experienced kibbutz leaders from other settlements. And in this case no wool could be, or would have been, pulled over their eyes. We needed their help, whether it was in economic or social matters. They had demonstrated their ability elsewhere and kept to accepted ethical practices. These veterans were privy to the deepest level of problems. They worked with us in the construction of solutions. Failure to provide them with genuine access would have defeated the very purpose of our invitation.

Genuine access may be contrasted with what can be called pseudo-access. Here 'permission' is granted to the researcher to study a problem of his (the researcher's) own choice. The question can be raised whether collaboration on problems posed by the researcher has the same driving force as collaboration based on pseudo-access. It may well be that problem-driven access and research is less likely to suffer the fate of irrelevance, or to be accused or quackery.[12] Chris Argyris (1958), examining the insider-outsider relationship, points out that:

if the research is not perceived by the subjects as need-fulfilling and meaningful, they may perceive the researcher as a 'tolerable long hair who will leave, so just bear with him for a while longer'. In this role, the researcher tends to receive more surface collaboration, more polite smiles, and is usually overwhelmed by data that, after careful analysis, are found to be primarily on the skin-surface level.

Another form of pseudo-access occurs where researchers are invited to discuss genuine problems, but at some stage the problem, as far as the insider is concerned, is resolved. However, despite its disintegration, either the problem-holder or the outsider is unable or unwilling to terminate the relationship and they proceed to create artificial problem-states and theories. For example, where the 'research' might be regarded as serving undeclared purposes unrelated to the problems under discussion. Research can sometimes be seen as a way of demonstrating executive seriousness of intent, of bypassing decisions, or of securing resources. A good strategy is crucial if such pitfalls are to be avoided.

A number of additional issues repeatedly arise when new work is to be undertaken. Some of the key questions are listed below without attempting to enter into substantial discussion. (Each question could be further subdivided and the implications examined.)

(1) *Payment and research independence*
What are the pros and cons of direct payment by the collaborating agency as against payment by a third party such as central government or research councils? What controls, if any, can funding bodies have over the products of the research?

(2) *Sanctioning*
Is there the need for a group of insiders from the collaborating agency to act as a steering group – the senior management team, a cross-section of staff, or some other group? If a sanctioning group is established, what should its relationships be with the project group? (see below)

(3) *The project group*
Who are the insiders who are most directly involved with the problem to be analysed? On what basis can the project group (those who will collaborate with the outsiders) be established? Can 'representatives' of groups of involved staff participate? Can the group contain different levels of management – and what are the consequences of so doing?

(4) *Confidentiality*
How can confidentiality be maintained between researchers and individual members of staff, and between the project group and other insiders? Under what conditions can research material be released to non-participants? What rules must be established for publication?

(5) *Collaboration*
How can we be sure that groups and individuals are genuinely collaborating rather than being coerced?

(6) *Method of work and feedback*
Is the analysis to be undertaken only with individuals? Will there be project group meetings? Is it intended to feed back reports to each individual, or to the group as a whole?

(7) *The research effort*

What are the advantages and disadvantages of one defined analyst working with the project group, as distinct from two or more researchers? How are the boundaries of research competence defined? How long will the research take? Is there some 'natural' length of time?

The list merely indicates several of the questions that need to be considered when establishing the contract for organizational access. The main characteristic of strategy is that it is concerned with issues and theories about the events that take place *before* the analysis of P_1.

The second component of social analysis – conceptual utilization
The phrase 'concept utilization and development' is used to describe the wide variety of theories, at varying degrees of specificity and testing, variously described as patterns, models, and concepts.

The main thrust of social analytical writing has – with the exception of the book of that name – been towards the development of concepts for the analysis of organizations. The fundamental tenet is the search for precision in the forging of scientific tools for the better understanding and design of social institutions; not precision for its own sake, but *clarity and precision that stems from the problems under consideration*. It is not necessary to elaborate further since this book has attempted to follow in that broad tradition. All that might be done is to emphasize that tools or models must pay their way. They must be subjected to the critical judgement both of involved outsiders from the field of social policy and administration, and to the broad body of practitioners with similar problems. There are models that impress academics who never have to deal with the problems that the models are intended to resolve. There are also models that impress welfare bureaucrats (I use the term non-pejoratively), but fail to pass 'the seven-year test', i.e. they failed to stand the test of time (Jaques 1976:viii).

Social analysts, in presenting their best efforts at model construction, are often in a mixed state of optimism and uncertainty. They can be confident that, if they have analysed the situation well, insiders may find the models helpful and begin implementation. Their uncertainty and anxiety arises from the – sometimes difficult to accept – tentativeness of these models.

The third component of social analysis – situational analysis
A third component of social analysis might be called situational analysis. It refers to theories of the *process* of problem-solving; to the steps taken in moving from P_1 to P_2 in the Popperian schema. It is, unlike

strategic analysis, concerned *only* with the problems of the insider, with the issues of the relationship between concepts and problems, that is to say:

(1) *When* should questions and concepts be introduced?
(2) *What* questions and concepts should be introduced?
(3) *How* should they be introduced?

The task of a theory of situational analysis would be to ensure that the problem is examined in depth and *explicated* in full. Explication will be defined as the process whereby problems are brought out into the open and eventually *presented in a form sufficiently precise to permit mutual rational control by critical discussion.*[13] It is part of the process through which tentative theories can be established by the conversion of background knowledge, myths, and values, into 'sufficiently precise' statements.

Explication threatens frameworks. It represents a risk and a potential challenge to existing structures; consequently it can be opposed or side-stepped. For example, Nevil Johnson (in an editorial commentary on a book by Sir Leslie Scarman) argues that:

. . . it is extremely doubtful whether we could in Britain provide for the effective protection of rights without making explicit certain conditions which would bind institutions, conditions which we have so far preferred not to define. (1975: 229).

Writing and the written document have a cardinal place in making problems explicit; in particular in complex organizations where verbal statements alone are insufficient. (We might note that written statements are often obsolete or irrelevant. So, the document can be seen only as a precondition and not as an automatic guarantee of open and explicit statements – choice will have to be made between the alternatives.)

Many organizational problems are not made explicit. It can be a time-consuming business and there may not exist the mechanism and/or the desire to embark on the process. Numerous problems are left untended, to smoulder and wreak havoc amidst the personal and collective health of social groups. Argyris (1980:205) refers to this as 'the inability of organizations to discuss risky and threatening issues, especially if these issues question underlying organizational assumptions and policies'. In cases where there exists the desire to explicate problems the external analyst has a useful role to play. Where problems are thought to be present but the desire is absent, there is little scope for collaborative 'insider-outsider' analysis.

Can situational analysis be distinguished from the personal ability of the analyst? Certainly disentanglement is not easy. Yet it is worth considering the possibility of developing an independent body of thought which might address itself to the sorts of issues raised by Rowbottom in his discussion of 'teasing-out requisite formulations' (1977: chapter 5). He provides both a brief general outline of the process and an actual case of 'teasing-out' in practice. He suggests that:

It is only by carefully examining people's typical behaviour, or by testing with them what their behaviour would be likely to be in certain critical situations, that the existing assumptions on which they work can be brought out into the daylight for review. (pp. 59–60).

Social analysts appear to employ a form of 'critical method' which involves confronting insiders with searching questions and examples. By so doing, the internal logic of his (the insider's) existing assumptions are placed under the severest testing that the ability of the analyst can master. (Here, we have the justification for distinguishing personal ability from the process itself.) The process is part of the 'mutual rational control by critical discussion' of the insider's theories, where the range and depth of testing reflects the analyst's personal ability, confidence and experience.

One of the most frequent criticisms of action-research is the failure of its practitioners as a whole, to explain or 'decode' how they actually proceed, 'even when one is able to observe them in action' (Clark 1972:66). Probably the absence of explanation is not unconnected with the complexities and difficulties of differentiating personal ability from a more generalized code of what actually happens.

Thus the talk of 'theories' of situational analysis is as yet optimistic. They barely exist. Perhaps in concentrating on concept building, and to a lesser degree on strategy, we are overlooking an important area for theory development. But reluctance to build a body of theory which discusses the process of problem-solving possibly also reflects the social analyst's prime concern with structure. In the face of the ever-pressing necessity to produce explicit statements about the insider's problems, the researcher is naturally reluctant to spend time on introspection, on self-examination of why a particular concept was introduced to a specific audience, at a specific time, and in a particular manner.

Values, problems and tentative theory

In the previous section I suggested, almost in passing, that the process of explication *converts values* into statements which can be controlled by 'critical discussion'. This relationship between values and explicit statements deserves additional comment. The 'place' of values has in fact presented many social scientists with severe problems. Thus, the frequent demand – 'to declare thy values' – would appear to be an irreproachable act of undeniable virtue from which the social scientist emerges an honest man, fit once again to look students and colleagues straight in the eye. Yet, is the declaration of personal values by itself valuable? What purpose does it serve? For example, is Peter Leonard's (1975) declaration that he is a marxist, relevant or not to the argument of his paper? Are we being informed that the author's self-confessed marxist perspective makes his argument more or less persuasive? Even on a purely practical level the information is insufficient since 'marxist' literature itself is so diverse that on any important issue we would need to raise a hundred questions. What sort of marxist, in what sort of situation?

Values are simply too significant to be treated in an offhand fashion. They may be likened to blood. No one would doubt its importance; but we prefer not to see it. We are neither bloodless nor valueless. Indeed we become worried – about blood and values – when, usually resulting from a problem, they surface to the light of day, and action becomes necessary. So, whilst values are the life-blood of everyday life, they become truly significant when there are interruptions in the routines of everyday life. Problems sharpen values wonderfully. As Etzioni declares: 'a commitment to a value that is not activating, which has no consequence in action, is really no commitment at all. [It is a person's action] . . . which reveals to others, and often to himself, where he stands and for what he stands' (1968:12)[14].

The demand for the declaration of values, in particular in the field of social policy and administration, might perhaps be more usefully regarded as manifestations of doubts about theories and their links with problems. This can be illustrated by Rex's example of studies in marital stability and industrial harmony. He criticizes many of the studies of marital stability for not making clear their value standpoints, since they 'are based upon the assumption that marriage as a lifelong union is desirable'. He points out that other authors have studied broken marriages from the point of view of the adjustment to separation of the parties. This is by way of repeating 'Myrdal's warning that such value-orientated studies are only truly scientific if the value standpoints from which they begin are made explicit' (1970:186; see also Myrdal 1972). Rex continues that 'there is no reason why anybody should not study the best ways of achieving marital stability, or industrial harmony, so long as he makes clear what he is doing'. But surely, the appeal to 'make clear what we are doing' might more usefully be regarded as a demand to explicate the link between problems and tentative theory. The best safeguard against the intrusion of concealed values lies in the explication of the full range of problems and the development of tentative theories which can be tested and acted upon. This is the safeguard against the 'unwitting influence of these values which shape the sociologist's selection of problems, his preference for certain hypotheses or conceptual schemes, his neglect of others' (Gouldner 1970:604–18). As Bottomore observes, Gouldner's solution to the problem (the 'expression of one's values as open and honest as it can be this side of the psycho-analytic couch') can lead somewhere else. It achieves the opposite of the position advocated by Wright-Mills: 'instead of turning personal troubles into public issues, he turns public issues into personal troubles' (Bottomore 1975:52).

A historical footnote

If social analysis represents the family, then *strategy*, *concept*, and *situation*, are its most prominent members. They have an independent and a familial existence which can be discerned in the early history of the family.

Jaques explains how social analysis is modelled on 'clinical research in psychological medicine' and how it

requires an individual or individuals in an organization, with a problem concerning the working of the organization, who seek the help of an analyst in determining the nature of the problem. (Brown and Jaques 1965:34)

The main phases in the work at Glacier 'as far as *method* is concerned' (emphasis added), are distinguished as:

(a) the phase of group discussions;
(b) the phase of exploratory individual discussions;
(c) the present phase of individual discussion and analysis backed by the systematic Glacier organisation concepts and an emerging theory of organisation. (p.39).

The first phase is illustrated in *The Changing Culture of a Factory*, which describes the period of collaboration between Glacier and the Tavistock Institute of Human Relations, when Jaques directed the research team from the Institute. By the time of phase (c), strategy and concepts were both recognized as independent bodies of theory. 'Strategy' was the developing methodology of access based on a psycho-analytical model, but restricted to work problems (p. 33). By 1958, Jaques points out that Glacier had policies, organizational concepts and procedures, which were sufficiently worked out for the company to establish its own management school (GIM Ltd).[15]

The third element, situational analysis, can be discerned in a number of paragraphs in 'Social analysis and the Glacier Project'. Thus, we read how Jaques describes the 'procedure' of social analysis:

I listen to the problem, try to get the sense of what it is about and, especially, try to listen for the more general principles which the individual may intuitively be stating but without recognizing it, since he is too near the matter and too familiar with it. . . . A second feature is that of looking for the spontaneously emerging solutions to problems, and helping to identify and conceptualise these solutions. . . . For me, informal organisation is at once a symptom of malaise, of organisational disease, and an attempt to overcome the disease. . . . I pay great attention to such symptoms, for often within them it is possible to discover the intuitive sense of people as to what ought to be done. (1965:43–4).

In these and other comments in the literature there is reference to something distinct from theories of strategy of access, or to concepts of organization. It is an account of the situational relationship of the outsider to the insider, an account of the *process* of problem-solving.

From social analysis to social science
So far, a research approach usually described by the title 'social analysis' has been outlined. Rather than regard this as a unitary methodology I have preferred to unpack the term into three component parts: strategy, concepts, and situational analysis. They will also enable us to move towards a critique of social analysis which, if better formulations of the research approach were available, might be more productive. There is by now a small body of criticism which would benefit from improved formulations. Disentanglement might avoid the publication of the sort of statement which claims that:

. . . when those who are 'social analysed' finally concur with their analyst about their time-span, their capacity or the capacity to which they should belong, a third party is left with little to judge whether the truth now stands revealed or the analyst has brainwashed his client. (Whittington and Bellaby 1979; see also Kelly 1968).

In this extract the phrase 'finally concur' is crucial. It is intended to create the necessary atmosphere for the almost explicit accusation that the social analyst has 'brainwashed' his client. Apart from anything else this presumes a great degree of gullibility and naivety on the part of staff in social services, health and other settings. This stance has been criticized by Giddens:

. . . institutions do not just work 'behind the backs' of the social actors who produce and reproduce them. . . . a common tendency of many otherwise divergent schools of sociological thought is to adopt the methodological tactic of beginning their analyses by discounting agents' reasons for their action . . . such a stance . . . implies a *derogation of the lay actor*.(1979:11, emphasis original).

Let us just emphasize again that *collaboration* means what it says, as part of the strategy of social analysis. Even if someone agrees to collaborate, they have total control over the written statement that might emerge from their interaction with the outsider. During the stage of situational analysis they can decide that they would prefer not to collaborate. But having agreed to collaborate, they are usually vigorous in defence of ideas and in pursuit of alternatives. What 'stands revealed' at the conclusion of the situational analysis is an explicit statement of an individual's perception of the key issues confronting him. My own strategy is to distinguish between these insider documents and my outsider analysis which combines the varying perceptions into what I call a *covering report*. The documents which have resulted from the discussions between insider and outsider, the stage of situational analysis, together with the covering report, will then form the basis of one or more group discussions.

The group discussion represents an opportunity for those who are collaborating with the researcher to examine together the alternative models (TT) that have been produced to cope with the issues (P$_1$). The group discussion is itself a forum for the elimination of errors (EE) and, as expected from the Popperian schema, a possible emergence of new problems (P$_2$).[16]

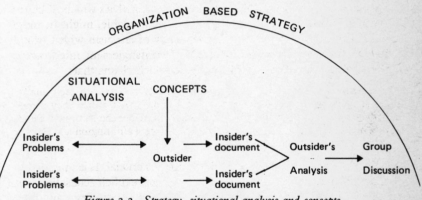

Figure 2.2   Strategy, situational analysis and concepts

This organization-based process has been referred to as moving from the *manifest* to the *assumed*, *extant*, and *requisite* situation. According to Wilfred Brown the definitions of these concepts are:

Manifest – the situation as formally described and displayed.
Assumed – the situation as it is assumed to be by the individual concerned. There may or may not be consistency between the 'assumed' and the 'manifest' situation.
Extant – the situation as revealed by systematic exploration and analysis. (It can never be completely known.)
Requisite – the situation as it would have to be to accord with the real properties of the field in which it exists. (1960:47–8).

The notion of passing through stages of understanding problems is undoubtedly useful, and we can certainly hold on to the idea of 'manifest' and 'assumed'. It is however the idea of 'extant' and 're-quisite' which is more problematic. Rather than utilize these terms I prefer to adopt the approach of the 'best' available tentative theory (with 'better' as defined earlier). 'Requisiteness' hints at prescription and a single answer to social problems. It is sometimes tempting to slip from an analytic to a prescriptive role. It is a traditional stance of social administration and is often what the insiders themselves want. The pressure to produce a rapid 'solution' can be intense. It would be foolish to claim that the boundary is always easily maintained and that there is never an (occasional) slip away from analysis. But a few painful excursions into the world of prescription usually serves as a salutory reminder to the over-zealous analysis. Ralph Rowbottom has discussed in detail the link between two different views of 'requisite' and the 'scientific products of social analysis' (1977; in particular chapter 8). His view of requisite is that:

it proposes that certain arrangements will generally prove to be workable in practice: that they will help rather than hinder people who are using them in the given circumstances to achieve their desired ends. (p. 106).

Utilizing Popper's idea of falsifiability, Rowbottom suggests that:

the requisite proposition is . . . *falsifiable*. Practice may reveal that inconsis-tencies do indeed exist . . . The test therefore is not just one of internal or logical coherence . . . but one against actual social reality as it is lived and experienced. (pp.106–7; emphasis original).

And most importantly:

Like the causal law, the requisite model is a general proposition of an 'if . . . then' form. *If* certain circumstances and needs X are given . . . , *then* arrangements Y are appropriate, suitable, requisite. (p. 107; emphasis origi-nal).

This softer view of requisite differs from the earlier and more emphatic proposition of Brown of 'the situation as it would have to be'. In his discussion of the nature of requisite, Rowbottom empha-sizes the 'scientific nature' of social analysis whilst stressing its inter-dependence with 'social reality'. There is a need, as it were, to defend the scientific credentials of getting too close to real problems.

In my own utilization of the Popperian schema I have not disting-uished between 'pure' and 'applied' research, or any other of the many classifications, in relation to the problems being addressed. It seems superfluous. Yet the question as to whether action and policy-orientated research is 'genuine' science is one that has often troubled its practitioners (see, for example, Cherns 1971: 63–72). In this course, they have not been alone. The spectre of 'true' science continues to haunt the corridors of social science, causing periodic fits of severe anxiety. But the action-researcher has faced the additional criticism that his concern with micro-issues, with the daily grindstone of institutional-based studies, prohibits the development of generalizable theories:

. . . the further we proceed down the list from basic pure research to action research, the more is utilization likely but the less generality is possessed by the results. (p.67).

It was partly in order to cope with this problem (generality) that the 'extended' strategy was developed. This is illustrated in chapters 12 and 13 where the orginal, departmental-based projects were then subjected to the critical evaluation of a wide range of involved parties in an extensive workshop and seminar programme. To this must be added the experience gained from other similar projects and the usual academic exchanges. The workshop programme however, has proved a distinctive additional, strategic approach, and is valuable in the testing and dissemination of ideas.

But is all this – strategy, situational analysis, concepts – 'science'? In the quiet of our own rooms, safe in the knowledge that no one is peering over our shoulders, we may be tempted to ask ourselves, 'does it matter?' Perhaps, like Wolin's (1968) political scientists:

few are interested in investigating for themselves the logical basis or the historical development of the sciences . . . wanting nothing more than to be allowed to get on with the work of empirical investigation . . . their hope is that the meaning of science has been settled.

But the matter is far from settled. The philosophers of science are themselves far from agreed about the nature of scientific explanation, and the previous 'standard account . . . has been subjected to damaging criticism' (Hesse 1980:vii). The Byzantine nature of the debate, with its charges and counter-charges, make it increasingly difficult for the policy-orientated researcher to know which tenets of the alternative model of 'true' science he is failing to emulate.[17]

One response of the social scientist to the problem of the nature of science is to reach for the calculator. This, it is thought, entitles the possessor to enter the fraternity of 'true' scientists, such as physicists.[18] But as Hayek, for example, argues, the field of physics (to which envious glances are often directed) does not deal with 'the interplay of a large number of such significantly independent variables as the individuals in the social order' (1967:3). We are unlikely therefore in the social sciences to obtain simple 'if . . . then' statements with the assertion that the conditions stated in the antecedent are satisfied at a particular time and place. More probably we may be in the position whereby theories can 'explain or predict only kinds of phenomena, defined by very general characteristics; the occurrence, not at a narrowly defined time and place but within a wide range of changes of certain *types* . . . (1967: 13). The 'worth' of such a theory (or 'models' as Hayek prefers to call them) is that 'it protects us from striving for incompatible aims' (p.17). We may achieve the explanation, not of individual events but merely of the appearance of certain patterns or orders; 'the understanding of the general mechanism which produces patterns of a certain kind . . . may provide important guides to action . . .' (p. 40).

A common failing is to take into insufficient account the complexities and consequences of theory construction in the realm of social institutions. This leads to demands for 'measurement' and 'evaluation' which may be incapable of realization. The 'models' that appear in this book cannot be 'evaluated' in the specific sense which is sometimes demanded. This does not mean that theoretical anarchy prevails; and that 'anything goes'. The rush for mathematical tangibility (and respectability) can result in a devaluation of the role of critical discussion. Models of organizational structures can be subjected to the intense testing of the good sense of practitioners and others competent in this field. This is one safeguard against 'grave abuses . . . pretentious, over-elaborate theories . . . and sheer quackery' (p.19).

The issues are both fascinating and important. Is he with Popper, Kuhn, Lakatos, Hesse . . . ? The dilemma facing the practising social scientist is that he or she has 'to get on with the work'. The only way through this might be to prefer that broader philosophical theory which seems to make sense in the context of their work. So I find that the Popperian schema, and in particular the proposition of tentative theory, is sensible.

Summary
In the light of the diversity of views regarding the nature of science itself, and the no less tortuous state of the debate concerning the communalities and differences with the social sciences, it would be unrealistic and unwise to argue the primacy of any one methodology.[19] A tentative approach to 'methodology' would appear to make good sense. Against this background I have suggested that one approach (social analysis), used to generate many of the ideas presented in this book, makes sense and can be differentiated into : (i) *Strategy* – the development and maintenance of access; (ii) *Concepts* – utilization and development; and (iii) *Situational analysis* – the process of explicating *problems*; The schema $(P_1 \rightarrow TT \rightarrow EE \rightarrow P_2)$ also seems to accord with, and provide an underlying framework for this approach; that is to say, the extended strategy of social analysis provides a fruitful approach in which concepts can be subjected to critical evaluation in individual and group settings.

This discussion, although it has centred on social analysis as a research approach, has raised many issues which are of concern to the whole enterprise of social science research. How can we secure genuine access? How can 'better' usable theory be generated? What is the relationship of research 'access' to usable theory? What is the place of 'values'? Is the policy-orientated researcher a 'true scientist'? It is not suggested that answers have been provided to such major questions. Again, in this chapter we have only peered beyond the boundaries of usable theory to allied contextual issues.

Notes

1. In order to avoid any possibility of misunderstanding I should like to make it clear at the onset that whilst I consider that social analysis has many virtues, it is not argued that it is the 'best' or only research approach. It happens to be an approach which I personally have had an opportunity of utilizing since 1971, and one which still appears full of interest. It is certainly not unproblematic or all-embracing. See Rowbottom (1977).

2. '. . . the very terms "methodology" and "method" are ambiguous' (Burgess and Bulmer 1981).

3. A useful discussion, including a comparative analysis, is to be found in Clark (1972). See also French and Bell (1973) and Suchman (1967).

4. I do not exclude the possibility of developing other components that could usefully be analysed; these three seem to be the most worthwhile at present.

5. The task of providing a comprehensive account has been undertaken by my colleague Ralph Rowbottom (1977).

6. I would wish to emphasize the phrase 'partial control' in this description of the attributes of grounded theory.

7. For the polemical reply, see Glaser and Strauss (1973: 259–62).

8. See Popper (1976) chapter 29 for a full discussion of these issues.

9. I think that this statement of the evaluation of theories effectively answers those critics who argue that 'Popperian science' is only concerned with 'intellectual glory' and 'cuts itself off from technological objectives'. These critics usually only take into account one or two of the six tests. See, for example, J.L.Cohen (1978).

10. These have been based on the Brunel Institute of Organisation and Social Studies (BIOSS), of which Elliott Jaques is Director. The researchers working on these projects might perhaps be considered as a 'paradigm community'. That is to say, 'a fluid group bound by overlapping conceptual and social beliefs' (Haraway 1976).

11. However, there is a certain tension evident in the first definition. Is it to gain scientific understanding 'and thereby' facilitate 'enacted change'? Or are these two paths, whose temporary co-existence suits both sides? (see, for example, Rapoport 1970).

12. For an important critique of the case that the answer to problems of access in bureaucratic organization lies in covert methods see Bulmer (1982: 250). 'Open entry may more often be negotiated than supposed.'

13. The phrase 'mutual rational control by critical discussion' is taken from Popper (1972: 44).

14. My own experience in the 'value cohesive' kibbutz community bears out Etzioni's position. See, for example, Billis (1973a).

15. These concepts were described by Wilfred Brown, the Managing Director, in his book *Exploration in Management* (1960).

16. For the role of 'group feedback' see Brown and Heller (1981).

17. I shall continue to use 'action-researcher' and policy-orientated researcher interchangeably. Neither of these descriptions is entirely satifactory. Perhaps 'collaborative-research' might do. On balance, the ungainly phrase 'policy-orientated' may provide the most adequate flavour of the social scientist who is prepared to come into direct contact with 'lived', 'experienced', social reality.

18. See Hayek (1967: 29–31) for a critique of what he calls the 'impotence' of statistics to deal with pattern complexity. 'The statistical method is therefore of use only where we deliberately ignore, or are ignorant of, the relations between the individual elements with different attributes, i.e. where we ignore, or are ignorant of, any structure into which they are organized.'

19. The major issues of the debate, together with references to the wider literature can be found in the works of Popper (already noted); in addition, see Ravetz 1971; Borger and Cioffi 1970; Lessnoff 1974; Lakatos and Musgrave 1974; Hesse 1980; and Kuhn (1970a).

3   The Bureaucratic Middle-Ground and Social Administration

The opening two chapters have considered the 'philosophical' and 'methodological' context of usable theory for the design and change of welfare bureaucracies. These terms provided a necessary 'shorthand' for describing two broad underpinning and interacting territories. In similar fashion we shall briefly examine in this chapter the 'disciplinary' context of our chosen field of study.

It will be recalled that we began in the Introduction by defining the bureaucratic middle-ground as an important part of that area that lies between the policies and norms of political institutions and the citizen in need. How have the disciplines of public and, more centrally for the ideas in this book, social administration approached the bureaucratic middle-ground? It will be suggested that they have focused their attention elsewhere and taken a rather wary stance. In their approach to the study of bureaucracy, public administrators have been much occupied with the problem of political control; whilst social administrators have been more anxious to examine the place of professional discretion. In the case of social administration, the focus has been more on the impact of organization on professional discretion. We shall also discuss the tensions between what has been called the 'social conscience' (policy) thesis and what I shall refer to as 'community' administration.

Next, we shall look at the closest neighbours of middle-ground studies. On one side we shall enquire what the key notion of 'quality of service' might mean for the citizen in need. And, as far as the other 'political' neighbour is concerned, we shall examine what relevance our ideas about the middle-ground might have for political control.

But first I wish to examine whether there might be any links between the discipline of social administration and a need which has loomed large in the preceding chapters. I refer to the need for 'definitional clarity'. After all, in attempting to grapple with the opening task of responding systematically to social problems, we have had to consider, for example, what might be meant by 'social problem', 'bureaucracy' and 'structure'. But since this need will certainly not disappear and can be considered chronic and pervasive, I shall offer a few thoughts on its links with social policy.

Social policy and the need for definitional clarity

Demands for rationality, conceptual clarity, and precision in the use of the language, are standard clarion calls. Isaiah Berlin appears to make a takeover bid on behalf of philosophy and philosophers when, in an essay on 'The purpose of philosophy', he claims that:

The perennial task of philosophers is to examine whatever seems insusceptible to the methods of the sciences or everyday observation, e.g. categories, concepts, models, ways of thinking or acting, and particularly ways in which they clash with one another, with a view to constructing other, less internally contradictory, and (though this can never be fully attained) less pervertible metaphors, images, symbols and systems of categories. (1980:11).

This task which I have lumped together under the need for definitional clarity is not, we may suggest, just of interest to philosophers. For as Berlin himself continues:

one of the principal causes of confusion, misery and fear is, whatever may be its psychological or social roots, blind adherence to outworn notions, pathological suspicion of any form of critical self-examination. (ibid.)

If he is correct – and I shall assume that he is – then what he calls this 'reasonable hypothesis' is of particular import for social policy and administration, whose origins are rooted in a concern for the causes of confusion, misery, and fear. So, at first sight it might seem surprising that several distinguished writers in the field have still found it necessary to exhort their colleagues and others to greater conceptual clarity. Thus, Pinker complains of social administration's 'persistent lack of conceptual and theoretical foundations' (1971:13), and 'terminological confusion' (1979a: 6). More recently Klein asserts that 'the first responsibility' of the social policy man 'is to worry about the meaning of words: to avoid the slipshod use of language which tends to creep into the debates about social policy' (1980). And Parker has expressed concern 'about the way in which social policy issues are discussed . . . a stock of ready words and phrases which . . . create powerful images . . . too imprecise for the purposes of careful analysis' (1981).

These continued demands for clarity may arise from a number of causes. Amongst these may be listed the tradition and comparative youth of social administration. More importantly perhaps, we might briefly pursue the possibility that the particular and chronic demand for definitional clarity in the theory and practice of social policy arises from the nature of its field of study, where there is a need to secure some temporary stability in a tumultuous world.

That there is a powerful need to 'group', 'classify', 'define' things and facts is a contention found in most areas of social science. For example, Durkheim and Mauss in their discussion on primitive classification (1973) provide one possible explanation by reference to the 'remote influences which . . . have left behind them an effect which survives and is always present; it is the very cadre of all classification, it is the ensemble of mental habits by virtue of which we conceive things and facts in the form of coordinated or hierarchized groups'. Berger and Luckman (1975:35), acknowledging their debt to the Durkheimian view of the nature of social reality, see ' . . . everyday life as an ordered reality. Its phenomena are prearranged in patterns that seem to be independent of my apprehension of them and that impose themselves upon the latter.'

Leach, the social anthropologist, emphasizes that:

Our internal perception of the world around us is greatly influenced by the verbal categories which we use to describe it . . . . We use language to cut up the visual continuum into meaningful objects and into persons filling distinguishable roles. (1976: 33–4 see also Leach 1981).

The psychologist Lewin, referring to earlier work by Vigotsky, regards the process of differentiating previously undifferentiated areas as 'a basic biological concept'. He continues by claiming that 'in an unstructured, or new, situation the person feels insecure because the psychological directions are not defined . . . the person does not know what action will lead to what result' (Lewin 1963: 72–4).

Authors from other disciplines have also, like Lewin, been much occupied with the apparent need for permanence and stability. Thus, Polanyi suggests that 'the craving to find strands of permanence in the tumult of changing appearances is the supreme organon for bringing our experience under intellectual control' (1969:114). The craving for permanence is what Schon calls the 'Stable State': 'belief in the unchangeability, the constancy of central aspects of our lives, or belief that we can attain such a constancy'. He claims that 'belief in the Stabale State is strong and deep in us. We institutionalize it in every social domain . . . in spite of our talk about change . . . .' (1973:1).

What we have called by the generic term 'definitions' may be more or less useful, and they may also be more or less impermanent. But useful or not, social life without them is inconceivable. It would be without identity, without change, and totally unproblematic. A more realistic expectation, in the light of the pace and complexity of life, is that clarification and construction will become increasingly urgent. *Social policy and administration with its focal concern with the business and difficulties of living must naturally be immersed in such clarification and construction.*

We might note in passing that definitional fuzziness or deliberate ambiguity can for a time be employed as 'colonial' tactics to encompass other definitions – quite successful if the competing explanations are weak. Thus, Pinker criticizes social work's claim to universality and omnicompetence originating in the Seebohm Report and suggests that the 'failure to put workable limits to social work has encouraged these expansionist tendencies' (1979b). On the other hand, an interesting paper by Alaszewski (1977) describes the way in which a profession (occupational therapy) has taken over and dominated an area of practice from more established groups and protected it from newcomers by widening the definition of its professional scope.

By stressing the unity of the patient and the dominance of patient-orientation over technique-orientation, occupational therapy can claim to be the dominant remedial therapy, and can claim to encompass technique-orientated professions.

So, it appears that if we set ourselves the task of responding to social problems in a systematic and less impermanent fashion, then we shall not only need usable theories of middle-ground bureaucratic structure, but we will almost certainly become involved in the process of definitional clarification. This process, widely noted in many areas of social science, may be regarded as part of our attempt to secure some temporary stability in a turbulent world. With these comments in mind we can turn and see how public and social administration have approached the middle-ground.

Public administration and the middle-ground

For academic public administrators the issue of *delegated decision-making* to bureaucrats rather than the *working* of the middle-ground has been a central theme. How can political control be maintained over officials dealing with large organizational machines? In a study of county boroughs in the late 1960s, Greenwood and his colleagues reported that: 'perhaps the most important fear of members over delegation to officers arises from concern lest they become ignorant of facts that they should know in order to fulfil their duties' (1969).

Both the 1967 Maud and the 1972 Bains Reports attempted to resolve the dilemma. The former proposed that officials would be largely responsible for 'administration', with the management board of councillors making policies. The Bains Report declared: 'it has been suggested that extensive delegation to officers is in some way undemocratic, but we do not accept this, provided that the terms of delegation are clear and specific' (1972). Bains found it 'disturbing' to find that five years after the Maud Committee had 'exploded the myth of policy being a matter for the elected members and administration for officers . . . many members and officers still see this as a sufficient description of their respective roles' (ibid).

One author has claimed that 'until the appearance of *Local Government Studies* only three years ago, the literature of British local government was largely innocent of theory (Baker 1975:21). Other writers have suspected the hand of 'management' at work:

> this type of theorizing normally favours an orderly chain of decision-making, realized through a grading of decisions according to their intrinsic import-ance, an allocation of decision-making responsibilities that is as clear and precise as possible, and a stress upon effective delegation subject to such performance tests as can be devised. These managerial notions are certainly out of line with the traditional system of local government which . . . stipu-lates that in principle all decisions are the responsibility of the part-time elected representatives. (Self 1971).

Even a brief excursion into the literature reveals the concern ex-pressed by writers such as Self and others, over the intrusion of a 'management' approach which does not take into account what they regard as the characteristic and distinguishing features of the political framework. Work by INLOGOV writers echoes the same point. 'This application of the ideas and concepts from the literature of organiza-tional theory to that of public administration is not a process which receives universal approval.' In their view 'what is needed is a measure of reconceptualization rather than rejection' (Greenwood *et al.* 1980: 8–9).

It appears that most public administrators have had little to say about delegation and control *within* the bureaucracy.[1] Issues of poli-tical control have taken pride of place, and much of the theoretical concern has revolved around the 'policy-administration' dichotomy. In an important paper which spans the public and social administra-tion boundaries, Michael Hill (1981) has challenged the policy/ implementation dichotomy which 'has replaced the politics/ administration one, without recognition of the fact that one mislead-ing distinction has merely been replaced by another'. He claims that the 'top-level battle . . . in the process of translating political aspira-tions into action has been given extensive attention while equally important phenomena which follow on after it have tended to be neglected'. In his search for 'new approaches' to top-down control, 'which is so fundamental to the maintenance of a liberal democratic political perspective', he examines a number of key issues. Of these, the question of discretion, professionalism, and the role of 'gatekeep-ers' may all, I would contend, be usefully analysed within the four-dimensional framework which will be presented in Part II. He sug-gests that local government has done rather better than central gov-ernment in making the politics/administration boundary more perme-able, and cites area sub-committees, joint working parties of officers and members, and performance review committees as supporting evidence for his contention. Hill concludes by acknowledging the considerable difficulty in suggesting solutions to the problems of the relationship between conventional political control and some wider concept of democratic control.

Other authors have focused on different aspects of the dilemma. Regan, for example, is primarily concerned with the absence of an 'accountable executive' in local government. He argues for a cabinet system in which councils would elect the mayor or sheriff with power to appoint individual members of the council to be the political heads of various council departments (Regan 1980; see also RIPA and PSI 1980). This, it is suggested, would overcome the problem of 'democratic accountability' – 'since *all* on a local council are responsible for both executive and legislative responsibilities *none* is clearly accountable for either. The public cannot easily apportion blame and credit for the stewardship of the council services when their elected representatives comprise a largely undifferentiated group' (Regan 1980: 9). Regan does not discuss, in this particular paper, bureaucratic accountability – whether or not blame or credit should be apportioned to officers.

Jones is also concerned about the consequences of diffused responsibility. He criticizes the notion of 'shared' or 'joint' responsibility, which is a 'superficially attractive' and 'high sounding' phrase which can too easily be used to 'justify evasion of responsibility' (Jones 1977: 7) A strong plea is made for 'locating responsibility, or at least the main responsibility'. Without such a clarification there is a 'challenge [to] representative democracy itself' (p.6).[2]

More recent literature indicates that the dilemma remains unsolved. Alexander points to the impact of the full-time councillor motivated by the desire 'to assume control of the authority's policy-making and policy-implementation' (Alexander 1982:121). These 'highly visible' councillors have begun to take 'the public acceptance of responsibility for the effects of policy . . . as well as the principles' (ibid). The potential dangers of such an approach were pointed out by Kogan and Terry (1971) at the time of the establishment of SSDs:

If local government is to become vital and real, councillors must get down to deciding what ought to be, and whether what ought to be is being provided by their department. They cannot undertake this work and 'manage' the department as well.

Much of this literature looks at the boundary between political control and bureaucratic work, from the 'top-down'. In Part IV we shall attempt to explore what relevance a usable theory of bureaucracy might have for the dilemma discussed in this section. For the moment we might note that in my own research into the middle-ground with directors and deputy directors of SSDs, the single distinguishing feature of the directorial role was the concern with an inner core of issues that directors felt could not be relinquished (Billis 1981c). This core concern was variously expressed by directors as:

'dealing with major issues of political sensitivity'

'protecting the political and professional environment'

'coping with issues that might hit the headlines'

Jones (1973) has suggested that there is a 'more relevant line of division: between what is publicly controversial or potentially publicly controversial, and what is not. Members are to handle the former, officers the latter.' These statements from SSD directors suggest that even this 'line of division' does not resolve the dilemma.

Social administration and the dilemma of professional discretion

A wary approach to organizational theory and the process of policy implementation can also be found in parts of the social administration literature. Here too the broad target is what John Smith, writing of the 1970 health and social services reorganization, refers to as 'this crass managerialism' (Smith 1979). Similar sentiments and unhappiness with the 'Weberian dominance' are expressed by Rose in a paper entitled 'Approaches to the analysis of social service organization' (1976).

Whereas public administrators' interest has been mainly in democratic accountability, social administrators appear to have focused more on the impact of inappropriate organizational forms on *professional discretion* (Thomason 1977). (However, a number of papers indicate public administration's growing interest in professionalism in local government. Laffin, 1980). The anxiety of many social administrators, especially those with a strong social work interest, is expressed by Gilbert Smith who, after outlining the 'main characteristics of bureaucracy', declares that:

it is clear that principles of bureaucratic organizations are in conflict with the standards of professional practice . . . . Whereas the professional very much values his autonomy, 'bureaucratic autonomy' is a contradiction in terms. (1979:25–6).

However, his analysis of bureaucracy is somewhat limited and would appear to be barely representative even of what I shall describe in chapter 7 as the 'prescribed-output' bureaucracies. I shall attempt to demonstrate in Part II that 'discretion' and 'autonomy' must in fact be seen in the light of a wide variety of bureaucratic models. Nevertheless, the professional versus bureaucracy debate is a real one that periodically ignites in a splutter of fury.

Whilst some writers are clearly more enamoured with the benefits of professionalism than they are with the evils of bureaucracy, there are many others who take at least a sceptical stance towards professional claims, and perhaps even regard with sympathy Bernard Shaw's declamation that:

All organizations of these anti-social interests tend to become conspiracies against the public. They maintain scarcity of professional services to keep up their prices, making entry difficult by unnecessarily prolonged apprenticeship, and examinations in discarded techniques, obsolete language, and irrelevant academic subjects. They resist all new techniques that supersede their own and impose new requirements on them. They persecute outsiders ruthlessly. The skill and knowledge they guarantee is, as to the skill, untested and often imaginary. . . . (1944:354).

Neither bureaucracy nor professions have escaped unscathed from the sustained attacks. (If both are regarded as social institutions based on tentative explanations for the resolution of problems, a theme developed in chapter 1, they will inevitably be subject to attack, and over the course of time, be threatened by alternative explanations.) Professionals for their part, have often expressed concern about the possible conflicts of values, functions, objectives, etc.

It is disturbing that agency values might be more influential as they may not necessarily be wholly compatible with professional values. (British Association of Social Workers 1977:24).

In contrast, Winnicott found it necessary to admonish social workers for sometimes talking '. . . as if the social services exist in order to provide a setting in which they can practise their casework skill. . . . Is the caseworker aiming at practising a professional skill, or serving the community?' (1970:61–2). Specht probably comes close to the core of the problem when, in an argument for the 'unitary' approach, he reminds his readers that the 'ultimate success' of the social welfare enterprise will depend 'on the extent to which the community values the totality of the services performed by social workers' (Specht and Vickery 1978:25).

It is this question of 'community value' which, I suspect, provides a more relevant and central approach to the 'professionals in bureaucracy' dilemma. Professions, however defined, must be able to claim – *and persuade someone to support them in their claim* – that they are in a distinct business and that they must respond to this in a 'situational' rather than a 'straightforward' manner (see chapter 5). For example, the continuing failure of social work, the core 'profession' of SSDs, to convince the public that it can do either of these things (witness yet another investigation recently into the 'social work task'), is a more genuine problem than that of the more emotive professional versus bureaucracy debate (National Institute for Social Work 1982). Were the core profession really confident in its claims the position might look different. But social work has failed to establish its 'business' – to capture and establish monopoly conditions for a time over specified problems and the inter-relationships between them.

To sum up so far, I believe it is not unfair to claim that, in general, both public and social administration have adopted a wary approach to the study of the bureaucratic middle-ground. Indeed, social administration can be said to have adopted a 'schizophrenic' stance, a claim which I shall pursue in the following sections.

The social conscience thesis

In considering social administration and the organizational response to social problems, we see that it is customary to attempt to create an atmosphere of optimism. Thus, we prefer to speak about departments of 'health', 'education', 'social service', 'social security', 'housing', – rather than departments for the resolution of ill-health, ignorance, social distress, insecurity, and homelessness. This optimism may be seen to reflect the same desire to create the illusion of permanency discussed earlier in this chapter. Yet it can be claimed that social welfare organizations are established to resolve severe problems; if so, it might be more accurate, if politically hazardous, to utilize the problem-based titles.

There is reluctance to see life as essentially problematic – and organizations in the field of social welfare as attempts to construct a less ephemeral and haphazard response. Whether we be practitioners in statutory or voluntary agencies, students, academics, policy-makers, donors or recipients, the goal-seeking paradigm appears to lead to a strong association with a desire to achieve ideal states. Indeed, the assumptions held about society by the writers of the most popular textbooks on social policy (in Europe and America) have been described as based on a 'social conscience' thesis or tradition. Writers in this tradition:

see the State as benevolent. The social services have as their aim the welfare of their users; the State provides the social services – the State has welfare as its aim. (Baker 1979).

Analysis of the social conscience tradition by Baker reveals the generally optimistic tenor of the main thesis. A benevolent state, a widening and deepening of our sense of social obligation, an increase in our knowledge of need, a belief in cumulative change in the direction of greater generosity and wider range, irreversibility of improvements, and a belief that the central problems of social welfare have been solved; these are analysed as the dominant assumptions of popular writers on social policy.

Despite the emergence of different interpretations, Baker suggests that the social conscience tradition will continue to be strong. Whether or not the 'tradition' is as coherent as suggested, there can be few doubts about the generally optimistic basis of the dominant tradition. Donnison, in an article in the same journal (1979), looks at a somewhat similar issue, the central assumptions held by Titmuss and his colleagues. Some of these assumptions were that:

● the growth of the economy and population would continue;
● inequalities in income would be modified by a social wage provided by social services and by progressive taxes;
● most of the electorate would support such programmes;
● the professions manning the public services were among the generally trusted instruments of progressive social change, and that their numbers would increase.

Once again, we can note the general optimism underlying these assumptions, although Donnison suggests that these have 'begun to crumble' since 1966, with the cuts in public expenditure associated with the end of post-war reconstruction, falling birth-rates and rising unemployment.

We cannot assume that the social wage or the taxes which finance it will grow – least of all that they will grow in egalitarian ways. 'Middle England' is not ready to be convinced by research and blue books that benign public services will – or should – create a more humane and a more equal society. (ibid.)

Almost inevitably, belief in a 'benevolent' state and the other aspects of the social conscience thesis implies comprehensive (large-scale) government intervention. The thesis thus sets an overall context or policy framework which may be contrasted with an approach to the middle-ground which I shall describe as 'community administration'.

Community administration
Despite the fact that many authors from Titmuss onwards have pointed to social administration's dependence on a wide variety of social sciences (sociology, economics, philosophy, political science), organizational theory has at most been a peripheral concern of social administrators. In searching for reasons for its lack of popularity, it would be difficult to argue that the present limited state of our knowledge about organizations could be a sufficient factor. After all, economics or sociology for that matter, are scarcely in a less parlous state; yet this has not hindered vigorous claims being entered on their behalf. I shall not pursue here the debate on the status and future of social administration.[3] Unwillingness to embark on a serious study of welfare bureaucracy may well be related to the tension between the need to resolve current problems and the belief in the attainment of future ideal states. Bureaucratic 'contamination' must be avoided at all costs. Even those who at first glance may appear to be risking contamination turn out to be engaged in organizational voyeurism,

eager to pass on risqué tales of bureaucratic life. The ensuing caricatures of welfare bureaucracies invariably come out unfavourably when
compared to any other solution.

What might be described as the 'community administration'
approach yearns for the beguiling beauty of 'smallness' and 'together-
ness'. Its adherents are in favour of 'decentralization', 'community',
'participation', 'teamwork', 'accessibility', 'co-ordination', 'collaboration'. Thus, it is claimed that:

In bureaucratic social service organisation *roles* of staff tend to be clearly
defined. Their relationships with users are typically meant to be detached,
void of personal feeling. (Hadley and Hatch 1981:148–9).

Furthermore, 'innovation within bureaucratic organizations is relatively rare . . . Most employees are likely to feel bound by their
tightly defined roles.' The large units of bureaucratic organizations are
compared with the small units of 'participatory', 'patch', organization,
where workers have 'flexible roles' and are 'empathetic' with clients
and where innovation is 'frequent'.

A number of questions come to mind. We might enquire, for
example, whether all bureaucratic organizations necessarily have
'large' units. And how large is large? What exactly is a 'unit'? Does it
include different bureaucratic levels? Are, for example, the home
helps headed by a home help organizer the 'unit', or the social worker
led by a team leader the 'unit', or the area team the 'unit'? Is five, ten,
fifteen, or twenty 'large'? Or, is it 'small'? What do Hadley and Hatch
meant when they argue for 'flat' organization? Does it mean there are
no hierarchical levels, or one or two, or what? The role of clients is
'expected' to be 'passive' in bureaucratic organization and active in
participatory organizations. Where are these expectations stated, or
where did they originate from? Are there no examples of departments
where client activity is encouraged? What is meant by organizational
'innovation'? The pioneering, careful, comparative study by Ralph
Kramer (1981), for example, casts severe doubts on the validity of
several of these assumptions – certainly as far as voluntary agencies are
concerned. Several other studies also point to the need for a cautious
and reasoned approach to the study of bureaucracy. Thus, Blau points
to five ways in which 'bureaucratic conditions generated favourable
attitudes towards change' (1963: 247). And Hall, utilizing earlier work
by Scott, suggests that 'conflict between professional and organizational norms is not inherent. . . . investigators of such conflict must
demonstrate that it exists' (Hall 1967; Scott 1965).

One of the major dilemmas that confronts the 'patch' protagonists is
that the participatory 'experiments' have emerged from the self-same
'inflexible' bureaucracies which they condemn! Recognizing the ques-

tionable logic of this argument, Hadley and Hatch (1981) attempt to recover their position by explaining that 'insofar as the [patch] team is deviating from standard practice within the local authority department, its development requires frequent explanation and constant defence'. In this organizational 'catch-22', even those bureaucracies that are grudgingly acknowledged to be capable of producing 'innovations' (such as patch organization) are still inflexible, since 'frequent explanations' are necessary. (We might ask in passing what is wrong with any series of important publicly-funded actions requiring frequent explanations?)

If we compare the above version of bureaucracy with the case studies of, for example, intermediate treatment and day care in Part III, it can be demonstrated that bureaucratic organization whilst it often has an abundance of problems also has the potential to be high-trust and effective. Those tens of thousands of dedicated staff who work with the most intractable of problems, especially in residential and day care settings, might justifiably take umbrage at the stigmatized role allocated to them in the community administration approach. Sadly, however, the disappointing thing for social administration, welfare bureaucrats and recipients, is that many of the criticisms of 'bureaucracy' *are* justified. The organization of work, be it on a large or small scale, is often complex and problematic.

In a helpful analysis, Gordon Rose has suggested that whilst there has been a movement:

back to trying to look at organizations as a whole . . . this is constantly breached in the social services field by the movement toward community care . . . which amplifies the modern trend towards combating the people-crushing organization. Thus the 'establishment' is seen as creating social problems by its discriminant perception and mechanistic reaction towards the under-privileged. [Rose denounces this view as] 'over-simplified' and 'biased' (1976).

There is, it seems, a chronic state of tension between the discipline's 'community' approach to administration and its social conscience policy partner. The former emphasizes smallness, while the latter implies comprehensive (large-scale) government intervention. Thus the area team – the key Seebohm concept – may be seen as an attempt to straddle the gulf between policy and administrative stances, an attempt to secure comprehensive welfare without 'bureaucracy'. So it is hardly surprising to read reports of the 'failure of centralized services' or to see that 'the Seebohm vision of social services departments in close contact with small communities has not become a reality' (Holman 1980).

A number of other authors have challenged aspects of community administration and pointed to the wooliness of several central themes. For example, Cohen (1979) has examined the disbenefits of 'community care'; and 'team work' has been explored in a joint project between the United States and the United Kingdom (Lonsdale, Webb and Briggs 1980). Self has pointed out that whilst most writers, politicians, and officials are 'decentralists in principle . . . this favourable sentiment seems often incapable of producing effective action' (1976:72). Smith and Ames have cast doubts on the Seebohm principle of the 'area team' upon which earlier hopes of community administrators were pinned. In their review of the literature they analysed several basic assumptions that form part of this tradition (1976). It is a tradition that has not encouraged serious investigation of the middle-ground links between policy and service delivery. A similar point is made by Webb and Hobdell (1980):

We certainly have not begun to construct the equations which would link various types of organisations and professional practice with the quality of service received by the client.

These authors have drawn attention to the interconnection between policies, 'types of organization' and 'quality of service'. It is to this last phrase, so important for middle-ground studies, that we now turn.

Quality of service
Can bureaucracies provide a 'good quality of service'? Or, are they all destined to treat their clients as 'passive' recipients?

I doubt that 'quality' can be severed from subjective judgement. Whilst tangible indicators such as bedspace, expenditure, availability of specific facilities, caseloads, occupancy rates, and so on, may be useful adjuncts to departmental decision-making, they must be treated with caution. (This is a bitter lesson which I have carried with me from my early days in a settlement which had the highest per capita expenditure and the worst food in the entire kibbutz movement!) An illustration of what quality of service is all about comes from David Donnison (1980) who seeks to answer the question:

What does the 'quality of service' mean? It's intangible, yet unmistakable. Working for the Plowden Committee (on primary schools), the Public Schools Commission and the Supplementary Benefits Commission, I have visited well over a hundred social security offices and scores of schools and hotels in several different countries. You sense the quality of service they provide within a few minutes of entering . . . And what about the good social security office? The man waiting to greet you at the entrance is neither obsequious nor offhand. He stops to have a word with a bewildered old lady and explains which waiting room she should go to before taking you up to the manager's office . . . . When you reach the manager, he and his team will tell you their priorities for the coming year. Pretty soon they hand you over to junior staff, some of whom are curious or critical about features of the service they're providing and are not afraid to say so . . . Everything about these services conveys the same messages. Their staff know what they're supposed to be doing. They care about their customers and see them as real people. And, they have pride in themselves and their work. That's partly because their managers care for *them*. They clearly explain what's expected of them, give them time and training for the job, make demands which are challenging but never impossible, and look after them if they get into real difficulties.

Donnison continues by describing situations where the 'grey anonymity of the civil service' works against that innovation which might lead to improved quality of service. 'Too often local office managers merely manage resources over which they have no control. Innovation seems risky. They cannot choose their own key staff, and their regional controllers exert only a little more influence in choosing them.'

This discerning account of the presence and absence of 'quality' of service will ring true to those who, for one reason or another, have been in a position to compare the functioning of many similar organizations.

It makes *a vital link between individual ability, the authority content of organizational roles, and desirable outputs such as innovation and good quality of service*. It is worth spelling out a few tentative propositions.

Quality of service can never just be a matter of non-human resources. It is the specific staff of organizations who are accountable for quality of service, and in particular those who are managing the client-impact workers. Are these roles explicit and agreed? Have they been given the authority to do the work? Or, like Donnison's office managers, have they no control over resources? Further, do they have the capacity? Or, are new recruitment and training patterns required? Finally, and possibly most important of all, do we actually know who precisely is responsible for establishing desired standards of service in what bits of the organization? Or, is this an unclear area where terms such as 'shared', 'joint', and 'team', serve to obscure the real issues of accountability and quality? Most of these issues will appear as topics for discussion in Part II.

Research experience recorded here and elsewhere indicates that the flavour and working of bureaucracy need *not* necessarily accord with the simplistic approach of community administration. It is neither necessary to make light of the problems of bureaucratic life, nor to diminish the work of all welfare bureaucrats with unhelpful stereotypes. As J.H Smith (1979) points out:

People who would elsewhere denounce attempts at simplistic classification as 'labelling' in this area cheerfully designate all large organizations as 'bureaucratic' and then move on to the next count on the indictment – 'professionalism', for example, or 'the casework approach'.

There do exist welfare bureaucracies that evidence qualities of flexibility, innovation, and care for clients and staff. Social scientists cannot airily dismiss them as 'accidents'. The search must be on in order to understand why some bureaucracies have more problems than others. Having furthered our understanding of the structure of bureaucracy and the individuals who work in them, it may then be possible to debate genuine choices in the nature of the response to social problems. As Thomas Kuhn felt it necessary to declare in his 'Reflections on my Critics', 'to explain why an enterprise works is not to approve or disapprove it' (1970a). Neither should analysis and theory generation be equated with agreement.

Summary

This chapter has focused mainly on the relationship between social administration and our chosen field of study, welfare bureaucracies. It was suggested that the discipline has a particular need to become involved with the meaning of words, a need which was already clearly indicated from our opening task of establishing a systematic response to social problems. This demand for definitional clarity may be considered to be part of a general desire for temporary stability.

We then noted that public administration has, in the main, concerned itself with the issue of delegated decision-making compared with social administration's focus on professional discretion. Whilst both disciplines have adopted a rather wary approach to the study of the bureaucratic middle-ground, social administration has adopted a 'schizophrenic' stance, torn between the *social conscience* and *community administration* traditions. We concluded with a brief comment on the 'quality of service', indicating its links with individual ability or *capacity* and the *authority* content of organizational roles – two central concepts of Part II of this study.

Notes

1. However, an important exception to this is Michael J. Hill's *The Sociology of Public Administration* (1972). See also R.J.S. Brown (1971) chapter VI for a critique of academic public administration's lack of interest in organization theory.
2. A powerful argument in fact for the sort of discussion that will be opened in chapter 8.
3. This debate can be traced in Titmuss (1958, chapter 1); Titmuss (1976: 21); Donnison and Chapman (1965: 26); Slack (1966: 39); Pinker (1971: 11–13); Carrier and Kendall (1977); Taylor-Gooby (1981b); Walker (1981: 225–50).

PART II

Usable Theory for the Design and Change of Welfare Bureaucracies

In this Part we return to the opening task: How can we make a systematic response to social problems? It will be argued that it may be necessary to establish an organization consisting of people who occupy roles – the building blocks of structure.

We shall suggest that three core dimensions of structure are *category*, *level*, and *authority*. To these must be added a fourth fundamental 'dimension' – individual *capacity*.[1] Each of these themes will be the subject of one or more chapters; here, a brief introduction only will be provided.

The process of *categorization*, or the *horizontal* dimension, may be broadly illustrated from the field of social policy and administration where we have divisions between what are generally considered to be, for example, 'housing', 'health', 'welfare', or 'educational' problems. Merely to list these divisions is to become acutely aware of the problems of definitional clarity. Nevertheless, there *is* a sense of different 'sorts' of work, of types of basic problems to be resolved that, it may be supposed, emanate from differences in objective things (Lorenz 1977: 7).[2] The analysis of horizontal boundaries can open up a Pandora's box. What is 'child guidance'? (Rowbottom and Bromley 1978) What is 'intermediate treatment'? (Billis 1976) What is 'educational welfare'? (Robinson 1978) And so on. Analysis of horizontal boundaries can lead to the questioning of current definitions upon which organizational structures are based (see the discussion of these issues in chapter 1). In chapter 4 we shall question the current definition of the work of Social Services Departments.

The second, or *vertical*, dimension to be considered is the 'level', or *stratum*, of work. These strata represent a hierarchy of discrete responses to problems, each stratum comprising a qualitatively different and successively 'higher' response. The theory identifies only five such steps, although recognizing the possible existence of higher levels.[3] The five strata listed in successive order and starting from the least complex are:

(1) Prescribed output
(2) Situational response
(3) Systematic service provision
(4) Comprehensive service provision
(5) Comprehensive field coverage

In chapters 5 and 6, the levels of work theory will be presented in detail, and in chapter 7 a typology of organizational responses will be developed. We shall claim that these theories throw new light on several social policy debates.

The third dimension, *authority*, needs to be identified precisely enough to suit the limited objectives that we have set ourselves.[4] It will be regarded as the adhesive which binds different roles together, the sanctioned right of role-occupants to actually translate expectations into actions.[5] In chapter 8 we shall present some ideas on the nature of authority and control and, in so doing, challenge current ideas about the nature of 'delegation'.

During the course of a study based on ten years' membership of a kibbutz, I came to the conclusion that the main stumbling block in the development of the settlement was something which might be called 'administrative talent' (Billis 1971). In later research a further attempt was made to analyse the nature of administrative capacity, which was defined as 'the ability to cope with the duties of strata of specific organizational posts' (Billis 1977).[6] Two 'conclusions' were presented which underpin the basic approach to capacity adopted in this present book. These were that (i) capacity varies between individuals, and (ii) its rate of development is different.

In chapter 9 we shall discuss further the nature of 'capacity' and what happens when it comes face to face with bureaucratic structure.

Notes

1. I am, in this analysis of organizational structure, builiding primarily upon a substantial body of work emanating from the Glacier-Brunel researchers (see chapter 10). The study of organizational structure is part of a major academic enterprise with an extensive literature. A useful introduction to the literature is provided by Tom Lupton, *Management and the Social Sciences*, 2nd edn. (1971). In organizational structure we might note the major work initiated at Aston University in 1961 (*see* the bibliography in Social Science Research Council Newsletter 35, October 1977). However, few studies of structure focus on organizational design and change, and of these scarcely any take modern welfare bureaucracies as a specific area of research. It would have been impractical to relate to that general body of organizational research and I have preferred, in the main, to set this book within the context of social administration studies.

2. The 'epistemological prolegomena' is a persuasive essay on the nature of the relationship between man 'as a physical entity, an active, perceiving subject, and the realities of an equally physical external world, the object of man's perception' (p.1).

3. These five levels, together with the typology in chapter 7, are also more precise than the 'technical' and 'managerial' systems of Talcott Parsons (see Parsons 1960:chapter II).

4. In this discussion we might just note Weber's classic analysis of rational legal authority in his *The Theory of Social and Economic Organization* (1947); and the critical appraisal of his views outlined in Merton *et al.* (1952). The section on 'Power and authority' in Ralf Dahrendorf's *Class and Class Conflict in an Industrial Society* (1972) is brief and useful. A comprehensive examination of the link with tradition from a political science standpoint which contains many references to the literature is Carl Friedrich's *Tradition and Authority* (1972). A 'social psychological' approach to the issues is to be found in Gerth and Wright Mills, *Character and Social Structure* (1970) (especially chapter 9). A more recent essay with numerous references is 'Power and authority' by Steven Lukes in Bottomore and Nisbet (1979).

5. More precisely authority has been defined as 'an attribute of a role which gives the incumbent the right to exercise power within socially established limits, and to apply to others positive or negative sanctions (rewards or punishments) depending upon the quality of their behaviour. It is thus the exercise of power in a manner which others have said is allowable and are prepared to support. (Jaques 1967: 39).

6. Part of this paper appears as chapter 14 in this book. See also Jaques (1967) and bibliography for his key works.

4 The Categorization of Welfare: The Case of Social Services Departments (SSDs)

Clarification of the horizontal (categorization) dimension of 'welfare' agencies can be exceedingly difficult. Often it has been unease surrounding this dimension that has dominated social policy debates. Indeed, it is rare to find a period without a major committee in session deliberating the nature of some occupational or departmental work.[1]

Is, for example, 'looking after' the elderly in residential institutions, residential social work, nursing, hotel-keeping, social care – or what? What is intermediate treatment, day care, social work, home help work, occupational therapy . . . ? Is 'looking after' the mentally handicapped in adult training centres social work, education, industrial training, or some distinctive activity in its own right? (National Development Group for the Mentally Handicapped 1977). Is looking after the mentally handicapped in hospital, nursing or social care? (Report of the Committee of Enquiry into Mental Handicap, Nursing and Care 1974). Are the mentally-ill living in group homes in the community, 'patients', 'clients', or 'residents'? Szasz suggests that:

the phenomena now called mental illnesses be looked at afresh and more simply, that they be removed from the category of illnesses, and that they be regarded as the expressions of man's struggle with the *problem* of how he should live. ('The myth of mental illness', in Szasz 1974:21).

He attacks the categorization of the problems of mental illness as medical when they are 'psycho-social, ethical, and legal deviations'. Another author, Robinson, points out that children with behaviour problems tend to be seen as 'bad' because of the difficulties caused for teachers in carrying out their tasks, while:

children who are isolated and withdrawn may hardly be noticed because they make fewer demands on the teacher. On the other hand, children whose behaviour is seen as bizarre, and especially those whose parents are known to suffer from psychiatric disorders, are often seen as 'mad'. (1978:63)

The social policy categorization questions are numerous and the implications many. For example, if the elderly in residential care primarily require 'nursing' then it may make sense to recruit nurses and to ensure nursing control of the home. In turn, nursing control of residential homes raises major questions, not the least of which is why they should be within social services departments. If however it is not indended to provide nursing care but something else which might be called residential social work, then recruitment and training will be of a different pattern. Residents may get a different service in nursing or residential social work dominated homes.[2]

But the dimension of categorization includes even more than the mainstream major service and department activities of the sort illustrated above. In the task of establishing an organizational response to social problems we shall probably need to employ staff in distinct *supporting*, or 'non-operational', roles to pursue activities such as finance, supplies, transport, secretarial, research, personnel and public relations. These, too, may be grouped together in a variety of permutations with accompanying problems scarcely less severe than the categorization of the operational activities.

Perhaps one of the few helpful statements that can be made about the categorization of activities is that it seems that there are certain activities that 'congeal' together, that 'make sense' as coherent roles. Thus, at the broadest level, the mixing of operational and non-operational activities has in practice often proved highly problematic.[3]

In view of the impossibility of analysing the horizontal dimension of all those agencies focusing on welfare problems, I have chosen to focus mainly on one major form of welfare bureaucracy, the SSDs in England and Wales, which represent the governmental hard core of service provision. I have been reassured of the possible wider relevance of these ideas by discussions with European social welfare managers and practitioners.

The chapter will probe into the general categorization of the broad work of SSDs. In so doing it will be suggested that *social breakdown* might replace 'the prevention of social distress' as a definition of that work, and that this can be differentiated from another cluster of social problems which will be defined as *social discomfort*. It will be claimed that this clarification can illuminate a number of social policy debates. The definition leads to questions about the present activities of the statutory agencies. It leads to questions about the meaning of 'prevention' in social welfare. It leads also to questions about the relative roles of the statutory and voluntary welfare agencies.

organizations which are described in optimistic terms and whose

SSDs: from 'the prevention of social distress' to social breakdown
Politically, it would seem, it is easier to argue for the construction of organizations which are described in optimistic terms and whose general 'objectives' are couched in acceptably vague phrases (noted in chapter 3). The influential Seebohm Report which led to the estab-

lishment of SSDs sways between statements of massive optimism and hard reality. Thus, in an optimistic vein,

This new department will, we believe, reach far beyond the discovery and rescue of social casualties; it will enable the greatest possible number of individuals to act reciprocally, giving and receiving services for the well-being of the whole community. (Home Office *et al.* 1968: para 2).

Perhaps most expansively of all, the Committee suggested that:

it can be argued that the basic aim of the social service departments is to meet all the social needs of the family or individuals together and as a whole.

It is difficult to posit a more all-embracing and unobtainable ambition. 'All the social needs' – what department could possibly fulfil the heavy burden of such an expectation? In a more realistic tone, the same report, in a major chapter arguing for the creation of a social services department, emphasizes 'social problems' and 'social distress'. Local authorities, it is suggested, 'must assume wider responsibilities than they have at present for the prevention, treatment and relief of social problems' and the present structure 'ignores the nature of much social distress' (paras 129 and 142).

Even during the period of rapid expansion of SSDs immediately after the Report, there was overwhelming agreement (in project and conference work) from staff in the new departments that they were primarily in the business of 'the prevention or relief of social distress'.[4] So, whatever the authors of the Report may have hoped in their more expansive moods, those doing the work adopted a more realistic approach to what was actually happening. But is social distress an adequate description of the horizontal dimension of welfare bureaucracies?

I shall argue that whilst this description has not been without utility, it may be too vague. Vagueness in itself need not be problematic, were it not for the fact that we may be deceiving ourselves into believing that we are providing something that we are not – a situation of dubious benefit for the community. Definitional analysis and clarification will not lead to a rigid framework – it will remain 'tentative' (see chapter 2). (Indeed, it can be argued that rigidity is the product of lack of clarity.) However, what might be achieved is greater internal consistency in agency boundaries: an achievement well worth attaining if the worst abuses of bureaucratic overlap in the various sectors of welfare provision are to be avoided.

I first became uneasy about the phrase 'the prevention of social distress' during work on a number of projects in day care, one of which is included as a case study in Part III. This unease was conveyed to a number of departments; but whilst it aroused some mild interest, they had little time or energy to pursue serious discussions (Billis 1975b). In those days a major issue facing departments and researchers was the development of organizational models capable of handling the large and growing range of activities. The pursuit of alternative definitions for the work of SSDs took second place to these other more burning issues. (The relationship between problems and explanations has been discussed at a more general or 'philosophical' level in chapter 1.)

In the past few years the environmental conditions within which SSDs function have changed dramatically. The pendulum has swung from extreme optimism to considerable pessimism regarding the potential role of SSDs in society. However, the underlying logic of my views about 'the prevention of social distress' has not changed despite the changed context of the debate. In the period 1980–82 several of these ideas about 'prevention' and 'social breakdown' were published. Of equal importance was the subjection of these ideas to 'critical discussion' (see chapter 2) by numerous staff from SSDs participating in workshops and courses.

This period of doubt regarding the horizontal boundary of SSDs and in particular the unease about the possibility of 'preventive' social services work coincided with a personal exploration of the relevance of several of Karl Popper's ideas for 'middle ground' research. A few of these themes (the relevance for organizational structure and methodology) have been discussed in Part I. However, I feel it is appropriate to note that these ideas, especially about problems and the development of theory, reinforced the more pragmatic doubts surrounding the actual functioning of SSDs.

In brief, it now seems to me that 'the prevention of social distress' no longer stands up to critical discussion. I shall argue that:

- the 'business' of SSDs is to cope with *social breakdown*;
- social breakdown may be distinguished from *social discomfort*;
- 'preventive' social services work is a misleading and harmful notion.

First let us consider *social breakdown*. By this I mean that *an individual is either already in an institution or, if no action is taken, is judged to require some form of institutionalization, within an explicit period of time*. Social breakdown may thus be regarded *as actual or imminent loss of independence* – the transfer of accountability for an individual's work, play, and sleep to an agency sanctioned by society.

The presence of a time boundary is an essential element in the definition of breakdown. Without this, every intervention in human situations can be claimed to be 'preventing' eventual undesirable states. Only by making judgements about the length of time before breakdown will occur can intervention be justified. Are we talking about breakdown which will occur within hours, days, weeks, months or what? The introduction of a time boundary may go some way to building greater realism and producing more effective work. It may move us away from over-ambitious and historicist approaches to welfare, according to which specific individuals or groups such as the elderly, displaying one set of problems, are judged to be on an 'inevitable' decline.

That it might be some notion of breakdown that actually underlines the actions of government welfare bureaucracies is suggested – at least in the British setting – in official statements; for example we read that:

The need to provide statutory child care services can be attributed generally to three causes – a malfunctioning or breakdown of the family, breakdown of education, or breakdown of health. (Barnes and Connelly 1978: 12).

As far as the elderly are concerned the primary objective of departmental policy is:

to enable old people to maintain independent lives . . . to help achieve this, high priority is being given to . . . measures designed to prevent or postpone the need for long-term care in hospitals or residential homes. (p.13)

Although the term breakdown is used in describing national objectives for the care of children, the description of departmental objectives with regard to the elderly comes nearest to our own usage; that is to say, breakdown as actual or imminent loss of independence. It might be argued that the concept has not changed since the time of the Poor Law. What has changed, and continually changes, is our perception of what at any time constitutes a state of breakdown.

I have so far suggested that *social breakdown* should replace 'the prevention of social distress' as a better definition of the horizontal dimension of SSDs. (The meaning of 'better' was discussed in chapter 2.) Here we might note that in making such a claim my contention is that social breakdown is 'more precise' and 'explains more facts' than 'the prevention of social distress' (Popper 1974a:232). This contention may however be more readily accepted if we proceed to distinguish social breakdown from *social discomfort*, for I believe that SSDs are attempting to respond to two different categories of need. Only by distinguishing the two can the claim to have provided a 'better' definition be reasonably judged. We can be helped in this search by the work of Maslow (Maslow 1970:27–41). In the following section we shall examine how his theories provide further understanding of social breakdown and also lead to a definition of social discomfort.

Social discomfort

Those aspects of Maslow's work that are relevant to the present discussion are continued in his writings on human motivation. In essence, he suggests that there are five sets of goals or basic needs which are arranged in a hierarchy of prepotency: physiological, safety, love, esteem and self-actualization. Maslow claims that once man's 'belly is chronically filled', then other 'higher' needs emerge and dominate the organism: these are the *safety* needs. The 'good society' ordinarily makes its members feel 'safe enough from wild animals, extremes of temperature, criminals, assault and murder, etc.'. Usually the need for safety is active only in emergencies such as 'war, disease, natural catastrophe, crime waves, societal disorganization, neurosis, brain injury, chronically bad situations'. Love needs, esteem needs, and the need for self-actualization in turn only emerge as preceding levels are satisfied. However, Maslow claims that most members of our society who are normal are partially satisfied in all their basic needs at the same time, and that the hierarchy is best described in terms of 'decreasing percentages of satisfaction as we go up the hierarchy of prepotency'.[5]

Despite the roughness of his analysis it still has implications for operational social policy. It is a bold attempt to present a hierarchically stratified theory of basic needs. Perhaps Maslow's theory – undeveloped though it is – may nevertheless breathe life into 'needology', in particular if basic needs are regarded as 'problems'.[6] For, as he pointed out, a satisfied or gratified need may be considered for all practical purposes 'simply not to exist'. So Maslow's hierarchy can be seen as a tentative theory of categorization based on the *severity* of the problem.[7]

It can be suggested, therefore, that in their concern with breakdown, SSDs are coping with the most basic of Maslow's basic needs – the physiological and safety needs. This statement takes us a little further by providing an additional theoretical explanation for the horizontal dimension of SSDs. When however, the physiological and safety needs are contrasted with the 'love' needs, we shall begin to see how the 'severity hierarchy' can be utilized by social policy-makers.

If both the physiological and the safety needs are fairly well gratified, then there will emerge the love and affection and belongingness needs . . . Now the person will feel keenly, as never before, the absence of friends or a sweetheart or a wife or children. (Maslow 1970:31).

I suggest that the phrase *social discomfort* might be useful in describing this group of needs which are less urgent than the physiological or safety needs, and that SSDs are providing services that, whilst they are primarily aimed at some of the problems of breakdown, also cater for *some* citizens whose major problem is social discomfort.

Consider the following example as related in a BBC programme.

Two elderly people were being interviewed after their local authority had decided to withdraw bus passes because of alleged 'abuse'. What, the interviewer asked each one, is the effect on them of the withdrawal of bus passes? In the words of one of those interviewed it was 'as if I had lost a friend'. For the other interviewee, because of her severe physical disabilities, the effect was much more dramatic; in her own graphic description, 'it was as if I was a puppet on a string' (BBC Radio 4, 17 March 1977). Both suffered, but for the former the problems were felt to be those that we have classified as social discomfort. For the latter, withdrawal of bus passes threatened her immediate possibility of independent living. She could be considered to be in a state of social breakdown.[8] This is an example of the same service (bus passes) being provided for two different states of need.

Research in other departments indicates that in several instances *specific* services are being provided for a group of 'clients' who in the main cannot be regarded as in a state of social breakdown. In particular, there exists a rather strange classification called the 'able elderly' (see the study of day care in Part III). What are the implications for recipients and providers of services if more than one category of need is encompassed by the same organization? Does it matter? These issues will be returned to later in this chapter. For the moment the discussion is restricted to the conceptual distinction between breakdown and discomfort.

There are a number of studies which examine that broad problem area which we have described as social discomfort. For example Hadley, Webb and Farrell, in their work with Task Force, provide formidable evidence that, for the particular group of elderly receiving services, 'loneliness' was the most pressing and dominating problem.

Many of those who said they were always or often lonely seemed dominated by the feeling. When the interviewer started asking questions on loneliness the old people often broke down and cried. (Hadley, Webb and Farrell 1975:40).

This, and other studies, suggests some connection between bereavement, the presence of neighbours, and feelings of loneliness. The profile of the typical Task Force client is a widow in her seventies or eighties, living alone in rented property, with one or two friends or neighbours (ibid., 42–4). She is likely, it is suggested, 'to feel lonely sometimes or often and is much more liable to loneliness than people in the elderly population as a whole'. The authors conclude that a 'substantial minority of the elderly population as a whole are isolated in that they had very small networks of meaningful relationships, some were very isolated in that they had no such relationships' (ibid.: 187).

These authors argue that, in addition to the value or ideological reason for state intervention, the true cost of extending the social services may be less than we expect because of the possible postponement of institutional care. Nevertheless, the cost consideration is secondary to the main case for increased domiciliary support – which is 'a merit in its own right' (ibid.: 188). (Whether or not the social services department is, as they suggest, 'the obvious candidate' for the provision of these services, is a theme that we will return to shortly.) However, if isolation *inevitably* leads to breakdown then the case for a separate conceptual category is considerably weakened. If it does *not* necessarily lead to breakdown then the distinction can be maintained with significant policy implications.

For the moment we are content to establish that it makes sense to define a group of problems that broadly flow from conditions such as bereavement, and this category can – *in its own right* – be the most pressing problem that an individual faces at a particular period. If this division into two distinct categories (social breakdown and social discomfort) is persuasive then we have moved a considerable way towards the replacement of our starting phrase 'the prevention of social distress'. There remains the task of examining 'prevention' in order that the entire early definition might be abandoned.

'Prevention'

'Prevention' is a much favoured political slogan. There is scarcely a report or Act on welfare topics that does not claim this desirable objective as an integral part of the proposed changes (for example Home Office *et al.* 1968; Home Office 1963 DHSS 1976 Phoebe Hall 1976). The desire for 'prevention' may be seen as part of that same search for permanence discussed in Part I. An increase in 'preventive work', it is claimed or hinted at, will lead to a decrease in those problems that the agency was established to resolve. It is an irresistible slogan of almost universal appeal. But whilst it has great appeal the concept also presents a considerable dilemma for the servants of welfare bureaucracies. If both problems (social distress) and some pre-problem stage called preventive work are included in the same agency boundary, there would appear to be a built-in predisposition for conflict. Time spent working with breakdown situations (such as residential care) must compete on theoretically unfavourable terms with the more attractive goal of prevention. Why bother with a theory that resolves only today's crises when an alternative 'theory of prevention' will stop or at least reduce the future flow of breakdown? The two theories must fight for dominance. Money and time spent on breakdown conditions represent that much less available resources for prevention. What should be the agency's priorities? Is 'preventive work' the 'same' as working with the inevitable crises? And a main question for the theme of this chapter: does the earlier distinction between social breakdown and social discomfort have relevance for the critical debate on the nature of prevention?

Despite its inclusion as a desirable objective in most social welfare legislation, there is probably general agreement that 'prevention' is used vaguely in this context. It is to the field of health that social welfare casts its most envious glances. There, the three concepts of primary, secondary and tertiary prevention are widely used. Their validity and utility in the health setting cannot occupy our attention here, but it can be noted that welfare administrators have not been able to transfer these definitions to the area of social distress. The Seebohm Committee preferred to adopt the concept of *specific* and *general* prevention. The latter was defined as:

Community-wide policies aimed at creating environments conducive to social well-being by improving work opportunities and conditions, by ensuring reasonable standards of living or educational attainment. (para 434).

The Committee provided two examples of general prevention, housing and services for the under-fives (nurseries, playgroups, home helps to families, family planning services). The extent to which certain of these examples fall within the definition of general prevention might be questioned, but the central issue is whether the whole category can be considered to be 'preventive'. Do the services not answer needs (housing, health, education, etc.) in their own right? The discussion is not merely semantic. It can be argued that failure to clarify what problems are actually being resolved, by subsuming them within some giant 'preventive umbrella', leads to confusion in agency boundaries and piecemeal service provision. Ill-health, homelessness, inadequate income, poor educational opportunities, isolation, all merit comprehensive organizational responses. It is difficult to appreciate the logic, or the benefits to clients, of the same action in response to need being considered as 'preventive' when undertaken by an SSD, and yet, as in the case of homelessness, 'merely' mainstream work when undertaken by the housing department. But in the light of the British experience at least, the whole argument that SSDs should be, or have become, involved in 'general prevention' sounds hollow. Departments are primarily engaged in coping with social breakdown. Indeed, it can be argued that the pursuit of this elusive goal – general prevention – distracts attention from their prime work.

It is the second of these definitions – specific prevention – which is of more interest. This is defined in Seebohm as:

Services focused specifically upon certain individuals or families at high risk to forestall distress for them or reduce its effects and its severity. (para 434).

Further examination of the notion of specific prevention shows that it is used to include a number of distinct situations: (i) individuals or families with problems; (ii) individuals or families 'at risk'; and (iii) individuals or families in 'at risk' areas. In fact categories (i) and (ii) are used interchangeably in the Report, and whilst in the paragraph quoted above there is a clear statement about services with the 'at risk' that will or might 'forstall' distress, the following paragraph speaks of the 'at risk' – 'whose problems are likely to generate further and more profound difficulties' (para 435). Later we find a plea for more help 'during periods when an individual or family passes through a transitional epoch and has to make *radical changes* in roles, adjustments and attitudes' (para 452). Clear examples are given – 'the school-leaver, the family in the early stages of formation, the worker approaching retirement, the bereaved wife or husband, and the discharged long-term prisoner' (para 452). Doubtless there are many other examples of periods of 'considerable change' which could have been added to a list which anyway – if it were to be given serious consideration – might place most of us as 'clients' three or four times in our lives!

In addition to those who clearly have severe problems (category i), and those in at-risk situations (category ii), a third category of 'preventive' work is identified which fits neither the community-wide nor the two specific preventive categories identified so far. It is 'community development' – 'a process whereby local groups are assisted to clarify and express their needs and objectives and to take collective action to attempt to meet them' (para 480). Community development is linked to the notion of areas of special needs – of 'problem areas'. The same question can be asked of community development as of general prevention. What are the problems that are actually being tackled? Do these problems sit easily within the work of SSDs?

Two objections to the 'preventionist case' have so far been presented.[9] One is that within SSDs the inclusion of work called 'preventive', together with work dealing with current problems, must lead to a conflict of interests and confusion over the priorities. Secondly, we claimed that much, and possibly all, of the work regarded as prevention is in fact a response to needs that should be tackled by their rightful names, be they problems of homelessness, education, poverty or whatever. These needs ought not to have to hide behind the skirts of prevention in order to be met.

Other objections have been raised by critics of the preventive arguments in other social policy settings. Illich has mounted a powerful broadside against what he calls the preventive 'disease-hunt' in medicine:

Diagnosis always identifies stress, defines incapacity, imposes inactivity, and focuses apprehension on non-recovery, on uncertainty, and on one's dependence on future medical findings, all of which amounts to a loss of autonomy for self-definition. It also isolates a person in a special role, separates him from the normal and healthy, and requires submission to the authority of specialized personnel. Once a society organizes for a preventive disease-hunt, it gives epidemic proportions to diagnosis. (Illich 1976:96).

Despite the difference in setting we might be ill-advised not to consider the parallels in the area of social welfare.

Cohen has raised serious doubts about so-called 'self evident' and 'well-established' beliefs in the field of penal policy. Amongst these he questions the notion that the causes of most forms of deviance are in society, and that 'therefore' prevention and cure must lie in the community and not in artificially created agencies constructed on a model of individual intervention (1979). He identifies three main problem areas of 'community' control: blurring, widening, and masking. Once again, there are interesting parallels for social welfare. Briefly, *blurring* refers to the increasing invisibility of the boundaries of the social control apparatus; *widening* describes the additions of new programmes which supplement or expand the system by attracting new populations; and *masking* concerns the way in which 'the benevolently intentioned move to the community may sometimes disguise the intrusiveness of the new programmes'. What Cohen describes as 'blurring' is of particular relevance for our present discussion. Intermediate treatment is used to illustrate the confusion caused by the community control movement's ideology of unclear boundaries. Thus, 'it is by no means clear where the prison ends and the community begins, or why anybody is to be found at any particular point'. He points out that the same treatment is used for those who have actually committed an offence and those who are thought 'at risk' of committing an offence. In the case of intermediate treatment the border between 'flexibility' and 'confusion' is dangerously fragile (Billis 1976).

Perhaps the most serious case against prevention is the weakness of the line from the theories to the problems they are supposed to resolve. 'Prevention', in any of its definitions, has meaning only if an unambiguous causal link can be posited between problem and effect. Does intervention in one form or another really solve the problem? (Once again, we are not arguing against intervention *per se* but the clarification of *what* problems are actually being resolved.) Thus 'preventionists' have claimed – as for example in the Task Force study – that relieving problems of isolation and that group of 'love needs' which we called social discomfort, should be part of the work of SSDs, because it would reduce more severe problems.[10] But if

Maslow's theory of the hierarchy of needs is valid, then satisfaction of social discomfort needs will lead to the emergence of the next need for esteem. Thus, according to this theory, the resolution of problems of social discomfort where those are the most pressing needs, will not necessarily reduce more severe problems.

We can now summarize the two alternative and competing theories of the appropriate work boundary for SSDs. The first we might continue to call the 'preventive' theory, although appropriation of this name – given the desire for optimism – may incorrectly invest it with an aura of the preferred choice. According to this standpoint, society has at its disposal theories which link a variety of pre-breakdown situations. Individuals and groups can be 'at risk' by virtue of making radical changes in role or by living in at-risk areas. Generally, the dominant 'preventive' theory is, however, that which suggests that SSDs should be dealing both with individuals facing social breakdown problems and a particular form of need which we have described as social discomfort.

In this section I have put forward an alternative theory which sees the main thrust aimed at coping with social breakdown by meeting physical and safety needs. The theory is given greater strength by positing a time boundary on the judgements made. In the following section we shall examine the extent to which this theory of social breakdown illuminates the boundary between governmental and non-governmental intervention.

Statutory and voluntary welfare bureaucracies

The analytical distinction made between social breakdown and social discomfort may help to illuminate the vexed question of the boundaries between the statutory and voluntary provision of welfare services. The nature of non-governmental voluntary agencies is now rightly receiving greater attention. Yet, despite the appearance of the 'Wolfenden' Report and the incresed research interest in the voluntary sector as a whole, knowledge of this important field of activity is scant (Wolfenden Committee 1978). Consequently, we shall restrict the discussion to brief comments about the present problems and the relevance of the concept of social breakdown to those problems

Politicians of all parties, spurred on by financial stringency, continually affirm the benefits of voluntary involvement in the welfare service. Why then, as is well documented, should statutory/voluntary interaction be so fraught?[11] Might the difficulties flow from unclarity surrounding the horizontal boundaries of the two sorts of agency? Can we indentify work that might be intrinsically appropriate for voluntary activity? So far, little headway has been made in discovering any such area. The Wolfenden Committee in its review of the role and functions of voluntary organizations states that 'the absence of systematic studies during the past 20 years is notable'. The Committee suggests that a key reason for our lack of knowledge is that 'the voluntary sector, however one chooses to define it, lacks clear-cut boundaries'. The problem is not resolved by the Report which prefers 'to place the voluntary sector in a broad context by distinguishing it from . . . the informal, the statutory and the commercial systems'. An earlier report from the Personal Social Services Council puts the matter bluntly:

We do not have a clear picture of what the voluntary contribution is, could be, or should be. (Webb, Day and Weller 1976).

This certainly seems a widely accepted representation.[12] Whilst, as we have already stated, full explication of the contribution of the voluntary sector awaits further research, it may be fruitful to approach the problem with the aid of the 'hierarchy of needs'.

It appears that, looking at the category which has been defined as social breakdown, there exists what might be described as a desire for a high degree of public accountability. In its crudest and most minimal form it is to be found in the unwillingness of advanced industrial societies to permit their citizens to rot on the streets or to endanger other citizens. Basic safety needs – of the individual and of those with whom he interacts – are regarded as the duty of one or other level of government. Children, above all, must be protected, and in their case the boundary is continually stretched until we have indeed the concept of a 'continuùm of care' (see chapter 13 for references to the concept of 'intermediate' treatment). As Wilensky and Lebeaux point out:

There is usually less resistence to investment in growth . . . the main handicap of the children of the poor is that they chose the wrong parents. And the chance of salvaging the child of the slum is perhaps greater than that of rescuing his parents. (Wilensky and Lebeaux 1965: xii).

The social breakdown of the 'normal' elderly is also regarded as a public responsibility. Here too the notion of prevention has reached out to embrace wider and wider groups.[13] We can thus make at least one generalization, and that is that the breakdown of members of society who are regarded as 'normal' is likely to be regarded by governmental agencies as very much their business. They will wish either to control directly or to have a strong monitoring mechanism over the bureaucracies coping with mainstream social breakdown. Governments might wish to manage these organizations themselves or to sub-contract the problem to the really 'solid' non-governmental bureaucracies whose public status and reliability are assured. Even in countries such as the Netherlands which have a tradition of private non-governmental welfare bureaucracies, vigorous measures are taken by government to ensure both minimum standards and strong links by virtue of financial support systems (see Kramer 1981: 19–35).

But there are a whole line of difficult classes of problems that fall within the definition of breakdown but that occupy an uneasy border territory between statutory and voluntary agencies. These are the problem categories that are in some way abnormal. They are, for example, the breakdown cases that drink too much, take the wrong sort of drugs, or get beaten up by their husbands. Drug addicts, alcoholics, battered wives – these are the sorts of groups that inhabit this particular border territory and where we can expect to find active voluntary involvement.

Other groups of the distressed are the victims of a different form of definitional warfare – in this case between the breakdown bureaucracies themselves. Who, for example, should be responsible for the mentally handicapped in residential care? The Jay Report presents another example of suggested change based on changing definitions of the nature of the problem.[14]

We might sum up so far by arguing that boundary problems (between state and voluntary sectors) are most likely to arise when parts of the latter sector enter the accepted, mainstream, high public accountability social breakdown field. As public definitions of what is regarded as breakdown change, so too will the interaction between the state and the direct-service voluntary organizations change. (Given that 'there is no guarantee that voluntary effort will necessarily materialize where need is greatest' (Wolfenden Committee 1978); there is a strong case for proposing that comprehensive coverage of social breakdown ought to be the responsibility of the state sector.

If the burden of social breakdown is to fall primarily on the statutory agencies, what distinctive role is there for voluntary welfare bureaucracies? It is here that the concept of social discomfort may be useful. Whilst this is a less urgent state of need, there is every reason why such need should be met. But is there any convincing argument that such needs could, or ought to, be met comprehensively by the state? The need for belongingness or love is real enough. It should be met by services and appropriate resources. It is important work in its own right. Perhaps it might more usefully be regarded as genuine 'welfare'. Do people whose most pressing, urgent need is social discomfort require their problems assessed and diagnosed by public servants? Might not this field of need be distinctive, appropriate and rewarding for voluntary welfare bureaucracies? But there remains to consider the unanswered question: does the clarification really matter?

Does it matter?

Explication of the categorization of welfare lies at the heart of social policy; it permits critical discussion and the development of alternative theories which still remain rooted in the attempt to solve the orginal problem. Theories of social policy can and do flourish in isolation from the direct field of action. But at some stage – if they are to contribute to the resolution of social problems – they must come down to earth and be capable of implementation.

There are additional reasons why clarification has a direct impact on service provision. For clients and staff of the bureaucracy it matters a great deal whether the nature of work is, or is not, made explicit. The less clear the definition, the more victims there may be of that border warfare referred to earlier. Vast numbers of people in trouble are involved in the disputes and, whilst we must accept that there will always be muddy and changing areas, there is no reason to accept the present dimension of the confusion. Research over many years in SSDs shows that as far as the elderly are concerned, for example, it is often a matter of chance whether they remain in the community and whether they get day care and domiciliary services, or whether they enter residential homes or hospitals.[15]

The identification of a new category – such as social discomfort – can also serve to sharpen discussion about the nature and extent of existing services. Thus, SSDs are providing a number of distinct services which are *mainly* geared to meet discomfort needs: typical examples are lunch clubs, certain work centres, holidays and outings, bus passes, playgroups, nurseries, telephones, TVs, good neighbour schemes, and some intermediate treatment schemes. The distinctive feature of these services is that they primarily facilitate meeting, talking, listening to other people; that is to say, they increase the possibilities for 'belonging'.

By meeting the less urgent discomfort as well as breakdown needs, agencies can appear in a more optimistic aura. They can appear to shed the reality of their work and gain political backing; for many breakdown clients carry little political clout whereas 'preventive work' offers a brighter future. We might repeat here our previous assertion that claims for 'prevention' have tended to take professional priority over breakdown cases if they are co-existing within the same department.[16] However, the fundamental dilemma for the agency is that it cannot shed its breakdown work. Coverage of discomfort or other non-social breakdown needs may thus be sporadic and partial although often launched with much publicity and banner waving. Those citizens in social discomfort – who receive services from the breakdown agencies – will need luck on their side.

Disentanglement of discomfort from breakdown reveals the SSD *déshabillé* in its early morning reality. Are the elderly in need who are most buffeted by the definitional tensions well served in the present situation? How long will discomfort clients continue to get even the present modest services if they have to compete in the same department with the more urgent cases?

So to answer the opening question of this section, clarification – painful though it can often be – matters. It matters to staff at all levels in the bureaucracy. It matters to the agency and the community. It matters above all to those at the receiving end.

Summary

This chapter has been devoted to an exploration of the categorization of 'welfare' as exemplified by the case of SSDs. It was contended that *social breakdown* (the loss of independence within an explicit period of time) could usefully replace vaguer terms such as 'social distress'.

Social breakdown was then distinguished from *social discomfort* (the need for love, affection, and belongingness), and the question was raised whether the latter inevitably led to the former. Following a problem-based approach, the reality of so-called 'preventive work' was examined, an issue which I have discussed in detail elsewhere (Billis 1981a).

Having defined social breakdown and social distress and raised doubts about the validity of *prevention* in social services work, the chapter concluded with a few thoughts on the boundary between the statutory and voluntary sectors. Is social breakdown being comprehensively responded to by the State? Is social discomfort a viable activity for the voluntary sector?

Finally, a few comments about categorization. In this part of the book we shall not pursue further the details of the turmoil in this horizontal dimension. In Part III categorization issues appear in several of the case studies. These are perhaps sufficient to indicate both their importance and the difficulties of analysis.

In the next few chapters we move on to present in more detail a tentative theory of the vertical (level of work) dimension, an area which has attracted less attention but which is of substantial interest if usable models of organizational structure are to be achieved.

Notes

1. At the time of writing this chapter, the *Barclay Report* (NISW 1982) had just been published.
2. See DHSS (1979). The Report noted that only a handful of the officers-in-charge of the 124 Homes visited considered that the task might include a 'rehabilitative aspect' – and few mention the 'encouragement of independence'. It notes that 95% of officers-in-charge and most other senior

staff have a nursing qualification. Is it surprising that nurses expect to nurse rather than 'encourage independence'?

3. Here I have in mind, as one example, the case of a research officer in an SSD who was also expected to spend half his time doing community work. This mixture of activities was abandoned in the light of the very different nature of the two areas of work. Another example is of an office-manager in a voluntary agency attempting to undertake visits and counsel clients. Small organizations, of course, appear to have little choice but to combine many activities in one role. Work so far with small voluntary organizations indicates, however, that they sometimes have more possibilities than can appear at first sight, e.g. services can be bought in or part-time staff employed rather than tacking on a wide variety of activities to one role.

4. Early research noted that the phrase 'social distress' is the best we have: '. . . to distinguish a certain sort of need from what is customarily classified as physical or mental health on the one hand, or on the other from those personal problems which have not yet reached the point where the social functioning of the person concerned had fallen below what at any time is regarded as a generally acceptable level' (Brunel Institute of Organisation and Social Studies, Social Services Organisation Research Unit 1974: Table 3.1).

5. Maslow's exceptions must be noted, in particular his hypothesis about 'increased frustration toleration through early gratification', e.g. that satisfaction of basic needs in the early years can lead to exceptional power to withstand present or future thwarting of these needs (1970:37).

6. Maslow's ideas may be contrasted to much of the current literature on need. For example, Nevitt who declares that: 'Apart from the most basic need for nourishment there are no overriding physical or sociological laws which will pre-determine the identification and selection of needs.' (Nevitt 1977:123). Indeed, she feels that since needs 'are only goods and services without price tags, there is little that social scientists can do with the concept' (p.127). Other authors have suggested that whilst 'academic commentators' might argue whether the concept is useful, 'for the decision-maker considering the question "What is need?" becomes unavoidable' (Jones *et al.* 1978:42). However, the same authors point out that 'the difficulty is in obtaining a consensus as to what constitute appropriate criteria by which needs can be ranked relative to one another' (p. 26). Neither of these commentators appear to utilize need as a helpful concept. See also Bebbington and Davies (1980). For a discussion of need from a marxist standpoint see Taylor-Gooby and Dale 1981: chapter 8).

7. The question might be raised as to whether failure to satisfy the 'less severe' needs, such as self-actualization can lead to breakdown. Despite the fact that inability to 'self-actualize' does apparently cause breakdown, it might be argued that this takes place only in societies that have more or less satisfied the basic needs of their communities. The response therefore to these 'higher level' breakdowns might be different; that is to say, non-governmental.

8. I am ignoring the question of assessment, and assuming that 'felt need' matches 'normative need' (see Bradshaw 1972).

9. We are all probably 'preventionists'. I am using the phrase to describe

those who claim that intervention in 'pre-problem' stages of social distress (in at-risk, situations, areas, or general prevention) will almost certainly reduce social distress.

10. More recent writers, such as the authors of the majority Barclay Report, continue to argue the virtues of prevention; this time the panacea is 'community social work' (National Institute for Social Work 1982).

11. In particular the publications of the Volunteer Centre; see Darville (1975) and Bruce and Darville (1976). The position in Scottish Social Work Departments appears similar. See the report by Ann Mitchell (1977). She refers to the 'insecurity' felt by some officers who 'are anxious about the dileneation of their own duties' (para 8.4).

12. However, at the time of writing there has been a spate of publications discussing the centrality of the voluntary sector in welfare provision; for example, Gladstone (1979); Hatch (1980); Hadley and Hatch (1981); Webb (1981); and Kramer (1981).

13. I am not ignoring the effects of the present economic recession. These ideas were in fact developed during the expansionist period of SSDs. They may be even less practical now, but they still dominate social policy. See, for example, Baker (1979).

14. As the Committee state quite clearly, 'Our answer to the problems of mental handicap residential care is contained in our model of the way in which society should respond to the mentally handicapped individual.' (Report of the Committee of Enquiry into Mental Handicap, Nursing and Care: 376).

15. This statement is based on project work and numerous interviews with staff dealing with these problems over the last nine years. It is commonplace to hear senior staff admit, for example, that there are still many residents in care who could have remained in the community. For a recent sad account of the problem see Goodlove, Richard and Rodwell (1981).

16. Research seems to support this contention. Thus, Holme and Maizels (1978: 131–2) show that social workers operate 'two systems of status hierarchy . . . low status client groups are allocated to the lowest ranks in the social services hierarchy'.

5 The Bureaucratic Grassroots

Irrespective of political system, large-scale organization appears to result in the well-known pyramid or hierarchic form of organization. Despite the search for alternatives most employment work is carried out within such structures (see chapter 1 and Tannenbaum *et al.* 1974). It is only a minority of the workforce who find themselves within non-hierarchical frameworks such as family businesses, partnerships, and co-operatives. The bureaucratization of the 'breakdown' business or, to put it more delicately, the development of human service agencies, has led to the establishment of similar hierarchical structures.

Perhaps not surprisingly, welfare bureaucracies have encountered considerable difficulties in handling the machinery of problem-solving. Bureaupathology can strike ruthlessly at 'mutual benefit associations', business concerns' 'service organizations' or 'commonweal organizations' (Blau and Scott 1963). It can permeate organizations staffed by social scientists or engineers. In small face-to-face organizations employing a dozen or so staff, problems may often be seen in personality terms. As, or if, organizations grow in size, it is easier to identify what problems are truly personal and what lie at a deeper, structural level. Recent research indicates that employees of small-scale voluntary organizations do not live in a problemless, organizational Garden of Eden.[1]

In chapter 4 we illustrated the nature of categorization by analysing the work of SSDs. Now we turn to the vertical boundary and face the immediate question of the absence of a generally accepted language which could serve as a basis for critical discussion. The customary organizational language is often crude. Thus, as the 'bottom' of the heap are to be found workers generally described as at the 'grassroots', on the 'shopfloor', in the 'frontline', at the 'coalface', and so on. Next, that vague group lumped together under the title of 'middle management'. Finally, 'top or senior management'. These three descriptions are not adequate for a serious analysis of hierarchical organization.

A more sophisticated analysis is attempted in the work of Tannenbaum who defines 'hierarchical position' according to the number of persons directly above an individual in the chain of command. Thus, social work assistants might easily be depicted as having at least six people above them in the formal SSD organization chart (see chapter

7). But, as the authors admit, there are a number of 'complications' which have to be met by further 'scores'. The criticism that may be made of this piece of valuable comparative international research is not dealt with by the various 'scoring' mechanisms. The authors 'rely on the official definition of the respondents' position, [however] in some cases respondents did not agree with the chart' (Tannenbaum *et al.* 1974). Those conversant with the usual high level of dissonance to be found in any organization between personal and so-called 'official' organization charts will be sceptical of the ease with which the researchers dismiss this problem.

In this chapter we shall endeavour to explore further the first two levels of work. The objective is to provide fuller definitions of the bureaucratic grassroots as a prelude to a consideration of several major social policy issues. The chapter contains explanations of:

● Stratum 1 where problems are taken as demands; and
● Stratum 2 where problems are treated as situations.

It continues with:

● a definition of the *client impact level*; and
● an analysis and models of the *initial impact* on clients.

Stratum 1 – problems as demands

Before describing the first level of work we must be careful to distinguish (at least) between (i) *job titles*, and the like; (ii) the work that is *actually* being performed; (iii) the personal *capacity* of the worker; (iv) the work that the organization *expects* to be performed. These distinctions will need to be borne in mind throughout. It is not restricted just to this description of Work Stratum 1. It is evident that the following discussion is not exhaustive, but it is hoped that it draws attention to the possible pitfalls.

Some titles are more misleading than others. For example, the title 'social work assistant' should be approached with caution. It seems to imply that the incumbent is expected to 'assist' someone in doing something – and to that extent may hint at a lower level of work than social work or the social worker. But research into what social work assistants are actually doing indicates that this is not so at an individual level, and that furthermore the organization may have very different expectations. Thus, it is not unusual to discover that not only are their titles misleading, but what they are actually doing, what senior management (if they have thought the matter through) expect them to do, and what they are capable of doing are all in disequilibrium (see, for example, Stevenson and Parsloe 1978; Holme and Maizels 1978; Parsloe 1981).

Other titles, particularly outside the welfare bureaucracies, may be more homogeneous and give a fairly accurate indication of the complexity of work both expected and performed. For example ticket collectors, bus drivers, machine operators, bank tellers, shop assistants, typists, assembly workers, porters, gas and electricity meter readers, refuse collectors, caretakers, car park attendants, postmen, telephonists, cleaners, guards, etc. The flavour of the work that these titles conjure up is of activities which are fairly 'straightforward', 'routine', or static'. Although it should be emphasized that these adjectives do less than justice to many of the jobs listed, which require lengthy periods of training, are highly skilled and demand considerable sensitivity. Nevertheless, *in most cases* – even in these examples which have been chosen deliberately to minimize ambiguity, this cautionary phrase must be added – the title accurately reflects both the organizationally expected *and* actual work. These are but a few examples of a massive area of work where *what* is to be done in terms of the kind or form of result to be achieved does not (or cannot) be decided by the worker. The problems that they are expected to resolve are regarded as demands.

The binding characteristic of Stratum 1 work is that the output is prescribed. The driver of the agency minibus is expected to arrive at the local day centre on time. The driver is expected to provide a safe and comfortable journey to a designated place. He will also, of course, be expected to have an understanding and supportive approach to his passengers. Drivers are not usually expected to make evaluations of clients' personal and social position and to recommend alternative services or therapy. Likewise, bank tellers are expected to receive and pay out money. We would look rather oddly at the teller who, when presented with a cheque to cash, proceeded to provide advice about the state of the customer's personal finances. We might also be startled if a typist from the pool returned our draft letter to a client or other agency with a suggestion that we would be unwise to send it given the current problems that the intended recipient was facing. This says nothing about the *capacities* of the individual workers who may well be capable of solving these and other problems of greater complexity. What is being suggested is that we deliberately construct enterprises where much, if not most, of the work is *expected* to be at this stratum.

The concept of Stratum 1 work can be expressed slightly differently by stating that *we know what the end-product is going to look like, before we start*. In many instances, such as in manufacturing, the end-product is tangible and is easily seen or envisaged. But there are large numbers of people engaged in Stratum 1 work in the public and private sector where, although the end-product is not tangible, it can be described in such detail as to make no difference to that end-product. Thus, the driver of our minibus is expected to produce a pleasant journey within the constraints, such as the rush hour, over which he is generally agreed to have no control. One journey to the day centre ought to be much like another, irrespective of the driver. If necessary, the upper boundary to Stratum 1 work could be described in a handbook which would guarantee an output identical, to all intents and purposes, to that of any other output in that category.

Although the output is prescribed, *the work as a whole is not prescribed*. Once again, a glance at the previous examples provide evidence of Stratum 1 work where significant discretion is called for within the prescribed output boundary. Our drivers, for example, will have their own *methods* of organizing their work; what speed to drive at to ensure a comfortable journey, how to handle the anxious or difficult passengers, and so on. It is because such discretion does exist that the word 'stratum' was originally chosen as the most appropriate to describe a distinct layer of work within which there would exist the possibility (if required) of distinguishing finer gradings of personal responsibility. Furthermore, although Stratum 1 workers are expected to work within the prescribed output boundary, it is often the case that they may also be expected to draw attention to 'unusual' or 'emergency' situations.

The construction of organizations where the expectation is that certain work will be at Stratum 1, also makes a fundamental statement about the way in which it is hoped that responses will be made to problems and, for the purpose of our discussion, social problems in particular. For, prescribed output work involves an expectation that (social) problems will be responded to as demands. And that these demands are isolated and repetitive. We return to this central theme when the full array of alternative responses to social problems is discussed in chapter 7. For the moment, prescribed output work might be depicted as in Figure 5.1.

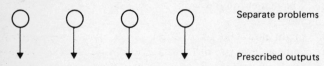

Figure 5.1   *Prescribed output work*

Stratum 2 – problems as situations
In the previous section it was claimed that it is possible to describe a stratum of work which is distinctly and qualitatively different from other work. We also emphasized that 'expected work', which forms

part of the structural dimension of a role, must not be confused with the actual performance or capacity of an individual in role, and that this in turn needs to be differentiated from the title of the role. Thus, in the case of social work assistants it was noted that the title could be misleading, since:

● the level of work that the organization *expected* them to do was not necessarily
● what they were *actually* doing, nor
● what they were *capable* of doing.[2]

It will now be argued that Stratum 2 work represents a conceptually different response to problems. That is to say, that the problems are not regarded as demands but as situations whose 'real needs' have to be investigated, assessed, appraised and judged. The binding characteristic of Stratum 2 work is (unlike Stratum 1) that we do not know beforehand precisely what the end-product of the work is going to look like. The very language of Stratum 2 is different and, whilst titles must still be approached with caution, they will usually, when referring to this level of work, not give the same impression of 'straightforwardness' that was observed in the discussion of Stratum 1 titles. This can be illustrated by looking at some of the examples given earlier, this time providing a Stratum 2 response.

We can confidently propose that when constructing the role of 'bank manager' there is envisaged an expected response to problems which is different from that of the bank teller. It might be assumed that the manager who responded in the fashion described as that expected of Stratum 1 would get short shrift from senior management. When approached for a loan the manager would be expected to investigate the relevant business and personal finances of his client, discuss the nature of his business, assess his ability to repay the loan and give broader financial advice. We (as the customer) and the bank (as the employer) *expect* the bank manager to respond in such a fashion. (It may be that bank managers are expected to work at higher levels; I have met too few in either a personal or professional capacity to comment.)

We might now take an example of a problem and illustrate how there can be at least two different responses. I have a severe headache. My GP isn't available, or I do not think it important enough to bother him; so I seek help from the local chemist shop. What response can I expect from the chemist's assistant behind the counter? (Let us assume that the chemist is not available, since this raises issues precisely of the sort that would repay examination at a later stage.) Well, from the person behind the counter I might reasonably expect to be informed which of the standard proprietary brands are in stock and how much they cost. With luck, I might also get a sympathetic word or look. Should I venture to ask which is the 'best' product for my particular ailment, I might either receive a somewhat embarrassed response or one that told me that 'they are all pretty good, but X – so they say – seems to be good value for money'. Chemist's assistants are not employed to diagnose individual needs. But should I now decide to approach my GP, I would hope to receive a very different response. What is the real nature of my headache? How long have I been suffering? Do I normally wear glasses? What is my emotional and physical state? Neither I nor the doctor can be certain when I enter the surgery, what will be the outcome of the visit; but I expect a response to my problem very different from that of the chemist's assistant. Once again, as in the example of the bank manager, all that is being claimed is that the expected work of the doctor is *at least* at Stratum 2 Such evidence as does exist points to the possibility that their work is probably at a higher level. But the main purpose at the moment is to demonstrate the difference from Stratum 1 work.

Thus, Stratum 2 work is concerned with judging the 'real' problem as distinct from the 'presenting' problem of those both external *and* internal to the organization. Externally, the problem will be those of clients, customers, patients, tenants – all those in fact who receive the outputs of the organization. Internally, situational responses may be expected in relation both to organizational problems and to subordinate members of staff. The expectation to respond in a situational response manner to other members of staff – to appraise their performance and ability, to understand their real needs – is an essential part of what has been defined as a *managerial* role.[3] Whilst we shall return to these issues in detail in chapter 8, we might here make a firm proposition of considerable importance in the design and analysis of organizations. *Managerial roles can only begin to emerge at this Stratum.* A managerial role can only be constructed at Stratum 2 (as illustrated in Figure 5.2), which necessitates explicitly responding to problems as

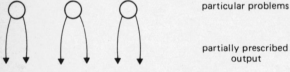

particular problems

partially prescribed
output

Figure 5.2   Situational response work

if they were 'individuals' with properties distinguishing them from other problems (or cases) in the category. Stratum 2 problems may be said to have an individual identity.[4] An important element of the managerial role is the requirement to 'judge' and 'assess' the performance of subordinates. Wilfred Brown points out that:

judging the performance of subordinates . . . is a very important part of the work of all managers. If assessment work is not done properly excellent subordinates fail to get increases of pay or promotion, inadequate subordinates stay in their roles too long, subordinates are left in a state of anxiety . . . in one way and another a great deal of tension, anxiety and even conflict, is generated. (1971: 79).

The development of the Work Strata theory has thrown new light on the place of managers in bureaucracies; the 'Stratum 1 manager' – it is postulated – will be a will-o'-the-wisp. Furthermore, we shall see that the theory offers an explanation for the chronic problem of the interaction between senior social workers and 'fully-fledged' social workers.

Basic expected work: the client impact level

In this section I shall introduce the concept of 'Basic Expected Work' in the belief that it may assist in an examination of several social policy issues.

Basic Expected Work (BEW) is defined as the minimum acceptable level of work of the organization, occupation or professional group. 'Acceptable' refers to the stratum of work sanctioned and expected by the governing body of the group concerned. BEW is not necessarily the same as the *lowest* stratum of work. These points, and the utility of the concept, need further elaboration.

In welfare bureaucracies, BEW may be regarded as the 'client impact level.[5] It is to be uncovered by asking the question: what is the organization's *expected* stratum of response to client problems? It is the 'public face' of the organized group. In manufacturing industry, BEW is often what is meant when talking about the 'coal face' or the 'front line' – Stratum 1 work concerned with the production of tangible products. In the field of social policy, answers to the question are far from easy. In the first place it can readily be seen that the impact level is not necessarily the lowest level of work in the welfare bureaucracy. The case of the experienced, 'fully-fledged' social worker, and the social work assistant, can be taken to illustrate this point. Let us assume that the client impact level of social work is, at least, at Stratum 2. That is to say that what Harriett Bartlett calls 'professional judgement' is being used.

In a profession the complexity and variability of the situations to be dealt with require the exercise of individual judgement by the practitioner in each new situation. Such judgement is a key operation in any profession (1970:140).

One model of the social worker/social work assistant interaction would then be where the assistant is, as the name suggests, working within boundaries set by the professional judgement of the social worker (who in turn in SSDs works within higher level boundaries). The assistant is then expected to perform prescribed output work with case accountability firmly in the hands of the social worker. So, whilst the lowest level of work with the client is Stratum 1, the impact levels may be said to be at Stratum 2, as illustrated in Figure 5.3.

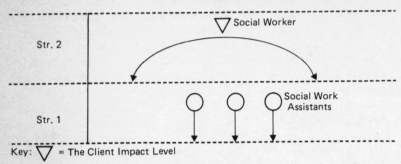

Key: ▽ = The Client Impact Level

Figure 5.3   A model of social worker/social worker assistant interaction

A similar distinction is, I believe, being made by John Cypher in his discussion of 'specialization'. He points out that:

> whereas many social workers will have been involved with the wide range of client needs at the stage of initial enquiries and, perhaps, in the making of preliminary assessments, nevertheless, given the number of cases which remain unallocated or are allocated to non-social work or assistant staff, *the actual provision of social work, in the sense of a full programme of skilled assessment, intervention and termination,* is more usually available only to children and their families. (1980:82; emphasis added).

Cypher's 'actual provision' is similar to my concept of *client impact*. It involves, in this example, case accountability remaining with the social worker and this in turn, as this author notes, requires work at all the points of assessment, intervention and termination. In passing we might draw attention to the allied problem of doctor-nurse relationships. Thus:

> Where a nurse participates in the process of abortion by medical induction, the treatment is nevertheless conducted by a registered medical practitioner as long as the process is initiated by a registered medical practitioner who remains responsible throughout for its conduct and control in the sense that any actions needed to bring it to a conclusion are done by appropriately skilled staff acting on his specific instructions, and he or another registered medical practitioner is available to be called if required. (*The Times*, 'Law Report', Queen's Bench Division, 10 November 1980).

This discussion of the relationship between social workers and assistants is obviously much simplified, and ignores the controversial problems raised by the absence of the horizontal boundary and an analysis of the activities in the social work role. However, for the purposes of the present discussion, it is sufficient to emphasize that the concept of BEW opens up the possibility of debating the actual strata of service being provided to the different categories of clients. What do we expect (and claim) our bureaucracies are doing in their interaction with clients? What are they actually doing? Even without entering a substantive debate there is now ample evidence to indicate that different client groups receive different responses.[6]

In concluding this description of the client impact level a final word of explanation is necessary before moving on to see how the concept operates in the context of reception and duty. It is not being claimed that a Stratum 2 client impact is 'better' than a Stratum 1 response; it is merely *different*. On the contrary, it can be argued that there are very good reasons (of equity and efficiency) that lead to a Stratum 1 impact being the preferred model. My main concern is to demonstrate that there *are* conceptually different responses and that these different responses can be shown to have their own implications, not only for the clients but also for the recruitment, training, and career development of staff, and for the control of their work.

The initial impact on clients
In SSDs many clients have become clients by virtue of passing through the reception and duty system of area teams. These systems vary even within the same department and numerous people receive services without passing through such a system. Nevertheless, the reception and duty system is a cardinal feature of departmental organization. If the concept of BEW is to prove useful, it ought to shed some light on the exploration of these initial impact systems. The descriptive account of duty officers in the Stevenson and Parsloe study, and Tony Hall's pre-Seebohm research into reception, provides the material for the following attempt at an interpretation in terms of work strata (Hall 1971:25–42).[7]

Hall utilized (with slight amendments) the Glacier concepts of manifest, assumed, extant, and requisite, in order to examine the operation of a local authority children's department in London.[8] Manifestly (the officially approved version), receptionists appear to be regarded as *aides* to the service providers:

> directing clients to the correct department or room, and informing child care officers and other personnel that a client has arrived to see them.

In fact the researcher noted the lack of any clearly communicated statement of functions, which resulted 'in the work of receptionists being based almost entirely on an informal code of practice'. Further discussions with key staff resulted in a summary of 'manifest reception functions', an abbreviated version of which is reproduced below:

(1) Receive visitors;
(2) Ascertain requirements, and either
   (i) attend personally to requirement, or
   (ii) direct visitors to seating area;
(3) When the children's department is required:
   (i) known clients – telephone offical, ask clients to wait or call back;
   (ii) unknown clients – complete 'record of enquiry form', telephone records and district office, and ask client to wait.

In the language of work strata it can be claimed that the receptionists in the children's department were (manifestly) expected to work at Stratum 1. The summary of functions contains typical Stratum 1 activities (sometimes associated with administrative sections) which could have been explicitly formulated in a modest handbook. There can be little doubt that (manifestly) receptionists were *not* expected to have an impact on the output. Whilst sensitivity, tact, and experience were also needed, it should not have mattered – in terms of whether service was received or not – which of the various receptionists saw clients. The BEW or client impact level of the agency was intended to reside with the professional social workers, the child care officers in Stratum 2 roles, as depicted in Figure 5.4.

However, Hall's examination of the 'ascertainment' duty of receptionists uncovered a significant difference between the manifest role and what many of them were *actually* doing. A number of examples are provided:

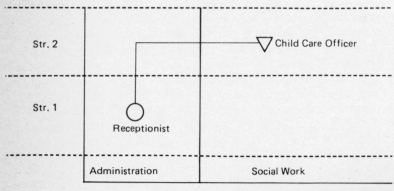

Figure 5.4   Reception as prescribed output

when a client informs the receptionist that she wishes to have her children received into care, this is, on the basis of the information given, the responsibility of a child care officer. The receptionist may, however, extend her function to ask *why*, and on the basis of the reply suggest that what is *really needed* is a day nursery placement. (Hall 1971; emphasis added).

It appears that receptionists also, in the absence of social workers, gave 'advice and guidance on the problem facing the client'. Hall sees these developments as a logical development of the reception role without, in that article, discussing the pros and cons of this development. In our terms the reality, as described by Hall, appears to be that receptionists had moved into Stratum 2 work (by asking the question 'why?' and attempting to move beyond the presenting problem), and were overlapping with the work of social workers.

I do not wish to discuss here whether there is an 'inevitability' about capable receptionists moving into a higher level of work. It may be that the agency had either 'over-recruited' (a common problem), or that it had failed to provide a suitable administrative career path for those receptionists well able to move to Stratum 2 administrative work. What will be contended is that it is neither necessarily a 'logical extension' of the receptionist's role, nor something which should be accepted without an explicit appreciation of the impact on clients.

Hall's study does not discuss in detail the duty officer role which is the complementary activity influencing intake into the system. This role is discussed in the more recent research into social service teams. Receptionists may represent the initial 'point of entry', but they operate within many different duty systems. It is commonplace for a variety of systems to co-exist even within the same department. The total entry system could involve the receptionist and a two-stage duty process; but it will be assumed that receptionists pass prospective clients over to someone called a duty officer. Such a duty officer, just to indicate the many possible systems, might be a team leader, a specialist intake worker, a basic grade social worker, a social work assistant, a trainee, or even a student on placement (see Stevenson and Parsloe 1978). They might be on duty by themselves or with colleagues. The period of duty might be a day in a week, a week at a time, or permanently as part of an intake team. They might be responsible for a geographical 'patch'. The referrals arriving to the duty officer naturally vary according to local conditions. But the organizational structure of the area (or department) also has a major impact on the work of the duty officer, since certain types of cases may be handled by specialist sections of the area team, and some categories may be deflected to voluntary and other agencies. Furthermore, the division of work between receptionists and duty officers varies. The horizontal boundary is far from clear-cut. Duty officers often handle 'routine' tasks such as:

filling in applications for car parking badges for disabled drivers and for a place in a playgroup or nursery, writing letters requesting clothing from WRVS and, in a few teams, noting down requests for a home help. (ibid:37)

In the light of these wide variations in the staffing and structure of impact systems (reception plus duty), it is hardly surprising to read of the diverse responses of duty officers to their work. Some officers said:

That duty was sometimes regarded as a 'note-taking exercise' or as 'simply information gathering' whereas 'what we should be doing is assessing cases and deciding whether we are in a position to help or not'. (ibid:41).

Two conflicting 'attitudes' quoted in the research were:

There are some people who would not accept the presenting problems as much as I do.

Compared with:

You have to get down to what the problem is, apart form the presenting problem.

The last quotation from the same research project leads back to the implications for the construction of welfare bureaucracies. It is taken from a worker discussing the great deal of 'autonomy' allowed to duty officers:

If you are asking whether I feel that it is a conscious decision from management that people in this office are quite capable [of exercising this discretion widely] – I don't think it is. I think it just happened.

These brief comments on the impact system pose in stark fashion the choice facing the senior officers of welfare bureaucracies: to let it 'just happen, or to make explicit policy decisions'. *If* the latter is to be the preferred course of action it will not be sufficient just to describe events.

The concept of BEW, together with the analysis of the horizontal boundary may, it is claimed, permit the beginning of some order in this confused area where potential client meets bureaucracy. Some of the ways in which models of impact might begin to be constructed are illustrated in Figure 5.5.

Several of these four models might be considered eccentric or absurd but, in the light of what has already been uncovered regarding the operation of duty systems, they are all to be found actually operating in departments. The representation of these models in the explicit form of Basic Expected Work enables hypotheses to be stated with regard to the consequences of adopting each model. The starting assumption will be that the individuals who fill the roles in the models

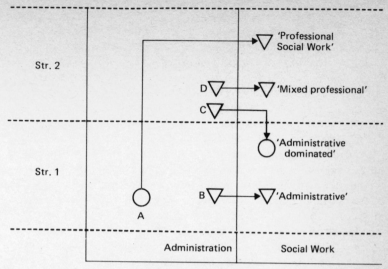

Key: ▽ = Basic Expected Work or client-impact

Figure 5.5   Impact models

are capable of working at the expected level of work.[9]

In Figure 5.5 Model A might be called the 'professional social work' model. Receptionists provide a prescribed output service working within straightforward criteria. They do not become involved in assessing 'the real' problem; that is the responsibility of the fully-fledged social worker to whom they pass on new clients. Neither are receptionists in this model expected to intervene in any manner which can significantly affect the situational response work of the social worker. All those passing through reception, and having been 'registered' as clients, have been assessed by social workers.[10]

The process described above might be compared with Model B – an 'administrative service'. Here, the person both enters the agency as a client *and* receives services on the basis of demand (within policy and resource boundaries) rather than situational response. Examples of this kind of service are more readily found in many day centres such as luncheon clubs and work centres for the elderly. Sometimes domiciliary services such as meals on wheels and home helps are also provided according to this model. It is perhaps worth emphasizing again that models of *expected* work, rather than the actual working of these systems, are being discussed. So, in suggesting that it is possible to point to departments operating Model B with regard to aspects of their day centre provision, we are claiming that this is an implicit policy. However, the prime concern of this section is the impact system in fieldwork area teams. The provision of day and domiciliary care, although occasionally falling within the purview of area teams, is probably best considered as part of the general 'impact dilemma' facing welfare bureaucracies, a dilemma which will be discussed in later chapters. In the fieldwork context, Model B appears to act – as an explicit policy – mainly with regard to specific client groups. Thus, the elderly may *consistently* receive services from staff (perhaps social work assistants) whose expected response is within Stratum 1.

Although Model C has been included as a theoretical possibility, it is difficult to find arguments for its adoption as an explicit fieldwork impact policy. It is an 'administrative dominated' model with the boundaries between reception and anything that might be regarded as 'social work' completely obscured. However, this model may be seen in operation in another setting: in the placement of the elderly into residential care (see chapter 12). Here, a Stratum 2 'administrator' may make the real decision whether or not a person is to be admitted into care, and pass the case on to a (lower) level worker to take care of the 'routine welfare' aspects.

Model D has already been identified in Hall's research mentioned earlier. Receptionists are given the possibility of making decisions affecting the 'output'; that is to say, giving advice and guidance, or persuading clients to take certain courses of action. The attraction of this model is that it protects the 'official professionals' and lessens their workload whilst enabling the administrator to make operational decisions influencing client services. Both administrators and social workers may be happy. The benefits for clients are less clear. If the receptionists can make key decisions on say Mondays, why bother with social workers for the rest of the week? What are the implications for clients faced with this model (which seems rather popular with GPs and their receptionists)?

Model D has been identified in situations where 'someone always has to man the fort'.[11] In this instance both administrator (and office manager) and professional 'social worker' were dissatisfied. The former wanted to concentrate on more interesting casework (and receive an appropriate higher salary). The latter was suspicious of the effects of professionally untrained (in the welfare field at least) office managers giving guidance to clients. Further analysis revealed that the agency did in fact have an alternative, but that it had been until then unwilling to face the policy option involved, that is, to narrow its field of operation.

Summary
I have in this chapter begun the discussion of the vertical dimension by describing the first two levels of work. *Prescribed-output work*

involves an expectation that problems will be responded to as isolated and repetitive demands. Level 2, *Situational-response work*, represents a conceptually different response. Here, problems are regarded as situations whose 'real needs' have to be judged.

The concept of *basic expected work* or *client impact level* has been introduced and used to develop models of impact systems. The concept will be further utilized in the following chapters.

Notes

1. For an account of some of the typical problems facing small organizations see Billis (1979) and Curran and Stanworth (1981).
2. We might further complicate matters by noting another 'dimension' – what people think they can do, which is often yet another difference.
3. A managerial role involves assigning duties and responsibilities, appraising performance and ability, and forwarding staff development. It implies authority to join in selection of staff, to prescribe work in as much detail as may be required, and to initiate promotion, transfer or dismissal. See chapter 8 for a more far-reaching proposition for the relationship of managerial roles to work strata.
4. We might note here cautious links with Saussure's view that 'identity is wholly a function of differences within a system' (Culler 1976: 28; see also de Saussure 1974).
5. Wherever the phrase 'impact level' appears, unless specifically mentioned otherwise, it refers to the *expected* work to be done.
6. This can be seen from the research of Stevenson and Parsloe (1978) and Holme and Maizels (1978).
7. A fuller account is provided in his *Point of Entry* (1975).
8. Hall refers to these concepts as quoted and refined by Donnison and Chapman (1965) from the original in Brown (1960). See also the early discussion of 'requisite' in chapter 2.
9. Should – as is not infrequently the case – it turn out that this is an optimistic assumption, it is also possible to make predictions regarding the consequences of the mismatch.
10. For a description and definition of registration and clients, see Brunel Institute of Organisation and Social Studies, Social Services Organisation Research Unit (1974).
11. I am referring here to research with a national voluntary organization with small regional offices providing services of a 'social welfare' type to clients.

6 The Higher Reaches of Bureaucracy

This chapter continues the examination of the vertical boundary of welfare bureaucracies. In large part the focus will move away from direct contact work with individual clients. Such contact work that does exist will usually entail expectations to perform additional (non-client contact) duties.

The higher levels of work to be examined (Stratum 3 and above) can often, but not necessarily, be regarded as 'middle' and 'senior' management. 'Not necessarily' because the sort of work that is in 'the middle' of one type of organization can be the 'lowest' level elsewhere. We shall continue to be concerned with 'expected work'; bearing in mind that this can be different from what is actually happening, or from individual capacity and personal expectations. Similarly we shall continue to argue that the different expected levels of work are qualitatively different. Expected work, it is claimed, can be analysed clearly into one or other of the defined strata. Stratum 3 is qualitatively different from Stratum 4, and that in turn is different again from Stratum 5.

After discussing these higher levels, the chapter introduces the concept of *Highest Expected Work* (HEW), or *societal impact*, which is meant to complement the concept of *Basic Expected Work*, or *client impact*, already introduced. It is also an essential component of the typology of organizations presented in chapter 7.

Systematic problem resolution – the beginnings of 'policy'
Whereas the first level of work responds to problems as discrete (prescribed output) demands, and the second level treats them as situations to which responses can only be partially prescribed, at the third level it is expected to go beyond this – to deal with them as a continuous sequence of situations. Workers at this level are expected to respond in a systematic fashion to a stream of work that has to be shaped into a framework for other situational response work to take place. In order to perform Stratum 3 work it is necessary to understand and take account of the inter-relationship of the defined situations – to be concerned with *ranges* rather than individual states. For the first time the word 'policy' can emerge as a description of this framework-setting activity. Indeed, a general point may be made that

a distinct organizational language can be identified as work moves from level to level. So, 'policy' is likely to appear as a descriptive term in Level 3 and above work. Jones (1973) has pointed out: 'What is one man's detail often involves another man's principle or policy'. Level 3 policy can set boundaries to the 'details' of Level 2 activity, and in like manner, it will often be bounded by higher level 'policy'.

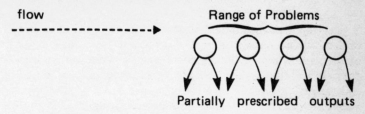

Figure 6.1   Systematic service provision (Stratum 3)

Figure 6.1 illustrates Stratum 3 work which we have called *systematic service provision*, and have defined as *making systematic provision of services of some given kind, shaped to the needs of a continuous sequence of concrete situations which present themselves*. Work at this level is of crucial significance for any study of social policy and welfare bureaucracy. For, to return to the theme of the opening chapter, 'design' and 'planning' require, as Ford put it: 'some general notions . . . which show the process as a whole, and review the relations of the separate problems to one another' (see chapter 1). In our terms they need a Stratum 3 response. *Social policy inevitably entails, at minimum, a Stratum 3 role somewhere.* A lower level response than this returns us to Weber's 'Kadi-justice', to a position where '. . . the judgement of the single case prevails' and to 'doing business from case to case' (Gerth and Wright Mills 1970: chapter 8). However, Stratum 3 work is still bounded by existing organizational provision; it is confined to dealing with flows or sequences of situations which arise from the given organizational provision.

In SSDs a typical Stratum 3 role may be the area officer. We might note here the great significance placed on the area office and its controller by the Seebohm Committee (see Home Office *et al.* 1968: chapter xix; also the criticism of the area teams by Smith and Ames 1976). They seem to have instinctively searched for what Jaques has called the 'key unit in the organization of all larger bureaucratic systems'. He suggests that 'if the Stratum 3-level organization is wrong, then the rest of the organization will inevitably be wrong also' (1976:313). Without entering here into any substantial debate on the success or failure of the area team concept (a debate that would take us into an analysis of the 'social conscience' tradition of social administration), the area officer role can be used to illustrate typical Stratum 3 expectations (see Baker 1979 and Billis 1981b). A main pre-occupation of Stratum 3 area officers is with the development, organization and introduction of client impact systems, of the sort described in chapter 5. It is at this level that arguments have to be mastered, and authoritative action taken, with regard to 'patch', intake, and all the other permutations of handling incoming cases to the department.

'Development' is another word like policy which often begins to appear at this level and, whilst it more often than not confuses administrative issues, it does conjure up a level of activity which is characteristically Stratum 3 – of initiative, of moving out, of searching and preparing guidelines for future action. Establishment of the Seebohm bureaucracies has been accompanied by numerous roles of this sort (see Billis *et al.* 1980).

The distinction between Stratum 2 and Stratum 3 cannot be too highly emphasized. New complex organizations, such as SSDs, may be particularly prone to lack of clarity, especially if they expect to attain in key areas of their work a BEW at Level 2 and beyond. A few examples may illustrate this point. The case study of intermediate treatment described in Part III is derived in large part from the department's initial ambition to combine in one role two different foci: a Stratum 2 *practitioner*, capable and experienced in working with children, and a Stratum 3 *coordinator*, capable of drawing together a number of projects and developing new ideas and policy initiatives. Workshops held with intermediate treatment officers from many authorities showed that this was not an isolated confusion.

The organization of work in residential and day care settings also offers many examples of the consequences of the lack of conceptual distinction between the two levels – homes and day care advisers may suffer from this problem. The study in Part III of the day care advisers illustrates in poignant fashion the personal suffering which can be partly attributed to conceptual unclarity. Other research rein-forces the general plight of so-called advisers (see DHSS 1979; Re-sidential Care Association 1982).

Yet another widespread example of confusion between Stratum 2 and Stratum 3 was to be found in the early post-Seebohm approaches to 'research' posts. Departments were unclear whether they wanted 'research officers' who were expected:

● to respond to some research situation themselves, and perhaps instruct others what data would be needed for a specific project (Stratum 2); or

● to provide a systematic research service, dealing with the continuous flow of departmental research need, and helping to formulate a policy to meet those needs (Stratum 3).

In some instances there may have been expectations of Stratum 4 work. Without pre-empting the discussion of the following section, we might just note that this would have entailed providing a comprehensive departmental research service encompassing not only the current flow of research needs, but also dealing with emerging, or as yet unmanifested, research requirements (Jones 1979).

The focus on social territory: Stratum 4

Although the word 'policy' begins to creep into organizational language at Stratum 3, it is more usual to associate it with Stratum 4 and above levels of response. At these higher levels there is no escaping the word. In its descriptive sense of setting guidelines for future action, it moves steadily to the centre of the stage. The stage, which is Stratum 4, is no longer open-ended and systematic, but 'comprehensive' both in terms of social territories and of services. And, although (social) policy can be usefully discussed in terms of a Stratum 3 response, it is more customarily used when describing what we are calling Stratum 4 or 5 responses.

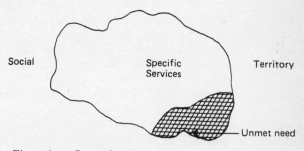

Social   Specific Services   Territory

Unmet need

Figure 6.2 Comprehensive service provision (Stratum 4)

Stratum 4, then, may be distinguished in sharp fashion from the lower, Stratum 3, response. The Stratum 4 role (see Figure 6.2) is expected to be concerned with a *defined social territory* and to *resolve the problem of comprehensively meeting needs for specific services throughout that territory*. Whereas the focus of Stratum 3 work is systems and frameworks, the Stratum 4 *comprehensive service provision* role is centred on searching out and making proposals for coping with 'unmet need', and gaps in provision. Inevitably, such proposals will entail capital investment, since decisions about the resolution of 'future' needs involve re-arranging or changing the resource configurations dealing with present problems.

However, Stratum 4 roles are unlikely to have *sole* responsibility for substantial capital investments of the sort which tampers with the particular kind of service which is well-established and sanctioned by the organization. This type of decision will probably lie with higher organizational levels (should they exist), or with the governing body.

The Level 4 welfare bureaucrats will be expected to ask the following sorts of questions, and to set in motion the appropriate systems: what is the extent of need for residential homes throughout the county or borough, or what is the extent of need for day centres, or home helps, or meals on wheels, or field social workers, or research facilities, or logistical services, or administrative support? They will be expected to produce comprehensive plans and budgetary proposals taking into account the implications for capital expenditure and staffing.

Typical Level 4 roles in SSDs are the various assistant directors to be found in those departments organized on a functional basis; that is to say, assistant directors responsible for fieldwork, or residential and day care, or administration (or any combination of these and other titles). This basis of organization is at present most commonly found in the London boroughs. The counties are more likely to be organized on a geographic basis, with Stratum 4 divisional directors, like their borough colleagues, responsible for specific kinds of services throughout the social territory. A Health Service example may be running a district nursing service. In Education Departments it might be assistant directors responsible for specific educational services, or the headteachers of comprehensive schools, or other complex educational establishments.

The position in Housing Departments raises interesting questions which are more easily dealt with later. However at this stage, it might be noted that Stratum 4 roles could be the directors of some departments, or the housing managers of others (see chapter 7 for a typology of organizations). In fact, the most graphic example I have of an expected Stratum 4 response occurred during a research project in a housing department of a local authority. The discussion took place in an office on the top floor overlooking most of the borough. When asked to describe his role, the housing manager rose and pointed to some distant horizons. 'Out there', he explained, 'I suspect there are housing problems which we are not meeting.' He was not referring to existing housing waiting lists or the existing flow of problems, but with suspected, emerging issues which he was groping to identify. Housing is a particularly good example, since the absence of Stratum 4 (and above) staff, capable of performing that level of work, may well contribute to the very evident problems of future years. (Not that I wish to suggest that there is a causal link between this and the housing disasters of recent years – the issue is far more complex – but *if* these roles are absent, then we should not be surprised if things 'go wrong'.)

The focus of Stratum 4 on 'social territory' has led to a number of questions and the consequent necessary distinction being drawn between 'social' and 'administrative' territories. Whilst much further research undoubtedly needs to be undertaken in this area, the distinction for purposes of analysis of levels of work is readily appreciated by role-holders at different levels. The problem is that geography as a basis for organization can appear at any level of work. Workers at all levels could in theory, and often do, have their geographic 'patch'. It is not difficult to think of examples. Thus, meals on wheels, home helps, and other domiciliary services could be so organized. Social workers can have their patches, residential homes could serve a specific community, area officers have their 'area', and so on.

The failure to distinguish between what might be considered 'real' social territories, consisting of people with interacting interests and problems well beyond the scope of one bureaucracy, and administrative territories which represent no more than convenient lines and boundaries drawn up at bureaucratic headquarters, dogs the discussion of welfare organization.[1] Often geography *per se* is seen as a 'good thing' and associated with notions of *gemeinschaft*. As such, it is both simplistic and misleading. When examining the bureaucratic organization the question must be: what level of response is expected to this particular geographical grouping?

Unless great care is taken in the design of organizations, it is not difficult to reach a situation whereby successive hierarchical layers all have a 'territorial focus' and the myth perpetuated that this 'focus' is in fact a comprehensive territorial responsibility. Without probing and obtaining *explicit* statements of the expected boundaries of decision-making to territorially focused roles, much frustration can be built up in a fruitless search for 'community'. This is specially pertinent at a time when SSDs are still searching for the realization of the Seebohm dream of 'community-based area teams'. The interest in the so-called 'patch' system which has been described as a 'quiet revolution' is likely to founder on the rocks of organizational confusion unless, amongst other things, the expected level of response is explicated (Hadley and McGrath 1979; see also the National Institute for Social Work 1982)

Field of need: Stratum 5
Stratum 5 work retains a comprehensive territorial responsibility for problems which appeared for the first time in Stratum 4. However here too, there is a clear-cut leap when moving from level to level. The change this time is to be found in the integration of the social territory

with an increased complexity in the expected service to be provided (or goods to be manufactured).

At any given period of social and cultural development the expected problems, which Stratum 4 roles were established to resolve, can be reliably described. We can readily comprehend what the services comprise and what sorts of facilities and staff are needed to deliver them, or to deliver additional services to relieve unmet needs of the same kind. Day centres for the handicapped, casework services for problem families, residential homes for the elderly, home helps, adoption and fostering services, these all conjure up images of well-understood services. The Stratum 4 role functions within a framework which is accepted and specified. Not so the Level 5 response. Now all that is defined as a framework is what we have called a *field of need*.

At Stratum 5 it is insufficient just to deal with particular problems in a systematic or even comprehensive fashion. All that and more, is required. The Stratum 5 role is expected to develop whatever comprehensive provision may be required in order to respond to (social) problems which have been categorized into titles such as 'education', 'health' and 'shelter'.

In chapter 4 we explored the difficulties encountered in implementing a particular definition of social distress and proposed a new categorization of *social discomfort*. No governmental bureaucracy has been created, in this country at any rate, to provide a Stratum 5 response to social discomfort. In theory, such an Orwellian bureaucracy could be established. Directors of social discomfort would be accountable for searching out all unmet 'loneliness' need in their authority, for researching into the issues and developing the necessary systems and procedures. They would be expected to interact with the other Stratum 5 directors. They would be heavily involved in negotiating with governing bodies and, like other comparable directors, would spend much time in understanding and working with the political systems.

The allocation of specific titles to a definite work stratum is hazardous and must always be preceded by the necessary words of caution. Titles themselves do tell us enough about the expected work, and little about the actual work. But for illustrative purposes, to give the 'flavour' of the level, it can be said that the chief officers of major departments in local authorities will be given a Stratum 5 brief. Similarly there are a number of national voluntary organizations whose officers are also encharged with Stratum 5 responses. The non-welfare field is of little interest to our main theme, but there, too, many Stratum 5 roles have been identified.

The Stratum 5 governmental bureaucracy is of particular social importance because of the planned or enacted tentativeness of its

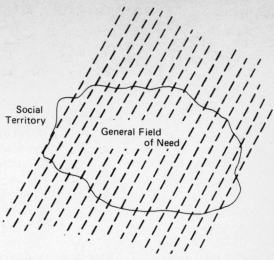

Social
Territory

General Field
of Need

Figure 6.3   Comprehensive field coverage (Stratum 5)

activities. In setting up these high level bureaucracies, comprehensiveness (both of territorial coverage and ranges of problems) is – if all goes well – achieved at the expense of increased uncertainty. Ruthless analysis of Stratum 5 boundaries is an essential precondition to even a modest degree of stability. The alternative of a more comprehensible (Stratum 4) agency is always available. Instead of SSDs we can establish agencies providing specific kinds of services such as homes and day centres for the elderly, children, handicapped, etc.

The Stratum 5 government bureaucracy is also very significant for social policy because of what appears to be an almost 'inevitable' overlap with other agencies making a similar level of response. Should educational welfare be in education or social services departments? What is the logic of the split in the provision for under-fives between SSDs and health authorities? What about the chaos in the position of the elderly in residential care and in geriatric wards? Should not 'leisure and recreation departments' be coping with some of the social discomfort services? What of the provision for the mentally ill? The questions are almost endless. The world of Stratum 5 agencies needs constant surveillance.

Figure 6.4 sums up the argument so far. Each level of work is bounded, although at Stratum 5 definitions of a next higher level remain speculative. But before briefly commenting on possible Stratum 6 responses to problems, we should yet again make the obvious point that *the desired response is a matter of societal choice and explicit decision.* The fact that SSDs may be used to illustrate the work strata

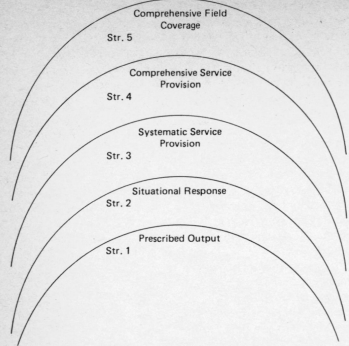

Figure 6.4   The boundaries to work

theory is *not* necessarily an argument for Stratum 5 responses to social problems. We shall introduce shortly the concept of 'highest expected work' and thus be ready for a complete exposition of organizational choices in the following chapter. If we do take SSDs for our main example, it is necessary to point out that above the director lies the governing body, the local authority and its social services committee. There is no higher level bureaucratic boundary to be found elsewhere. (Although one director of an SSD did claim that his chief executive 'acted as if he were in a Stratum 6 role', the overwhelming majority of the many directors with whom these issues have been discussed in research workshops and projects do not see themselves in a similar position.)

Beyond Stratum 5
It seems that, whilst higher levels of response may well exist, the Stratum 5 response represents the highest level at which *independent* social institutions can easily function. It appears (from discussions with staff from large-scale companies, multi-nationals, and local and

central government) that beyond Level 5 it is difficult to maintain a separate organizational existence. The links begin to feel very fragile. It would seem that comprehension and control of Stratum 5 boundaries lead to a preference for an 'independent company' operating level. Stratum 5 roles, which form part of even larger industrial and commercial complexes, demand seats on 'the board'. Those multinationals that have been analysed illustrate that links remain with Stratum 6 and whatever lies beyond that.

The limited observations that can be made indicate that in one multinational at least, the Stratum 6 role has the power to close down what we have called the field of need. And when it is remembered that in this example a 'field' consists of perhaps 20 or 30 huge (Stratum 5) industrial complexes, each occupying large encompassed territories with dozens of individual plants and hundreds or thousands of workers in each complex, and each such industrial complex dominating the economic and social life of its local town or territory; it can be appreciated that it is a very powerful role.

A Stratum 6 role would probably act both on the national and international stage, and naturally interact with heads of government and international financial institutions. Heads of State and their ministers would be intimately concerned with the implications of major decisions and there would be much two-way traffic. In the UK the appointment of heads of major nationalized industries (which must be assumed to be at least at that level) is usually the subject of considerable national interest and can invoke great parliamentary controversy. But so much for bureaucracy's stratosphere. Perhaps a Stratum 6 social welfare service-delivery organization exists. So far I have not had the opportunity to explore it.

Highest expected work: the societal impact

In the previous chapter the concept of Basic Expected Work (BEW) was defined as the minimum acceptable (sanctioned) work level of an organization, occupation, or professional group. In this chapter a complementary concept is introduced, that of the *Highest Expected Work* (HEW) of an organization.[2]

HEW may be seen as representing *the total or societal impact which those who established the organization have implicitly or explicitly sanctioned*. HEW is easily appreciated when examining proposals for the establishment of new statutory organizations. Thus, in the creation of the English and Welsh Social Services Departments, the HEW was clearly intended to reside in the role of the 'principal officer'. The Seebohm Report attempted to define the nature of the role and the quality which would be demanded of the officer. He must be capable of looking outwards, well beyond the limits of his own department and authority, and well into the future. He will face problems different from those facing heads of existing established departments. . . . He will have to survey the needs of the area and plan the deployment of workers to meet them. . . . He must be able to command the confidence of members, to persuade them to provide more resources for the services, to maintain a reasonable balance between the demands made on behalf of different groups in the population . . . [he must] consider further adaptation and the introduction of new methods to meet developing needs in a society which is undergoing rapid economic and social change. (Home Office *et al.* 1968: paras 618 and 619.

This extract from the profile of Seebohm's expected principal officer corresponds well to the definition of Stratum 5.[3] The ambition of the Committee was to establish departments which would be headed by a person capable of coping with a high degree of task and environmental complexity. A person who would be capable of coping with 'future needs' of an entire social territory. And the detailed description in the Report of the expected political interaction of the principal officer, and the high priority placed on the ability to win the confidence of other senior officers and fight for resources, are all examples of the Committee's intentions that the department would be a genuine 'creative innovation' (Schumpeter 1947).

Whilst the Report is careful to warn principal officers to take 'care not to become remote from the problems of workers in the field and those whom the department is trying to help', there is a vast difference between this proposed role and that of the 1946 Curtis Report's lengthy profile of the Children's Officer who would:

be a specialist in child care . . . [she] would be the *person* to whom the child would look as guardian . . . [she] would be so well known in her area as the authority on children's welfare questions that individual difficulties and problems would be brought to her as a matter of course. . . . Her essential qualifications, however, would be on the personal side. She should be genial and friendly in manner and able to set both children and adults at their ease. (paras 441-6 in Watkins 1975:428-9).

The Children's Officer of the Curtis Report is envisaged as what might be called a 'specialist practitioner' (Stratum 3) (Billis *et al.* 1980: chapter 8), but in the 'large county' it was accepted that she would be unable 'to know and to keep in personal touch with all the children under her care, and she should therefore aim at allocating a group of children definitely to each of her subordinates'. In this and other passages it seems that a Stratum 4 HEW was envisaged. (We may note in passing the changing pronouns that took place in a quarter of a century from the 'she' in the Curtis Report to the 'he' of Seebohm.) We have here the recognition that in 'larger' social territories it is 'impractical' for the Children's Officer to do the specialist work herself, and the consequent necessity to 'allocate' or 'delegate' work.

The Curtis Committee faced the problem of the differentiation, often reluctant and painful, between HEW and BEW roles. No such dilemma faced the full-blown, post-Seebohm, bureaucratic structures. It was almost unthinkable that the new principal officers would actually work with clients, at most they must not become too remote.

In the next chapter the relevance of HEW and BEW is seen for the development of a full range of responses to social problems.

Summary

In this chapter we have attempted to translate the vague notions of 'middle' and 'senior' management into clear-cut levels of decision-making. *Systematic service provision, comprehensive service provision,* and *comprehensive field coverage* have been defined and illustrated. We have noted how certain words, such as 'policy', and 'development', seem to emerge at different levels of expected organizational response.

Finally, the concept of *Highest Expected Work*, or *societal impact*, was introduced as a preliminary to the presentation of a typology of organizational responses in chapter 7.

Notes

1. The unresolved issue of the definition of 'community' looms large here, and is deliberately avoided. It is one of several bogs which, I feel, it is wiser to circumvent than seek a way through. See, for example, Bell and Newby (1971); (National Institute for Social Work 1982: See also Appendix B).

2. It is most straightforward to restrict HEW to bureaucracies and to the typology that appears in chapter 7. It is possible to discuss occupational groups and professions in the light of HEW – for example, its relationship to controverdial ideas of professionalization, careers and training – but this is rather peripheral to the main theme of this chapter.

3. However, some paragraphs of the Report have optimistic and high expectations going beyond the present analysis of Stratum 5; but the broad expectation is as quoted.

7 Alternative Bureaucratic Responses to Social Problems

In this chapter the concepts introduced in earlier parts of the book are brought together to produce a typology of alternative bureaucratic responses to social problems.

The typology illustrated in Figure 7.1 provides social policy-makers with a variety of alternatives. It makes explicit a tentative theory of organizational choices for welfare provision. Examples will be provided of the different types which, following the main themes of this part, it is suggested, can actually be constructed as deliberate and explicit policy. For convenience, the models are grouped into three headings: (i) the prescribed output bureaucracies; (ii) the situational bureaucracies; and (iii) the developmental bureaucracies.

After outlining and illustrating the typology there follows a discussion of several important implications. Is it necessary to implement all the layers in each model – or can 'partial' models exist? What, in other words, are the consequences, if any, of omitting levels in organizations? The issue has been found to be of particular significance for the non-governmental sector of smaller organizations with more limited resources. Finally, we consider the problem of 'hybrid' organizations, a subject which is returned to in the case study of day care advisers in chapter 11.

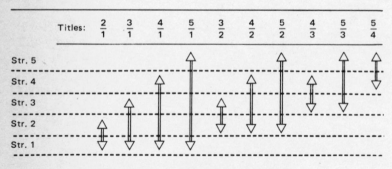

Figure 7.1   Typology of organizational responses

A typology of bureaucratic responses

The production of a theory of stratified problem-solving, together with the concepts and basic and highest expected work, provide the possibility of developing a typology of bureaucracies. For, following the work strata theory, all bureaucracies must have BEW roles at either Stratum 1, 2, 3 or 4; and their HEW at Stratum 2, 3, 4 or 5. It is a fairly straightforward step to move from this proposition to the full-scale typology of Figure 7.1.

We shall examine the different models of response indicated in the typology and attempt to provide examples from social policy areas. The models will be examined under three headings, those bureaucracies where the basic expected level of work is (a) Stratum 1, (b) Stratum 2, and (c) Stratum 3 and above.

The prescribed output or 'demand' bureaucracies

Of the ten possible models suggested in Figure 7.1 several have a client-impact level (BEW) at Stratum 1. They differ from each other in their expected societal-impact (HEW), which is at either Stratum 2, 3, 4 or 5. Because it is necessary to have a means of differentiating among these four models it is proposed to describe them as $\frac{2}{1}, \frac{3}{1}, \frac{4}{1}$, and $\frac{5}{1}$, in accordance with the titles in Figure 7.1.[1]

The $\frac{2}{1}$ bureaucracy

Looked at in ascending order of complexity we start with a rather dubious claimant to the category of 'bureaucracy' – the $\frac{2}{1}$ model. Although it falls within our definition, and for the sake of tidiness is included in the range of possible models, doubt must be expressed as to its vaibility. These doubts arise from the nature of Stratum 2, situational response work, which represents the highest level of problem-solving in these organizations.

As previously described, Stratum 2 work is expected to cope with particular problems and situations. It still involves, as Weber put it, 'doing business from case to case' (Gerth and Wright Mills 1974). It excludes the possibility that the role-holder is expected to develop policies spanning categories of situations. This presumably, if it is done at all, falls to the lot of the governing body. Freestanding, *independent*, $\frac{2}{1}$ bureaucracies (that is to say, organizations with a 'director' reporting directly to the governing body) are consequently dominated by the personality of the director or head who happens to be in post. It is not a model which is likely to be espoused by local or central governments anxious to implement more systematic responses. It is, however, a model which can be seen in the non-governmental (voluntary) sector, especially in the growing category of small-scale agencies totally, or nearly totally, dependent on government funding.

Although legally independent, they exist to provide services which are either paid for *pro rata* or on an annual grant basis by local authorities. These are fragile social institutions demanding vigorous and knowledgeable intervention from the legal governing body, if anything more than an ephemeral existence is to be maintained.[2]

A typical example of a $\frac{2}{1}$ bureaucracy is an agency working with the single homeless, employing about half a dozen full-time staff, including an 'administrator', and a further ten or so 'volunteers'. (It is more accurate to regard these volunteers as low paid employees.) Discussions with staff and residents in the agency's three hostels, and an examination of their public statements, demonstrated that the interaction with residents (the client-impact level) was expected to be straightforward help and assistance. Indeed, dealing with anything that smacked of 'judged' or 'real needs' would have been contrary to the agency's declared philosophy.

This project revealed many problems facing staff and the management committee. The former felt they were working in a vacuum with inadequate guidelines. The historic philosophy of the agency did not match up to their actual work experience and there was no person or body capable of developing more relevant policies. In fact, there was not one but several Stratum 2 roles, with no clear-cut director of the organization. This situation, too, will be familiar to those working in the voluntary sector. The 'administrator' was given a Stratum 2 brief and had no authority over the other Stratum 2 workers who had their own distinct area of work with direct access to members of the management committee.

It may be that these $\frac{2}{1}$ organizations are more helpfully seen as 'nascent bureaucracies', well worth analysing as a separate category. At any rate, whilst they cannot be discussed to any great extent in this book, they proliferate in the voluntary sector and in all likelihood play a significant role in the overall provision of social welfare services.

The $\frac{3}{1}$ bureaucracy

The $\frac{3}{1}$ welfare bureaucracy remains concerned with a prescribed output impact on clients. The organization confines itself to dealing with problems coming to it for resolution within existing organizational resources. As with the $\frac{2}{1}$ bureaucracy it is perhaps easier to appreciate its characteristics and qualitative differences from neighbouring models by stating what it does *not* do. Thus, there is as yet no role which is expected to take a social territorial view. And any 'concern' for unmet need will remain just that, and not be capable of implementation. These expectations, and the necessary role structures and resources to perform these activities, remain the prerogative of bureaucracies with HEW at Stratum 4. On the other hand, unlike $\frac{2}{1}$ bureaucracies, the $\frac{3}{1}$

organization *is* expected to develop policies and procedures which go beyond treating problems as separate. Also, unlike the $\frac{2}{1}$ bureaucracy, a distinct managerial level may emerge in order to control the client-impact work (see the argument in chapter 5 which proposes that managerial roles, as defined, can emerge only at Stratum 2 and beyond).

The managerial role structure is partially illustrated in Figure 7.2. Since, in addition to the managerial outline sketched in Figure 7.2, many other types of roles can also be built into bureaucracies to assist the director and managers, it can be seen that the $\frac{3}{1}$ organization need not be small. It can employ several hundred workers.

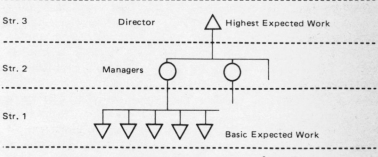

Str. 3   Director   Highest Expected Work

Str. 2   Managers

Str. 1   Basic Expected Work

Figure 7.2   Managerial role structure of a $\frac{3}{1}$ bureaucracy

Prior to the passing of the 1970 Local Authority Social Services Act establishing Social Services Departments in England and Wales, this type of bureaucracy may have been represented by several of the former welfare departments. $\frac{3}{1}$ welfare bureaucracy can now mainly be seen (in this country) in the voluntary sector. One such example is of a small agency with about 12 paid staff attempting to provide a befriending and advisory service for one-parent families. Other examples are to be found within the housing association movement.

The Netherlands, with its non-governmental and 'entrepreneurial' system of social welfare, has many $\frac{3}{1}$ bureaucracies. Thus, an example of a very large agency is a home help service mostly staffed by about 800 part-time home helps managed by 26 'leaders', under the director of the agency. Functioning within city boundaries, but not expected to take a comprehensive view of the home help provision for the territory, the agency would appear to be clearly of the type we have described as $\frac{3}{1}$. Obviously, such large numbers were only possible because of the part-time nature of the workforce and the conscious use of a battery of staff officers surrounding the director.[3]

A less extreme example also comes from the Netherlands. It is of a small religious-aid organization running a home for battered women with children. With 70 staff, the Home contained 30 adults and 65 children. In the market-dominated system of that country, the Home had previously catered for unwed mothers. The changing social climate, and the increasing divorce rate, had led to a fall in the number of clients and the organization had changed the category of problems it wished to resolve. The 'market' – in the words of the organization's director – 'now became women in crisis situations'. Most of the funding was provided by the Ministry of Justice and the local authorities. Essentially, it was a 'reactive' organization, intent on survival by dealing with its chosen category of problem. It did not have either terms of reference or ambition to encompass the problems of battered women and their children in its area; but was primarily concerned to develop policies that would persuade central and local government to continue their support and thus ensure the continued employment of the agency's staff.

The dominant question for social policy in a Stratum 3 (HEW) dominated world is who then provides the comprehensive territorial (local, regional, or national) impact? Consideration of the Stratum 4 and above organization leads us to the heart of social policy dilemmas.

The $\frac{4}{1}$ bureaucracy

The $\frac{4}{1}$ bureaucracy also provides prescribed output services. The client-impact level remains straightforward, based on mathematical norms of equity rather than professional assessment of need. But unlike the lower level bureaucracies, the societal impact level is now territorial. The governing body establishes the directorial role with comprehensive responsibility for a social territory, a point which was discussed in chapter 6.

The political system is particularly prone to spawning bureaucracies with 'comprehensive' obligations to a specific electoral population or of groups within that population. Often, the comprehensive expectation of bureaucratic endeavour is enshrined in the law. There may well be a natural desire for politicians to demonstrate their concern for the electorate by creating bureaucracies with comprehensive social impacts. So politics and politicians are a stable element of the work of Strata 4 and 5 roles in welfare bureaucracies.[4] 'Handling' the politicians is a basic skill to be learnt by all aspiring higher level bureaucrats.

The housing departments of local authorities provide many examples of $\frac{4}{1}$ bureaucracies. Their Basic Expected Work is often concerned with defined tangible products, with the technical maintenance of housing estates and the compilation of waiting lists for council housing according to prescribed criteria. The top work revolves around the precise notion of 'houses'. In so far as housing departments continue to provide services according to prescribed criteria and maintain their societal focus on specific kinds of services, the exemplify the workings of a $\frac{4}{1}$ bureaucracy.

We might here repeat the distinction between social territories and 'administrative' territories drawn in chapter 6. The former consists of bounded territories of people with interacting problems and interests ranging well beyond the focus of any one bureaucracy. The latter are administrative devices established by a bureaucracy to attain more efficient and effective work. But even within genuine social territories it would be hazardous to assume that the highest expected work of government bureaucracies is *necessarily* Stratum 4. Analysis must start from the level of response to be made to social need.

The $\frac{5}{1}$ bureaucracy

The leap from a Stratum 4 HEW role to Stratum 5 can be illustrated by the pressure on local authority housing departments to be concerned with a comprehensive housing service – with expectations to encompass a much wider range of provision than just with 'houses' (see, for example, Central Housing Advisory Committee 1969; Institute of Housing Managers 1972).

Work with several large housing associations suggests to me that they too have ambitions to move into a broader response for social need, extending beyond the development of new housing units and the management of existing tenancies. Their 'ambitions' – it is too soon in these particular cases to call them expectations – extend into what might be called the 'housing welfare' business.

The $\frac{5}{1}$ bureaucracy is most clearly seen in large-scale manufacturing industry where the end-product is unambiguously tangible and prescribed. The $\frac{5}{1}$ government bureaucracies may tend to be less clear-cut organizations, the breadth and complexity of their operations leading to lack of clarity at the 'sharp end'.

$\frac{5}{1}$ agencies are frequently established when central government wishes to maintain direct control over prescribed output services (such as social security, insurance and pension services), and where equity is a dominant consideration. The client impact level is bounded by the political necessity to guarantee equal financial treatment to huge numbers of citizens in a vast number of changing situations. The rule books become ever more complex and the organization is under constant pressure to build in additional 'supervisory' grades to maintain equity at the front line.[5] The client impact level requires large numbers of Stratum 1 workers, and the $\frac{5}{1}$ organization appears to be the largest independent bureaucracy and, as can be seen from Table 7.1, even fairly modest spans of control can lead to very large numbers of employees. We need to remember also that those figures represent

Table 7.1   Possible $\frac{5}{1}$ bureaucracies according to varying spans of control

Work level	A		B		C	
	Span of control	Employees	Span of control	Employees	Span of control	Employees
5	5	1	7	1	8	1
4	8	5	8	7	12	8
3	10	40	12	56	15	96
2	12	400	15	672	25	1440
1	—	4800	—	10 080	—	36 000
Total Employees		5246		10 816		37 545

only the work levels and make no attempt to represent the lengthy grading structures or web of role relationships (see chapter 8).

It is not difficult to understand the difficulties encountered in carrying out work in $\frac{5}{1}$ welfare bureaucracies. Engaged in a general field of work there will be multifarious activities which need to be controlled by hierarchies which are invariably lengthy, with a strong tendency to build in excessive layers of management in order to maintain quality control at the client-impact level. It is little wonder that these bureaucracies can be described as 'mechanistic'.[6] Without great care in their design the popular conception of 'bureaucracy' is all too easily a just perception of reality.

We might sum up this category of welfare bureaucracies with a Level 1 BEW by describing them as 'demand' agencies. They are expected to attempt to produce a series of identical services. Rules and procedures have to be developed to ensure equality of provision. Clients are 'processed' on the basis of 'just' demands on resources. They have an individual identity only in 'exceptional' cases. As the exceptions grow, the laws and agency policies must be continually re-appraised and adjusted. Discretion of front-line bureaucrats must never be allowed to move over the Stratum 2 boundary. To avoid this 'professionalization' of the bureaucracy, the rule books will tend to expand and require constant pruning if they are to remain manageable.

The situational response bureaucracies ($\frac{3}{2}$, $\frac{4}{2}$, $\frac{5}{2}$)[7]
This group of bureaucracies can be constructed to offer what might be called a 'professionally based' response to social problems. Unlike the group just described, the professionally based agencies do not take

problems as demands; but as situations to be assessed. Many of them $(\frac{3}{2}, \frac{4}{2}, \frac{5}{2})$ will also employ Stratum 1 workers to assist and support the Stratum 2 client impact workers. It is this set of organizations which is most commonly thought of when social work dominated agencies are under consideration.

The $\frac{3}{2}$ bureaucracy

Research in a pre-Seebohm Mental Health Department provides an example of a $\frac{3}{2}$ bureaucracy.[8] Although the theory of work levels had not at that time (1971) been developed, the original interviews are easily interpreted in work strata terminology.

Terms of reference of the project were 'to further understanding of the nature of the work being undertaken and the organizational relationships in the department'. Seven members of staff collaborated in the analysis. Each was interviewed at least once and their individual perceptions of work, organizational relationships, and unresolved or ambiguous issues were cleared for circulation to the other members of the collaborating group.

The analysis revealed both areas of general agreement and also numerous issues of unclarity. Of the latter, some problems were specific and of little current interest, others remain unresolved a decade later. Of these, several have either been mentioned or will be discussed in later chapters. (Other areas of disagreement analysed in this 1971 project included the familiar problem of the position of administrative staff who were not part of the mental health department, the role of social workers on sites outside the department's direct control, and the role of the deputy – yet another chronic problem.) The areas of agreement included perceptions of the main managerial line of the department whose resources were: 4 social work teams with a total of 20 social workers, 2 domiciliary occupational therapists, 3 adult training centres for the mentally handicapped, a training school, a hostel for mentally handicapped persons, a hostel for the rehabilitation of mentally ill persons, and flats for the rehabilitation of mentally ill persons. The administrative staff were based at headquarters.[9] The key roles are illustrated in Figure 7.3 in terms of work level analysed retrospectively from the original individual reports.

It should be stressed that the seven staff interviewed were from what was called the 'social work services'; heads and staff of hostels and centres were not included. Had they been so included we might have run into the 'hybrid' situation discussed later in this chapter. With the benefit of hindsight, the exclusion might be regarded as a major omission in the attempt to understand the work of the department. Still, despite these cautionary comments, the main thrust of the

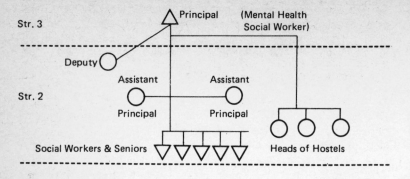

Figure 7.3   The organization of a mental health department

department at that time was undoubtedly to establish the client impact at Stratum 2, with the principal mental health social worker
operating at Stratum 3. (We might also note the consensual view of all
participants that the principal did in fact 'manage' 23 staff.)

That the HEW was Stratum 3 can be seen from the description of
part of the role of the principal, namely 'to ensure that resources are
made available to deal with referrals concerned with the possibility of
an admission of mentally disordered patients to hospitals'. She met
this duty by setting up appropriate systems such as rotas, joint
arrangements with other local authorities, and delegating work to the
deputy. There was also a 'community social work' duty involving the
care of persons suffering from illness, and the after-care of such
persons. She was accountable for setting the resources within the
budget and establishing limits, and for controlling this work. In order
to achieve these purposes the staff establishments were divided into
four social work teams on a geographic basis.

As part of the 'preventive' duties of the agency the principal had
also established various links (systems) of working with hospitals,
GPs, child guidance and child health clinics. In addition, the principal
had 'a duty to stimulate and generate ideas on the development of the
mental health service in the department'. This gave rise to a range of
typical Stratum 3 activities very similar to those undertaken by today's
'development officers':

● to arrange conferences of various kinds;
● to negotiate a change of venue for psychiatric clubs;
● to build up volunteer reserves; and

● to organize the internal furnishings, décor, policies and staffing for a new hostel for mentally subnormal children.

The client-impact level emerges from analysis of the roles of mental health social workers. Thus, one social worker felt that he had discretion (within policy) concerning:

● the frequency of visits to clients;
● what action to be taken;
● when to close or transfer cases; and
● applications to hospitals.

At the conclusion of this project the researchers raised a number of issues 'for further consideration'. Most of them were about the discretion and control of what I have now called the client-impact work.

The $\frac{4}{2}$ bureaucracy

The $\frac{4}{2}$, and indeed the $\frac{5}{2}$, agencies share the client-impact characteristics of the organizations just discussed. The $\frac{4}{2}$ agency provides specific kinds of services throughout the social territory. Unlike the $\frac{3}{2}$ organization it is unlikely to be a face-to-face group where director and staff are well-known to each other and co-ordination between top and bottom is rapid. The gap between the professional grassroots and the agency director has significantly increased. There will be a growing tendency in this type of bureaucracy to intersperse additional grades and to treat them as real levels of work and control. With the emergence of a 'senior management' group the 'professional versus management' split can emerge. Many Stratum 4 bureaucracies are likely to have Stratum 3 sites dispersed throughout the geographical territory with the consequent emergence of the problem of headquarters control over peripheral units.

To cope with its comprehensive terms of reference the $\frac{4}{2}$ organization may need a substantial number of support roles to help the main operational managers carry out their functions. It may need to appoint, or buy-in, specialist research and development resources.

Many pre-Seebohm county children's departments would have fallen within the $\frac{4}{2}$ model, and numerous national voluntary agancies have such terms of reference. We can draw on early research to explore the characteristics of one of the former county children's departments.[10] This particular project was based in two large areas within the county. The objectives of the research at that time were to elucidate the main types of work, the role relationships, and client problems. Whilst there were significant differences of individual perceptions, a simplified outline of the department would appear as depicted in Figure 7.4. With a main operational 'line' or children's officer, deputy children's officer, assistant children's officer, principal

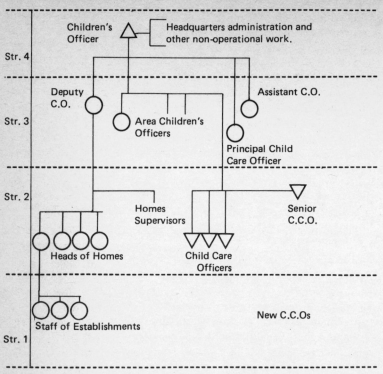

Figure 7.4   A pre-Seebohm county children's department (partial representation)

child care officer, area officer, senior child care officer, and child care officers, the research revealed many problems of role relationships.

Child care officers expressed a rather diplomatic 'unclarity' as to whether certain matters should be referred to the deputy, the assistant, the area officer, or the principal. Thus, the child care officer would 'approach' the deputy children's officer on matters relating to residential care, the assistant children's officer on financial expenditure, long-term care, and instituting proceedings, the area officer on short-term care and approval of foster parents, the principal child care officer on matters relating to casework technique in particularly intractable cases.

For those who hanker after the 'good old days', reports of that earlier research make salutary reading. The belief that lengthy hierarchies arrived with the Seebohm Report is rapidly dispelled. It is evident that the precursors of SSDs did not do at all badly!

The $\frac{5}{2}$ bureaucracy
This type of agency appears to represent the fulfilment of the

Seebohm ambition – an agency charged with comprehensive coverage of a field of need ('social distress') and staffed by highly trained professionals (see Home Office *et al.* 1968: chapter XVIII). The internal construction and organization of SSDs is described extensively elsewhere (see Brunel Institute of Organisation and Social Studies, Social Services Organisation Research Unit 1974: Billis *et al.*1980) and the case studies in Part III provide a few examples of the functioning of various parts of these departments.

We have already, when discussing the societal impact in chapter 6, illustrated the expectation which Seebohm held of the social services 'principal officer'. Research with social services directors and their deputies indicated that they considered themselves broadly fulfilling many elements of the Seebohm role, in particular its 'outward looking' focus.[11] All participants in the project emphasized their involvement with the corporate management teams of their authorities, with chief officers' groups, and with planning groupings of the health authorities. Great emphasis was placed on the 'political' aspects of their work. One director described his own main focus as 'moving the department forward by working with the political system of the social services committee and of the County management system'. Another saw his 'main function' as 'revolving around budgetary and political issues and being concerned with the protection of the political and professional environment of the department'; as being 'involved in any decision where the department has no established policy and/or which is likely to hit the headlines'. The director of a large county described his 'significant commitment on outside issues', with a main strand of work the 'oversight of the planning function' and yet another part of his work 'probing, challenging, and questioning'. Their responses were generally in accordance with a Stratum 5 response to problems, where management of the environment (field of need) of the department is a predominant duty.

The fieldwork side of a typical London borough might be organized as in Figure 7.5;[12] a county organization is depicted in Figure 7.6.[13] The SSD received 11% of the county budget (the second largest share compared with the giant's share of 66.7% for education). Of the Department's budget of £11,474,300, half was allocated for residential care (including administrative costs) and of this about £2½ million was allocated for the elderly in care. The department employed about 3000 staff in some 80 different locations; of these more than a thousand were employed in the residential and day care services, 490 in full-time posts in the home help service, and 258 were fieldworkers.

An example of a national $\frac{5}{2}$ organization might be the Department of Social Welfare in Cyprus. This is an interesting organization and we may note here the 'all-professional' nature of the service, indicating a

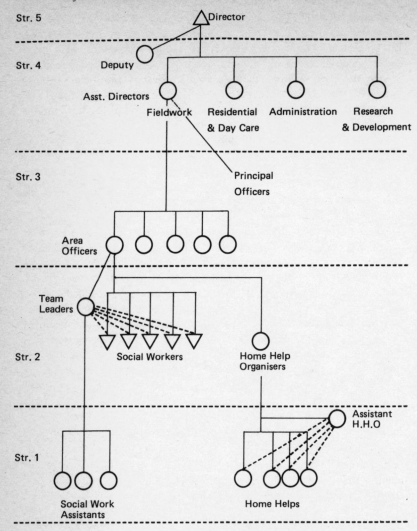

Figure 7.5   Fieldwork organization of a London borough

BEW at Stratum 2, and the comprehensive field (social welfare) coverage of the Ministry. The Department is divided at headquarters into sections covering (i) public assistance, related services and services for the elderly; (ii) personal services and services for children and the family; (iii) community work; and (iv) research. The country has a population of about 600,000 and the basic administrative units are the five districts headed by district officers. The Stratum 2 social workers are generalists operating a patch system and managed by

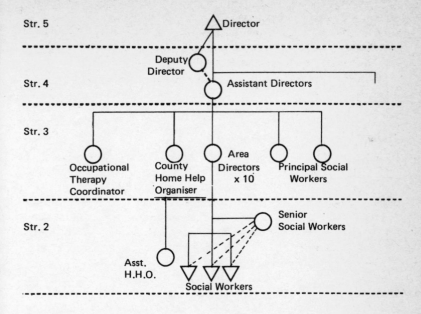

Figure 7.6   Fieldwork division of a large county, 1979

specialists reflecting the headquarter's division of functions attached to the district. The fascinating feature of this structure is the explicit and planned rotation of posts which goes on at each level and which ensures that those reaching the higher reaches of the bureaucracy have a wide knowledge of many aspects of the Department's work.[14]

The developmental bureaucracies

The defining characteristic of the developmental bureaucracies is the high level of work (Stratum 3 and above) expected at the client-impact level. This leads to characteristic tensions and fragility arising from the difficulty of maintaining 'managerial' control of the Strata 3 and 4 workers. Indeed, it can be argued that such *governmental* welfare bureaucracies are unlikely to be established. For the implications are that the front-line activity is carried out by highly trained professional staff who do not have caseloads allocated to them; but will be dealing with flows of problems (possibly stemming from the allocation of slices of territory) and organizing their own systems, procedures and priorities for dealing with categories of problems. These professionals will naturally expect a say on (but not carry accountability for) policies affecting the social territory. They will not respond favourably to extensive hierarchies and artificial chains of command. They will wish to become involved in developmental aspects of their profession, contributing to journals and participating in wider issues than the individual case. They will resent the contention that they can be managed by anyone other than a more experienced, capable professional.

The establishment of direct service agencies of this kind on a bureaucratic basis is a political gamble. It is also questionable whether community (political) sanctioning could be obtained for the degree of discretion associated with Stratum 3 and above client-impact work. It could perhaps only arise where the evidence of benefit to the community is so self-evident that the professional can in fact almost dictate his own terms. These service bureaucracies would reflect the highest degree of professional knowledge and training, with public confidence that their practitioners could be given an almost free hand. With the possible exception of medicine, it is difficult to see which social policy areas are candidates for this privilege. It may be that a few highly specialized organizations or institutes of practitioners may gain the necessary reputation and backing; but this will represent only a tiny fraction of the welfare provision.

It could also be argued that the maintenance of a few highly specialized centres is an essential precondition for the healthy development of the situational response agencies, providing them with the necessary research inputs for continuous professional advance. Anthea Hey has suggested that there is also a need for higher level (than Work Stratum 2) practitioner work in SSDs in order for there to be 'any opportunity for the development of new practice theory which is derived from actual practice' (Billis *et al.* 1980: 79). It may however be questioned whether, for the reasons outlined above, this higher level practitioner work could become widespread and accepted as the BEW of a governmental bureaucracy.

Developmental government bureaucracies may more readily be found in the advisory, research and co-ordinative agencies in the 'indirect' welfare business; that is to say, those agencies that are not providing services to the community, but nevertheless form part of the welfare network. These higher level bureaucracies may also be found in the non-governmental sector, which is not subject to the same sorts of political pressures.

An example of a $\frac{5}{4}$ (HEW might have been even higher) agency may be taken from discussions held with the head of a department within the Ministry of Social Welfare of an Eastern European country. It appears that the role of the Ministry is to decide on 'conceptual matters' in social care, since the main welfare system is at the level of work organization. For example, the rapid increase in the rate of divorce to 30 per thousand had raised the problem of the stability of the family. Policy options were (i) to make divorce more difficult (rejected as unrealistic); (ii) an educational programme (rejected as taking too long); and (iii) provision of a consultancy service.

This last possibilty was the preferred option, and marriage advice centres were established on an experimental basis. This proved successful and a proposal was put to the Government to establish advisory centres in each region. At the top (HEW) the role of this department was to provide a comprehensive coverage of ideas and policy throughout the field of 'social welfare'. The Basic Expected Work was at Stratum 4 and was expected to cover specific kinds of services within that field, organized on the basis of divisions for such areas as the family, children, and substitute family care.

Another $\frac{5}{4}$ agency is exemplified by a voluntary organization in this country. There is little doubt that its expected societal impact, as demonstrated by the role of its director, is at Stratum 5. Working primarily as a pressure group within a general field of need, its influence is at national and even international level. Its major reports are the subject of government interest (and worry). The director and senior staff are regular participants in television and radio programmes. The director is in constant interaction with Ministers and senior political figures. It employs a range of outstanding experts, each expected to make national contributions in their own specific field of expertise. They are aided in this by Stratum 3 researchers. It is difficult to do justice to this organization without providing more specific details, but it may be partially represented as in Figure 7.7.

I have so far attempted to demonstrate how the typology of possible organizational responses to social problems, illustrated in Figure 7.1, can assist in understanding and designing welfare bureaucracies. There remain, however, several points which require immediate clarification: (i) the question of 'missing' levels of response; (ii) bureaucratic choice and change; and (iii) 'hybrid' responses.

Missing levels of response.
Early research by the SSORU identified the 'missing level of management' as a prominent problem for SSD work in residential settings. With the development of the work strata theory it became possible to explain more thoroughly the nature of the problem, which could also be seen as a possible concomitant of major organizational restructuring. Since residential organization has provided many examples of this phenomenon, it will serve to illustrate the general proposition.

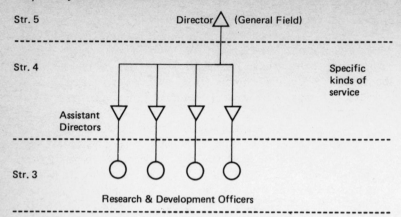

Figure 7.7   A national pressure group

(Although it should be pointed out that administrative sections of the departments have also suffered from the problem of a missing level.)

The position in residential organizations can be rapidly stated. In the first place the integration of residential work into SSDs has not been easy. Problem-based research workshops continue to attract many participants worried about standards of care and the development of systematic policies. These issues are dealt with in detail elsewhere (Billis *et al.* 1980: chapter 5; Billis 1982). Analysis of numerous departmental structures often throws up the sort of position illustrated in Figure 7.8.

In this illustration it has been assumed that most heads of homes are expected to work at Level 2, a proposition which has been tested many times. (There will also be Heads expected to work at higher levels, and perhaps a few even at Stratum 1; however, this is not central to the present analysis.) It should also be remembered that there may be some 60 or more heads in a medium-sized department. Many departments appointed what are called 'homes advisers': headquarters posts with unclear lines of authority over the heads they were supposed to be 'advising'. These advisers were rarely seen as managers by the heads in question – hence the identification of the missing managerial level.[15] It became clear, even without the aid of a theory of levels of work, that departmental and community accountability was based on a very slender thread. The heads could become a law unto themselves, rightly questioning the vague notions of accountability held in the department.

The Work Strata theory enables us to move beyond a missing level of 'middle-management' – to a statement about the *sort* of work that was expected and the consequences of its omission. Thus, it became

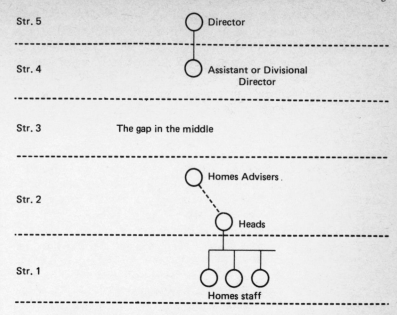

Figure 7.8   The organization of residential work within an SSD

possible to state that it was 'systematic service provision' which was required, a role or roles that would deal with patterns of service for a range of homes. Without this, not only is public accountability nebulous, but it is difficult to believe that anything that could be called residential 'policy' can exist. But cannot, it might be asked, the assistant director or divisional director (the Stratum 4 staff) fill this gap? Well, the difficulty with this as a possible solution is that these Stratum 4 staff will usually be too far from the grassroots activity in the homes, and have neither the time nor the appropriate organizational vantage point to make a satisfactory job of the systematic service provision. And should they nevertheless become very involved in the lower level work, we shall not be surprised to discover that strategic planning and other Stratum 4 work is being neglected.

To return to the typology in Figure 7.1, we can make the following proposition. In the first place some models $(\frac{2}{1}, \frac{3}{2}, \frac{4}{3}, \frac{5}{4})$ do not have the organizational space for a missing level. We are thus left with six remaining models $(\frac{3}{1}, \frac{4}{1}, \frac{5}{1}, \frac{4}{2}, \frac{5}{2}, \frac{5}{3})$ as candidates for constructional problems of the missing level. But it has already been argued that the most popular government welfare providing models will be $\frac{4}{1}, \frac{5}{1}, \frac{4}{2}, \frac{5}{2}$ because the others have either too low a level of societal-impact for social policy implementation, or too high a client-impact for easy political control. These four types will consequently need closer scrutiny and, as a rough guide, *particular attention should be paid to the Stratum 3 roles* – the only one to appear as a possible missing role in all four models.

There are also other reasons why Stratum 3 may be particularly problematic, reasons which arise from what might be called the 'mathematics of bureaucratic change', something which will be examined in the following section.

Bureaucratic choice and change

The prime purpose of the typology of responses is to provide the possibilty of social policy choices in the construction of the bureaucratic response. (It can hardly be claimed that institutional changes in the field of social welfare have to date been based on any very explicit models.) But other purposes of the typology might be *to increase understanding of historical changes in institutional structures,* and *to assist inter-organizational co-ordination and planning by providing a model for comparative analysis.*

From the argument so far, we can suggest that, when creating new organizations, such as at the time of Seebohm, $1 + 1 + 1$ does not necessarily equal 3. It cannot be assumed that taking a children's department, mental health and welfare departments, results in just one 'larger' department: it does not and might better be represented as in Figure 7.9.

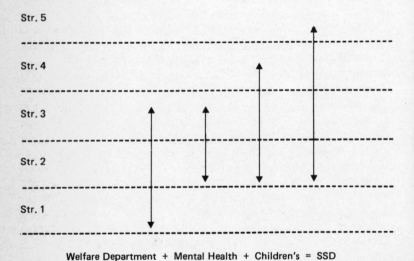

Str. 5

Str. 4

Str. 3

Str. 2

Str. 1

Welfare Department + Mental Health + Children's = SSD
Department   Department

Figure 7.9   Seebohm mathematics

In this figure I am making an assumption about one prime characteristic of SSDs which by now may seem unrealistic. This assumption, that the client-impact level is at Level 2, is in accordance with the social work dominated ethos of the departments. It is however a questionable assumption which demands further consideration (see chapter 4). Nevertheless, this example will have served its purpose if it does no more than illustrate that social policy innovations that necessitate institutional change require serious analysis. With our tentative theories of organizational structure we can 'predict'[16] many of the problems likely to occur if, for example, there are missing levels of response or false 'managerial' levels (see chapter 8).

In the previous section one example was provided of a missing Level 3 role. Another explanation for the missing middle level of management is that it can occur as a product of 'qualitative' organizational change. ('Qualitative' in the sense that the model itself changes as in Figure 7.9. Organizational change, of course, does not necessarily imply a change of BEW and/or HEW.) One phenomenon of organizational change arises from two prime forces. In the first place (as with SSDs) a director is appointed with extensive duties ranging well beyond those that went before. A senior 'management team' is appointed. The hierarchy becomes longer. Secondly, significant parts of the new organization are scarcely affected by the changes. Much of the grassroots work carries on as before, albeit in a different agency setting. In the case of SSDs this was particularly true of the work of the large number of staff working with clients in residential care. Thus, at one end of the organization are to be found a mass of grassroots workers 'attached' to the client base; whilst at the other end the senior management of the new agencies lengthens and stretches, and sometimes disappears from sight. The end-product can be two substantial ends with a very thin middle, the chewing gum effect (see Billis 1981a).

A second purpose of the typology might be in the area of inter-organizational planning and co-ordination. We can note here how the levels of work theory were utilized in one major project involving the Social Services and Education Departments of an English county (see Billis 1974 and chapter 9 of this work).

An important step in this project, which was attempting to develop a policy for the future of the Education Welfare Service, was the identification of the comparative levels of posts and decision-making in the two departments. An outline of the levels in the two departments that emerged after discussions with project participants is provided below in Table 7.2. It led to proposals for what were considered to be realistic mechanisms for joint planning in which the appropriate levels in one department meshed into the equivalent level in the other department.

Table 7.2   *Levels of decision-making in an English county*

	Education Department	Social Services Department
Stratum 5	Director	Director
Stratum 4	Senior assistant directors Assistant directors, area officers Heads of large comprehensives	Assistant directors
Stratum 3	Most heads	Area officer
Stratum 2	Teachers Education welfare officers	Team leaders Social workers
Stratum 1	Education welfare officers	Aides

Hybrid responses: tension at the coal-face

My contention is that the organizational typology does further the possibilty of social policy choices in the construction of a bureaucratic response. Despite the fact that it might – to those not accustomed to the intricacies of organizational reality and design – appear unduly complex, the typology does less than justice to the real problems of bureaucratic organization. In other words, there are, not surprisingly, a further set of problems that have emerged from the process of 'error elimination' in the application of the theory (see the discussion in chapter 2).

Whilst there are limits to the degree of specificity and technical detail appropriate to this particular book, one set of problems must at least be noted. I have referred to this as the issue of 'hybrid responses' and its development is outlined in the case study of day care (chapter 11). In order to round off the present exposition of alternative responses, the problem can be briefly stated here.

The typology portrays one main response. But even in the examples already provided, and certainly in the field as a whole, there are what we might call 'hybrid' models. Thus, an office of an SSD might have two main operational responses. There would be the fieldwork staff where the general expectation would be that a situational response (Stratum 2) model would be implemented; other staff, providing basic services such as meals on wheels and home helps, might be operating a demand (Stratum 1) model. In addition, Stratum 2 fieldwork staff would probably have assistants of one form or another. So we could well invisage a hybrid model as depicted in Figure 7.10.

That models of this sort are widely found cannot be denied. Much remains to be understood regarding the working of organizations and

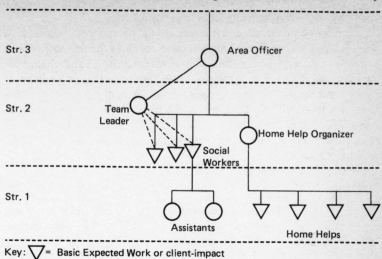

Key: ▽ = Basic Expected Work or client-impact

Figure 7.10   A hybrid operational response in an area office (partially illustrated)

part-organizations (such as area offices) where two different Basic Expected Work levels are to be found. Are there significant implications for the management of work and the delivery of services? What about career development, training and future prospects for the two different groups of operational workers? Thus, research in progress lends weight to the proposition that it may be difficult for Stratum 3 HEW operational units to function effectively with two internal coalfaces – or client impacts. In the six area teams under consideration in the day care study, the home help sections appear to function more or less as independent services. These are major issues which I can do no more than note for a future agenda.

Summary
Ten models of possible organizational responses have been presented based on choices of client and societal impact levels. I have attempted to provide examples from a variety of welfare settings in order to illustrate the utility of the typology. These models are, of course, 'one dimensional'. They do not take account of the permutations of activities (the horizontal dimension) of bureaucratic construction. However, it is not, I think, unfair to claim that the horizontal dimension receives most of the attention from practitioners and policy-makers. This is understandable in the light of – amongst other things – the occupational and professional interests that are concerned with these explanations and their control. So, in concentrating in these last three chapters on the vertical (level of response) dimension, some amends

may have been made in the imbalance of concern.

The chapter continued with reflections on the consequences of *missing levels of response* and moved on to consider the relevance of the typology for an understanding of bureaucratic choice and change. It was suggested that it could further our understanding of *institutional change* and assist *inter-organizational co-ordination and planning*. The chapter concluded by reflecting on the unresolved problems of what were called *hybrid responses*.

In chapter 8 we move on to consider the third dimension of organizational structures – authority.

Notes

1. In this and the following sections I am, of course, discussing role-structures. For brevity and to avoid repetition, I have omitted the word 'role' in much of the exposition and merely refered to $\frac{2}{1}$, etc. 'organizations' or 'bureaucracies'.

2. In this and the other examples drawn from the voluntary sector, I am drawing on research undertaken in the Programme of Research and Training into Voluntary Action (PORTVAC).

3. The European examples are drawn from workshops held with managers of European Social Welfare Agencies in 1978 and 1979.

4. The political involvement of Stratum 4 and 5 roles is not confined to welfare bureaucracies; see Rowbottom and Billis (1977).

5. I am using 'supervisory' as a general descriptive term.

6. The well-known division of Burns and Stalker (*The Management of Innovation*, 1961) into 'mechanistic' and 'organic' systems of management does not distinguish between the various structural types as described here. The absence in their work of a structural typology raises doubts about the validity of the conclusions. Much of their analysis can, however, be translated into level of work concepts. Consider, for example, the discussion on treating the market as a 'sink into which a firm tries to pour applications of techniques known to the firm' (in my terms, a Level 3 response) and 'treatment of the market as a continuing source of needs, actual and potential, which the firm tries to satisfy' (Level 4), p. 68.

7. An alternative term to decribe these bureaucracies might be that used by Cloward and Piven – the 'professional bureaucracies' – in chapter 28 of Kramer and Specht's *Readings in Community Organization Practice* (1969).

8. This research was undertaken as part of the brief of the Social Services Organisation Research Unit (SSORU). A general account of the work appears in Brunel Institute of Organisation and Social Studies, Social Services Organisation Research Unit (1974).

9. For present purposes we shall ignore the role of the medical officer of health (the superior of the principal mental health social worker) and the wider provision of which the mental health department formed a part. This might have raised the HEW, but it did not form part of the original research, and for illustrative purposes the mental health department can be treated as a single bureaucracy.

10. For a full account of the early research of SSORU see Brunel Institute of

Organisation and Social Studies, Social Services Organisation Research Unit (1974).

11. This is based on (unpublished) research undertaken with directors and deputies from seven local authorities, including counties, metropolitan boroughs, and London boroughs (Billis 1981c).

12. I have omitted residential and day care. Role relationships are included primarily to convey a sense of 'strong' (managerial) and 'weaker' (staff and coordinative) roles. (For details of role relationships, see chapter 8.) Also, I have not attempted to analyse where the BEW is in all the parts of this organisation. For an analysis of 'control and assistance' in a London borough, see also chapter 8.

13. This is extracted from Oxfordshire County Council (1979). It should be noted that this is not the most typical county organization. More popular at this time would be a split into geographic divisions at the level below the Director (Stratum 4). The allocation of posts to work strata does not, of course, appear in the original document.

14. This brief report is based on an account given by a senior member of the Ministry at a United Nations Social Welfare Workshop.

15. I have somewhat simplified the presentation in that there may be Stratum 3 principal officers in the charts. But they are usually too few in number to realistically 'manage' the Heads. I have also omitted the lines to headquarters 'administrative' sections, who often get involved in residential matters, and thus further complicate an already confused situation.

16. For a discussion of 'prediction' see chapter 2.

8 Authority, Delegation and Control: Towards an Alternative Approach

We have, so far, discussed the horizontal (categorization) and vertical (complexity) dimensions of organizational structure. In this chapter attention will be given to what was earlier described as the 'adhesive' which binds one role to another – *authority*.

Expressed rather differently, authority will be analysed as the sanctioned right, not only to influence the work content or *construction* of roles (the what?, how?, where?, when?, with what?, and how well?), but also the suitable *filling* (the movement into, continuation in, and movement out of) roles. In this chapter the possible complexity of organizational construction will almost be displayed. (A fuller exposition awaits the discussion of individual capacity in chapter 9.)

We then proceed to discuss the one-manager-per-stratum thesis (see Jaques 1967). It has proved very helpful in understanding several of the serious and pervasive pathological aspects of bureaucratic life, particularly the tendency of large organizations to create artificial layers of 'management', and the problem of unclear accountability.

The chapter continues by considering the extremely difficult question of the *delegation* of authority and accountability. Utilizing the concepts of *client* and *societal* impact, an alternative *structural* approach to organizations is developed in which the *control* of work is distinguished from the *delegation* of work. Doubts are cast on several current organizational models, and the possible implications for welfare bureaucracies are explored.

Pluralistic authority[1]
In this section we shall examine the third dimension of organizational structure – authority. We might begin by making the point that in all complex organizations, and even in very small ones, some roles have more authority 'attached' to them than others. Of course, to say that a role is very authoritative, or 'strong' is always to make a statement about its *relationship* to another role. To declare, as we shall later wish to, that a role is *managerial*, is to declare that it stands in a managerial relationship to certain other specific roles. Indeed, the occupant of one role may have the sanctioned right to exercise strong (managerial)

authority with regard to some roles, and weaker authority with regard to yet others. In other words, it is not unusual to find one person expected to exercise a number of different authority relationships towards different staff.

Fortunately, there appear to be certain types of roles that appear frequently in a wide variety or organizations so that it is possible to talk of 'general patterns' which can provide guides to action' (Hayek 1967 and chapter 1 of this work). In order to utilize more easily some of these general patterns I have grouped them around their relationship to the *construction* and *filling* of roles – the main areas of bureaucratic authority. In considering the main elements of construction particular attention will be paid to those questions that are held to be vital by employees and commonly subject to unclarity. These elements are:

What shall be done?   When should it be done?
How should it be done?   With what should it be done?
Where should it be done? How well is it being done?

These questions can be recast in terms which are perhaps more familiar. Thus, the question – what should be done? – requires a statement about the *assignment* of work. Does the role in question have attached to it the authority to assign work to other roles? The answer to the 'how' question necessitates explanations about the authority to set *methods* and procedures. The next question (where?) invokes statements about the *deployment* of staff – has the role authority in this sphere? When should work be done? This requires statements about the *programming* aspects of roles and authority in aspects such as issuing detailed plans, obtaining information, and overcoming obstacles. Next, the authority to *allocate resources* (the 'with what' question); here we need to know whether the role-holder is given authority to disperse the resources so that others can do their job. Finally, how well is the work being performed? The answer to this question leads to an evaluation of the *quality* of work.

The second arena where authority is required is, it is suggested, in the *filling* of the role; that is to say, the authority to influence or determine the *movement into* role, the *continuation in* role, and the *movement out* of role. The principal elements are:

movement into – selection
continuation in – induction
              – training
movement out – development
              – promotion
              – transfer
              – dismissal

Table 8.1 *Pluralistic authority in a bureaucracy*

Authority with regard to	ROLE TYPES						
Filling the role	Mana-gerial	Pres-cribing	Super-visory	Co-man-ager	Staff	Moni-toring	Co-ordi-nating
Selection	√		/	√			
Induction	√		/				
Training	√		/				
Development	√		/				
Promotion	√	/	/				
Transfer	√	/	/	√			
Dismissal	√	/	/				
Constructing the role							
Assigns tasks	√	√	/	√	/		/
Methods	√		/		/		
Deployment	√		/		/		
Programming	√		/		/		/
Resources	√				/		
Quality	√	√	/	√	/	/	/

KEY: / = influence   √ = major influence

It will be quite usual to find, especially in the larger bureaucracies, posts established which have influence in different parts of the above elements of filling the role. Only one role, however, will expect to have authority over all aspects of the construction and filling of other roles; that is the managerial role. Other common role-types are supervisory, staff, prescribing, monitoring, co-ordinating, and co-management. All of these have some degree of authority in role construction but not all have authority in the filling of roles, which can be regarded as the more sensitive of the two arenas of authority. Comprehensive discussions of these and other role-types are available in the publications of the Social Services Unit and the Health Services Organisation Research Unit. Consequently, I have attempted in Table 8.1 to represent only their main characteristics by way of illustrating the pluralist nature of authority 'attached to roles' in complex organization.

In order to avoid detailed analysis of the shades of authority, the account has been restricted to the authority to 'influence' and the authority to have a 'major influence', including the right to make final decisions. In discussions with staff the same point is sometimes made by referring to 'thick and thin lines' of authority with respect to the various elements. A broad level of analysis is often enough to point to ways of resolving problems; the practitioners themselves being more able to fill in the precise details. The cardinal rule might be expressed as: *providing sufficient definition to match the level of the problem being considered.* Some problems of authority may be handled at the 'thick and thin' line level; others may necessitate a finer spelling out of role components. My own research experience indicates that in this area the *realization* that authority is multi-faceted, and that organizations can be analysed in pluralistic rather than simplistic 'line and staff' notions, is often *the* major step forward. (Those, by the way, who doubt that social science concepts can exist and for a time prove fruitful, need only consider the entrenched nature of the 'line and staff' notion.)

One role that has constantly repaid detailed analysis has been that same role which constructs and fills other roles, i.e. the managerial role. This is hardly surprising given its pivotal position in bureaucratic organization. What is surprising is the way in which analysis rapidly decreases the number of 'managers' and increases the number of staff officers, co-ordinators, supervisors, and the like.

The development of the levels of work theory has added force to the more established analysis which utilized the authority-based role types (see chapter 10). These ideas, together with the concepts of societal and client impact presented earlier, will enable the development of an alternative model of bureaucratic organization. In the following section I shall suggest that there exists considerable confusion regarding the nature of authority (and accountability) and that this can be ameliorated by an analysis based on linking the concept of managerial authority to level of work. However, by itself, even this analysis is helpful but incomplete. To move a little further forward to the development of an 'alternative' model, we shall need in succeeding sections to outline what appear to be the current dominant models.

The manager, level of work, and accountability: confusion and analysis

The value of the concept of the managerial role in lowering the manifest height of bureaucracies will be examined in chapter 10 in relation to research in a home for the elderly. The same chapter will also describe part of the background to the development of a theory of levels of work. Here we can note that, building on the earlier work of Elliott Jaques, it rapidly became clear that by combining the concepts of role and level a proposition could be made that the 'thick' managerial line should cross a work stratum boundary. In other words, managerial relationships between staff, it is claimed, cannot be sustained within the same level of work. Staff doing Stratum 2 work cannot 'manage' Stratum 2 workers. Similarly, Stratum 3 workers

Next Work Stratum

Figure 8.1   *The straw boss*

cannot manage Stratum 3 staff, and so on. (It has already been suggested in chapter 5 that no managerial roles can exist at Stratum 1.) Should attempts be made to create by administrative fiat, managerial roles in situations such as that illustrated in Figure 8.1, then it is predicted that bypassing, frustration, and organizational overcrowding will occur.

The proposition shown in Figure 8.1 rests on the contention that the requirement on the manager to both construct and fill subordinate roles must necessitate a qualitatively higher level of response. A so-called manager who is not expected (and able) to make this higher level response will prove to be that most miserable of bureaucratic inhabitants – the 'straw boss'.

The one-manager-per-stratum thesis has been of particular use in analysing the continuing problem of the relationship of the team leader and fully-fledged social worker. If social workers are expected to work at Stratum 2 then – it is claimed – they can only be managed by a Stratum 3 worker. But analysis of the role of many team leaders illustrates that they too are expected to work at Stratum 2.[2] Their lot is not a happy one. On the agenda of problems presented by them for discussion, the questions of 'supervision' of experienced social workers and specialists, and accountability and authority, usually occupy pride of place. Different participants in one group of team leaders from different local authorities expressed many anxieties, for example;

- how to handle the supervision of experienced social workers and specialists;
- the meaning of accountability (this senior felt 'sandwiched between fieldworkers and the management team');
- the control of a group of highly specialized workers who 'had got rid of their last senior';
- doubts about the possibility of evaluating work;
- 'unreal expectations' and overwork; social workers had 'cut their previous senior into little pieces and he had left';

- the 'role' of the senior;
- the lack of priorities in work;
- the role of social work assistants.

This same group of team leaders utilized levels of work in examining their own situations over a period of three months. They also discussed with their staff how they (the staff) saw the team leader role. For many seniors the exercise proved highly illuminating and, they claimed, lowered the anxieties created by unreal expectations. For, from a general position as depicted in Figure 8.2, the situation began to emerge as in Figure 8.3.

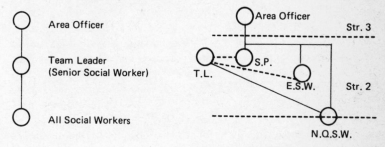

Key: Team Leader (T.L.)
       Senior Practitioner (S.P.)
       Experienced Social Worker (E.S.W.)
       Newly Qualified Social Worker (N.Q.S.W.)

Figure 8.2   Team leader role (before clarification)   *Figure 8.3   Team leader role (after clarification)*

The team leaders started to analyse the authority links between themselves and distinct groups of social workers; ranging from thick lines to the newly qualified workers, to what they called 'reporting' relationships with experienced workers, and 'on demand' relationships with senior practitioners. More detailed analysis would have required a rather different forum, working in the various authorities with most of the area teams. But the number of team leaders who continually and independently produce similar lists of concerns, and who respond in similar relieved fashion to the levels of work analysis, must indicate that the proposition has significant explanatory powers.

There are, of course, numerous unresolved questions even in the outline case given so far. The degree of unanimity among team leaders that they were essentially doing the same level of work as the experienced social workers, and that, when looked at closely, they did not feel themselves to be managing these staff, leaves as the next obvious problem the question: who does *manage* social workers? (That local authority social workers are still expected to be managed by someone is scarcely contentious (Rowbottom 1973).[3]) The only contender as manager would appear to be the area officer.

The other major question concerns the position of the newly qualified social workers. Here the question that would need to be answered is: what is *their* expected level of work? If there is an initial period during which the worker moves slowly into Stratum 2, then a case could be made for the team leader really managing these new workers. But what happens when the boundary is crossed (Stratum 1 to Stratum 2), and how does the transfer of accountability take place? The work of other researchers amply confirms the lack of clarity on these matters. We have just noted the dilemma of the team leader. Stevenson and Parsloe point to the confusion as seen by the grassroots social workers.

> To whom one was accountable, what accountability meant, particularly if 'things went wrong', how team leaders could know enough to make accountability a reality, were all questions raised by social workers and their team leaders. They recognised that they could share their worries with the supervisors but were not sure what this sharing meant. Was it just a way of receiving some psychological support in the same way that one receives support from colleagues? Or does sharing with the supervisor in some way hand on accountability and place a responsibility on the team leader to direct the work being done? What was obvious was that even when social workers recognised these issues few had been able to clarify their confused ideas and feelings, either by discussions within their agency or in training. Most evaded the issue, and for some, particularly those in hospitals, the question we asked 'to whom are you accountable?' seemed to defy an answer. (1978: para 8.79 p. 218).

The position in the higher reaches of SSDs would appear to be little better. A comparative study of the inter-relationships between directors and deputies of SSDs in six departments revealed a worrying picture of uncertainty about their relative spheres of authority (Billis 1981c).

In only one department, where the deputy was acting as the functional head (the fieldwork division), was the position reasonably clear (Figure 8.4B). Elsewhere the general picture was that the formal organization charts showed a single thick line between directors and their deputies, with a further thick line between the deputy and the rest of the senior management team (Figure 8.4A). In not one instance was this consistent with the actual working relationship as perceived by directors and deputies. In most departments the actual working arrangements seemed to place the Deputy in a staff-officer role (see Table 8.1 and Model C above). In several deparments, directors and their deputies, thought that some form of 'co-management' (Model D) was operating; with directors responsible for 'external' affairs, and

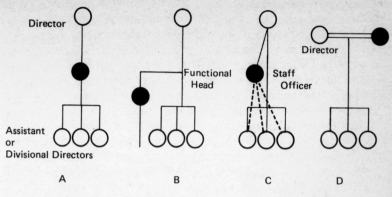

Figure 8.4   Four models of the role of deputy director [●]

deputies the 'day to day' management. Overall, senior management teams could not be sure who, at the very top, was accountable for what. In another department during a two-year research project involving the director, deputy, and four assistant directors, feelings were uncovered which brought to mind Jaques' description of 'paranoiagenic' institutions:

in place of confidence and trust they breed mistrust and weaken social bonds. They cause men of goodwill to despair about the duplicity of human nature without seeing the extent to which social institutions are calling forth the worst in men and supressing the good. (1976: 6–7).

In individual discussions members of the senior management group were bitter about relationships with their colleagues, the way in which the group failed to co-operate, and their image to the rest of the department. Just some of a long list of comments were:

'The senior group is seen as a dustbin.'

'We are played off one against the other.'

'We have a situation of private armies.'

'The Deputy doesn't have a real role.'

'I feel I can't get any co-operation.'

'People break the rules and do their own thing.'

'We're looked upon with a great deal of scorn.'

This unhappy state of affairs might be summed up by the statement made by a member of staff who declared that 'there is a lack of structure and formality in the way we manage'. Although this example might be extreme, it is probably not unique.

The position in other countries has also given commentators cause for concern. Indeed, in the United States two authors go so far as to talk of 'the crisis of accountability': 'the current crisis in social services is a crisis of credibility based on an inadequate system of accountability' (Newman and Turem 1974).

In these few examples I have attempted to illustrate the confusion which often surrounds the delegation and control of work. In so doing, another concept – *accountability* – has unobtrusively crept into the discussion. I have interchanged the terms authority and accountability for the reason that the latter requires the former in order to be translated into action. It *is* possible to have either without its partner, but it is not difficult to demonstrate the logical and practical disbenefits of such an arrangement. *Authority without accountability leads to dictatorship. Accountability without authority leads to impotence.* The case study of day care (in Part III) illustrates the impotence of middle management. The 'chewing gum effect' (see chapter 7), and the power of the authoritative head of home without explicit lines of accountability, illustrate the path to dictatorship (Billis *et al.* 1980: chapter 5).

Enough has perhaps been said to demonstrate the confusion, and to illustrate the possible utility of the different role-types – in particular the managerial role – when taken in conjunction with the concept of level of work.

We may now move on to the next stage in this development of a 'better tentative theory', or model, of bureaucracy.[4] First we shall discuss the *direct appointee* and the *directorial egg* models and their links with the idea of *delegation*.

The direct appointee model

In the direct appointee model (see Jaques 1976:chapter 4), the membership or elected governing body of the organization have decided to enter bureaucratic territory by employing one person. This, as I have tried to demonstrate in earlier chapters, is a major option confronting those who wish to grapple with the task posed at the start of this book: how to respond systematically to social problems. As work increases the governing body may decide to appoint additional workers *and maintain its direct control over all such paid staff*.

This is not a model that is generally to be found in the governmental welfare sector, where the social problems to be tackled are many, and the geographic areas substantial. It *could* however be implemented if, say, the problems were highly specialized and not too frequent. It is a model, for the same reasons, often found in the voluntary sector. For example, an agency working in the field of homelessness with five paid members of staff each with a 'direct line' to various members of the executive committee is illustrted in Figure 8.5 (PORTVAC 1979a).

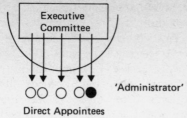

Figure 8.5   Direct appointee organization

It is evident that these 'single-handed' roles in Figure 8.5 – if they are above Stratum 2 – will often be doing many things that appear to be routine and of a lower level of work. These might include answering the telephone, typing letters, addressing envelopes, filing correspondence, making tea, cleaning the office and so on.

In the case of Stratum 2 and above roles, it is likely that, if the task is not actually in contact with the grassroots (whether this be clients, or research data, or administrative processes), the higher level bureaucrat will frequently need to 'dip into the water' to maintain contact with these activities.

These direct appointee organizations are not necessarily without their problems of authority and accountability, despite their small size. Thus, in the example illustrated in Figure 8.5, one of the workers was designated the 'administrator'. Whilst it seemed that he had some authority over the other workers, this was certainly not managerial, and they all had a 'direct line' to various members of the executive committee. In these circumstances, which only emerged during a 'social analytic' project (see chapter 2), it was difficult to discover who was accountable for what. Much time and energy were expended in day-to-day co-ordination and control of work. There was no mechanism or individual role, and little surplus energy, to discuss deeper issues of policy.[5]

The directorial-egg or 'directorial' model
This model sees the growth of bureaucracy as spawning from the single 'directorial egg' as a result of increasing work and the delegation of work.

Historically, a manager was a person who was put in charge of a venture by a company of people who, in order to finance it, had joined together and subscribed the necessary money. . . . if he required the assistance of others in his task and chose subordinates to whom he could delegate some part of his work, then his function corresponded to the managerial position . . . His delegation of part of the work in no way affected his total responsibility . . . . He was, in fact completely answerable for any failure on the part of his subordinates. (Brown 1960: 72).

This view of the growth of organizations through the delegation of part of the work of the person in charge was not confined to the industrial setting. This is evident from the way in which the Curtis Report (see chapter 6) envisaged the work of the children's officer in the large county where, because of the impossibility of knowing all the children 'under her care', she would need to 'allocate' a group of children to subordinates. The Committee was trying to resolve the dilemma of complex organization in which it is no longer realistic to assume that the director will actually deliver the client-impact services. Thus the acknowledgement that a 'group' of children would be allocated to subordinates.

The unanswered questions are then of level of work and accountability. Was the children's officer, of what was called the large county, to be held accountable for the children allocated to her subordinates? Furthermore, what was the logic of appointing a highly skilled practitioner if, as far as the children are concerned, the service would not be received from the children's officer but from subordinate staff? One answer to these questions has been in the development of a variant of the directorial model which we may call the 'practitioner-king' (or queen-bee model. It may be that the organization of hospital clinical work is of this type. The consultant does 'consultant' level work (say, Level 3 or above) and other lower level work is 'delegated' down to subordinate doctors as depicted in Figure 8.6.

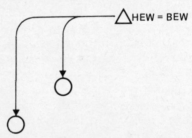

Figure 8.6   The practitioner-king

This would appear to be the model held by the Curtis Committee. Somehow, the person at the top (the children's officer) retains accountability for his/her patients although most (perhaps all) of the work is carried out by subordinate staff. But this thesis is under attack. The problem to be resolved is: *what real impact are the clients getting?* A Working Party set up to examine the organization of hospital clinical work stated that 'the specific tasks carried out by doctors of different grades in the hospital service has (sic) never been clearly defined and there is no consistent pattern'. They continued with the sharp comment that:

Many consultants consider that, in their NHS work, there are certain tasks which should only be done by subordinate doctors although it is not clear whether this view is shared by their patients. The nature of these tasks has not been defined, but the consultants' concept of 'non consultant' work appears to include not only resident on call work, and routine technical tasks . . . but also more sophisticated work peculiar to individual specialities. (King's Fund Working Party 1979: 35–6).[6]

Model 8.6 presents several difficulties. Some are evident from the King's Fund discussion of the consultant's role and are difficulties which I feel are endemic to this model of doing work. The practitioner-king or queen is expected to be responsible for higher level (in this case 'consultant') work, and to provide *that level* of work to all the clients arriving at the portals of the kingdom for treatment or care. Undoubtedly there are many situations where the delegated work model is viable and reasonable; but it would seem that a logical precondition must be that the director can in reality control the impact on all those clients on his case list (see chapter 5).

The practitioner-king model, because of the restricted number of clients it can serve, is of limited value in the discussion of large-scale coverage of welfare problems. A further limitation of this model is its dependence on practitioner-kings, who are likely to be in short supply. This model does however have the important virtue, in theory at least, of a clear statement of accountability. Both societal- and client-impact are vested in the practitioner-king who unequivocally carries accountability for that work.

However, most welfare bureaucracies do not operate in *practice* as if the societal- and client-impact were integrated in one role (like the practitioner-king variant) but, in the manner of the typology in chapter 7, they implicitly *differentiate* the two impacts. The director of social services, unlike the hospital consultant, is *not* expected to deliver the client-impact. Most governmental welfare agencies, like their industrial counterparts, appear to follow the mainstream directorial model. And here lies their major dilemma, for in this mainstream model, whilst the director is not expected personally to deliver services, all work is still held to be *delegated* from him and he is held accountable for that work.

That the directorial model is probably the dominant local authority organizational paradigm may be exemplified by the following extract from the section on the delegation of powers to chief officers in an English county. The Council 'delegates' powers to chief officers who:

may authorize the exercise of those powers by other officers in his Department . . . provided that (i) the Chief Officer shall himself retain responsibility for any action taken by any officer so authorized to act in accordance with such powers, and (ii) the Chief Officer shall not authorize any other officer to delegate further any power delegated specifically to him by the Chief Officer. (Oxfordshire County Council 1980).[7]

In this example 'sub-delegation' is apparently restricted to one step downwards. We might doubt the reality of this limitation when the list of delegated powers to the SSD director of the above department is examined. Apart from the fact that much departmental activity does not appear on the list at all – and we might wonder where it rises from – those powers that are listed are so vast that the reality of the limitation must be questioned.

The Inquiries which have stemmed from the continual welfare 'scandals' – in particular the Maria Colwell case – illustrate the theoretical weakness of the directorial-egg model (DHSS 1974b). According to the precise letter of the directorial model the director, if not the Council itself, must always 'retain responsibility' for the actions of subordinate staff. Whether these subordinate staff, and the various levels of superiors between them and the director, should also be held accountable is unclear in this model. Nevertheless, the directorial model, in all its forms (including the practitioner-king variant) does possess the apparent virtue of being able to pin-point who 'carries the can' – it is always the person at the top. Any alternative model, such as that which will be developed shortly, will also need to provide answers to the questions of authority and accountability. However, before attempting that task, it does seem necessary to engage in some form of skirmish with the ubiquitous notion of *delegation*.

Delegation: definitions and speculations

Bearing in mind its widespread appearance both inside organizations and in the literature about organizations, it might be expected that a rigorous definition of delegation, or delegated authority, is readily available. The fact of the matter is that inside organizations the term is, as we have already illustrated, much confused; and in the organizational literature the term is usually absorbed as one of many 'self-evident' concepts.[8] But if practitioners are facing difficulties this should always serve as a warning to commentators that the self-evident usage is no longer acceptable. That delegation in social welfare is a confused term is all too easily demonstrated. What then might be said by way of clarification?

We begin with a definition that contains some virtues and considerable difficulties.

Delegation: 'The investing of one person with appropriate and sufficient authority *to act for another*'. (Curzon 1979: 95, emphasis added).

Linking delegation to authority is a useful first step. Certainly, to speak of 'delegation' in any sense without providing the authority to perform the delegated action would bring us back to the unsustainable position of accountability without authority. The considerable fly in this ointment is, however, the phrase 'to act for another'. Taken literally, it must mean that the 'delegate' has as much authority as the main delegating institution or person granting the authority. If X is to act fully on my behalf, he must have exactly the same authority as I possess, since if he does not he cannot be said to be acting in every respect for me. If X, my deputy, can act as if he were me – as is claimed by many directors of SSDs – then the local authority and the social services committee must have sanctioned this form of 'co-management' of the agency (see Figure 8.4D). But it is doubtful whether such sanctioning is to be found in any authority.

The 1932 'Committee on Ministers' Powers', discussing the nature of delegated legislation, pointed out that: 'The power to legislate, when delegated by Parliament, differs from Parliament's own power to legislate.' So, whereas Parliament could provide for the boiling of the Bishop of Rochester's cook to death, 'any power delegated by Parliament is necessarily a subordinate power, because it is limited by the terms of the enactment whereby it is delegated' (Home Office 1932: sect. 3). If this is transferred to the context of organizations, we might make the following preliminary proposition: that no role contains the authority to delegate its own level of authority. 'Delegated authority', *if it is to retain any meaning at all*, implies the delegation of a lower level of response to problems and accompanying authority.

In fact there are those who have firmly rejected the idea of 'delegated authority' and the directorial model of organization. As long ago as 1926, Mary Parker Follett argued that 'final authority' is an illusion.

I do not see how you can delegate authority, except when you are ill or taking a holiday. And then you are not exactly delegating authority. Someone is doing your job and he has the authority which goes with that particular piece of work. Authority belongs to the job and stays with the job. (1973: 120).

Actually, it is not clear whether, even in the two examples provided (illness and holiday), authority can be 'delegated'. From interviews with directors and their deputies it seems that the former's absence would have to be considerable before the latter could take on the authority of the director's role (Billis 1981c). Certainly, the usual period of annual leave, or an illness of equivalent length, would be unlikely to lead deputies to accrue 'directorial' authority. Nevertheless, Mary Follett's main argument is persuasive. She criticizes what we have called the directorial-egg theory of organizational growth as coming from an 'historical' rather than an 'analytic' outlook.

We look back and see that when a business begins in a small way the head has many duties which after a while, as the business grows, are given to others. This has made people think that these duties by right belonged to the head, but that he has found it convenient to delegate some of them while, as a matter of fact, the convenience is just the other way round. There are in business certain separate functions; the smallness of a business may make it convenient for one man to fulfil them all, but they are still separate functions . . . But the separation of function does not mean delegation of authority. (Follett 1973: 120).

I could not attempt, nor is it my intention here, to produce a comprehensive analysis of 'the rise of bureaucracy'. The prime intent is to examine a few of the dominant models (direct appointee and directorial, including the practitioner-king), as a prelude to further model building. So, we shall merely note these two opposing views of organizational growth while continuing to pursue the main theme of delegation. I am also anxious to avoid an arid form of 'analysis' of the word 'delegation', which loses contact with the real problems. Perhaps therefore, we might sum up this discussion and move forward.

It seems that the dominant directorial model of organization draws its strength from something like the lagal definition of delegation quoted earlier. For it will be recalled that the county council regulations permitted chief officers to 'authorize the exercise of those powers by other officers in his Department'. The phrase 'those powers' are in turn taken to be those *same powers* that were 'delegated' from the county council. In this directorial model there is no explicit account taken of the 'separate functions' which, as Mary Follett points out, tend to form independent roles. Nor is any account taken of different *levels* of decisions which are bounded by higher level roles or institutions which have established these roles.

In view of these limitations and the operational problems listed earlier, it seems that, at the very least, the legal definition of delegation could be rewritten in a somewhat more useful fashion for organizational utilization. It might be redefined as: the investment of one person with appropriate and sufficient authority to do their work (and not 'to act for another' as appeared in the original definition).

However, it is tempting to succumb to the temptation to abandon 'delegation' completely and to see whether an alternative model of welfare bureaucracy can be developed. In fact all the ingredients for such a model – which I shall term *structural* – have already been presented. It remains to draw them together.

A structural model of welfare bureaucracy
The basic elements of this alternative structural model were in fact presented in the previous chapter. Thus, at some level, distinct client-

impact work is taking place. This is *controlled* by one or more levels of managerial roles which move upwards to the director of the agency. This model also provides an alternative view of the growth of bureaucracy to that which sees it spawning from the single directorial egg as a result of increasing work and the delegation of roles. For the concept and definition of bureaucracy presented here *already explicitly includes the differentiation of client from societal-impact.*

The establishment of most welfare agencies usually takes into account not only that there will be a director, but also that defined services will be offered to the agency's clients. In SSDs, field and residential workers, day care workers and domiciliary staff, are all interacting with thousands of clients. It is a patent absurdity to pretend that the director is the actual provider of all services and that these staff in some way are acting only with 'delegated' authority from the director. In like fashion the concept of a 'school' has built into it the roles (at least) of 'teacher' and 'headteacher'. The prison has its governor and warden. Factories have their shopfloor, and factory, managers, and so on, throughout the different bureaucratic settings. Thus, Basic Expected Work roles contain authority which is *not delegated from above; but which exists in its own right as part of the defining structure of organization.* So the line from client to societal-impact is one of managerial control, and not delegation.

However, managerial control roles can need 'side-ways' supporting roles, assisting managers in their control activities, and not down-wards through the main operational line. For example in some SSDs, area officers do not, according to this analysis, 'delegate' work to Stratum 2 social workers; but *control* social workers with the *assistance* of team leaders whose roles have authority to perform certain duties *vis-à-vis* social workers, as represented in Figure 8.7.

Neither area officers nor team leaders, and certainly not assistant directors or the director, are expected to carry the area caseload 'assisted by' social workers. It is the client-impact troops who carry the cases which have been 'allocated' according to policy and prefer-ence by team leaders and area officers as part of their 'control' duties.

In this alternative exposition, therefore, *control* and *assistance*, not delegation, are the key concepts. We must add that large bureaucra-cies will probably need both control and assistance roles.[9] The point being made is *the need to be clear which of these types of role are operating.* For without such clarification it cannot be clear where authority and accountability actually lie. Is the social work assistant 'assisting' the social worker who retains accountability? Or is he or she providing the client-impact work (at a lower level) which is controlled by the social worker? Are deputy directors controlling the work of assistant directors? Or are they assisting directors in the performance

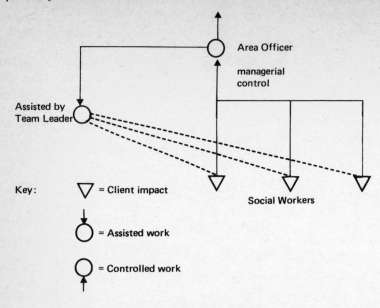

Figure 8.7   Control and assistance in an area office

of their (the directors') role? For clients, assistant directors and others at the receiving end, the distinction is critical.

But to illustrate more adequately how these concepts of control and assistance might operate, and also in order to re-examine the wisdom of several well-known metaphors (about bucks stopping and cans being carried), it may be helpful to outline several organizational features of the operational services of a London borough social services department as it might appear according to the foregoing analysis.

In this much simplified structure, societal-impact is vested in the role of the director. There is a hybrid client-impact (see chapter 7) of social workers and home helps whose work is controlled and managed by area officers and home help organizers. Because neither area officers nor home help organizers can cope on their own, they require assistance from team leaders and assistant home help organizers respectively. In this model, as in Figure 8.7, social workers are expected to respond at Stratum 2, but they have no assistants to help them. The team leader is not managerially controlling any operational staff, but is co-ordinating a group of social workers. This co-ordination involves (see Table 8.1) work in the area of task assignment, programming and quality control. The line of control moves directly from area officers to the assistant director (fieldwork) who needs the assistance of prin-

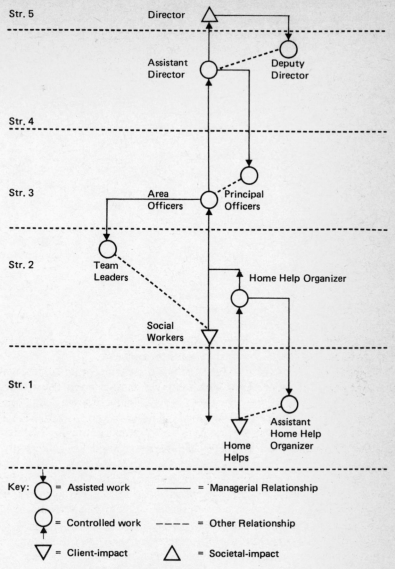

Str. 5 — Director

Str. 4

Str. 3 — Area Officers / Principal Officers

Assistant Director / Deputy Director

Str. 2 — Team Leaders / Home Help Organizer

Social Workers

Str. 1 — Home Helps / Assistant Home Help Organizer

Key: ○ = Assisted work   —— = Managerial Relationship

◗ = Controlled work   ---- = Other Relationship

▽ = Client-impact   △ = Societal-impact

Table 8.8   Control and assistance in a London borough SSD[10]

cipal officers, one of whom acts as staff officer *vis-à-vis* the area officer. The line of control leads from assistant director to the director who has a deputy assisting (mainly) as a staff officer to the four assistant directors.

There is no overwhelming virtue in this model compared to others that could be constructed, for example, with different client-impact work. Thus in some places the home help organizer/home help relationship might have to be redrawn – with the home help organizer assessing need and making a Stratum 2 response and the home help assisting the organizer in her work. (Although, in view of the large number of clients, it is a moot point whether a genuine Stratum 2 client impact could be sustained.) The possibilities are many. The advantages of this form of model building are that it enables statements of client and soicetal impact, and lines of accountability and control, to be made explicit.

So, who is responsible, for example, when 'the liner hits the rocks?' Sir Maurice Dean (1969), participating in the widespread debate on 'accountable management' which followed the publication of the Fulton Report, pointed out that although 'the captain is responsible':

However, in the subsequent inquiry no-one suggests that he alone should be interrogated. The inquiry would range into the adequacy of navigational equipment (especially if the ship had been navigating in fog) and the skill of the staff.

With the benefit of the discontinuous analysis of levels of decision-making we could – if we knew enough about it – go rather further and analyse which roles were accountable for what level of decision-making on the liner.

The social welfare ship is continually foundering – is the captain always responsible? According to the 'directorial egg' theory (where all work is delegated from the manager) the temptation is to answer 'yes'. The more complex model presented here casts considerable doubt on this way of approaching the apportioning of blame in the steady stream of welfare scandals.

Instead of the all-responsible captain, we suggest that people in roles are accountable for the level of decisions (complexity or vertical boundary) and group of functions (categorization or horizontal boundary) expected in that role. Should analysis of the scandal reveal lack of boundary clarity we know to whom to turn. It would indeed then be the next immediate constructor of roles (the immediate manager) who could be held accountable. Should the inquiry reveal that the boundaries to the role were reasonably explicit, but that an error of 'judgement' was made *within* the role, then the role-holder is accountable. Should the inquiry reveal that the *system*, that is to say the policy for handling the range of cases within which the tragedy fell, was faulty or non-existent, then the blame can be placed at the Stratum 3 role-holder. Should the tragedy be merely a symptom of a *specific service* failure, for example the lack of comprehensive policy or plans for a client group, then following Figure 8.8, we should be looking to the assistant director. Should the inquiry reveal a mesh of inter-divisional chaos ranging across more than one division and throwing doubt on the coverage of the department as a whole, then it is to the director that we turn.

Above the bureaucrats stand the politicians. For what are they accountable? Regan, in his inaugural lecture (1980), has gone as far as describing the local authority council as a 'Headless State' in which the absence of a highly visible and powerful political executive diffuses responsibility and makes it difficult for the public to apportion blame and credit. It is not my main concern to examine the interface between the political and bureaucratic systems (see chapter 15). It does seem however that, although Regan is making a valid point, failure to differentiate the role of elected representatives and *their* political executive from bureaucratic executive action, also makes it difficult to 'apportion blame'. Presumably, governing bodies – in this case local authorities – can at least be held accountable for the decision whether to send a liner or a raft (or something in between) to ride the welfare seas. Theirs, too, is the accountability for appointing the captain. The demarcation between the political and bureaucratic system has been expressed as follows:

It is for elected bodies and office-holders – parliament, ministers, local councils, committee chairmen – to determine and approve the volume and distribution of public spending and the level of services it sustains . . . It is not for them (public employees) to determine the scope of the public services or the quantity of money to be raised in taxes to finance them. (*The Times*, leader, 13 June 1981).

There is one further complication in this analysis of authority, and that is the problem of 'referral upwards' of matters of doubt. What happens when a worker refers an issue to a 'superior officer'? Is the original worker, or the superior officer, then accountable for any consequent action? It is not surprising that the Stevenson and Parsloe research uncovered much confusion over this matter. Without knowing whether the referral is to a controller (manager), or an assistant of one sort or another to the manager, it is not possible to give a clear-cut answer. The referral of issues to so-called 'superiors', who may have accountability without major authority, is often no more than 'take-it-or-leave-it' advice-seeking from senior colleagues. It is difficult to see how these matters can be sorted out without generally agreed and explicit statements of authority and accountability. In the structural model presented here I attempted to come to grips with issues which the directorial model does not appear to be able to resolve.

Summary
We began by analysing bureaucratic *authority* into its component parts

and presented a table of role-types of *pluralistic authority*. These roles ranged from 'strong' *managerial* to weaker *monitoring* and *co-ordinating* types. We then saw how the proposition that managerial relationships must cross a work level might illuminate several chronic problems of current organizational models.

In order to develop more fully an alternative approach – the main elements of which have appeared in earlier chapters – it was considered important to explore the nature of the dominant organizational models. After noting that the *direct appointee* model is more often found in the non-governmental sector, we considered the *directorial* model and one of its important members, the *practitioner-king or queen* model.

It was suggested that a concept of *delegation* underpinned the directorial model which saw all authority and work stemming from the top managerial role. Accordingly, in this paradigm, accountability for all work also flows to the top. We challenged the validity of this model and proposed an alternative *structural model* in which *client-impact* roles are explicit and *controlled*, and in which there can also be a variety of roles giving *assistance* to the main operational lines.

In the following and final chapter of Part II we shall consider the way in which individual initiative and ability might fit into this structural account.

Notes

1. The pluralistic nature of authority was noted at least as long ageo as 1926 by Mary Parker Follet in her discussion of 'Pluralistic Authority' (see Fox and Urwick 1973: 125).
2. The following comments are based on personal work over the last seven years with between 100 and 150 senior social workers (team leaders) from some 30 authorities in an extended series of workshops. The following account is of one such series with senior social workers, all of whom were designated team leaders.
3. The basic contention appears to be valid even when tested in workshop discussions (1983) with staff from the most 'decentralised' of departments.
4. For a definition and discussion of 'better' and 'tentative theory' *see* Part I, chapter 2.
5. For a discussion of the relationship between management committees and paid staff in voluntary agencies, see Harris (1983).
6. The Working Party utilized a number of ideas which have emerged from BIOSS research, including the Work Strata Theory.
7. I am leaving aside for the moment the place of the local authority elected representatives. The idea that they can be held personally accountable for the actions of all the many thousands of staff seems to me to be even more far-fetched.
8. However, important discussions are to be found in the political science

literature. See, for example, Birch's three main usages of representation (1971: 15).

9. Assistance roles involve those included in Table 8.1 and, of course, go well beyond the standard 'line' and 'staff' dichotomy.

10. I have included in Figure 8.8 only the Fieldwork Division and, even within this, numerous categories of staff have been excluded in order to preserve the main theme. The list of exclusions is lengthy – hospital social workers and their managers, intermediate treatment and other specialists, fostering and adoption sections, court officers, social work assistants, family aides, administrative staff co-managed in the division – and so on.

9 Individual Initiative Meets Bureaucratic Structure

How can we combine that degree of individual initiative which is necessary for progress with the degree of social cohesion that is necessary for survival? (Russell 1970:11).

The 'problem', as Russell put it, 'is one of balance; too little liberty brings stagnation, and too much brings chaos' (p. 37). A structural account of welfare bureaucracies presented so far can appear to fall into what has been called the 'hyper-structuralist trap', 'which deprives "agents" of any freedom of choice and turns them into the "bearers" of objective forces which they are unable to affect' (Miliband 1970). Any such impression must be firmly squashed. First, there are no 'objective forces' in this account, but tentative theories.[1] Second, the emphasis on structure has been an attempt to ensure its place as an equal partner with personality explanations of organizations. I can recall too many examples of suffering in organizations which had belittled structural factors to regard the issue with equanimity. Somehow Russell's 'balance' has to be found at the level of organizations. This emphasis on structure is an integral part of a concern for the preservation and development of individual initiative in work. Although they have not occupied a prominent place in this presentation, ideas such as trust, responsibility, commitment, goodwill are never far from the surface as honourable occupants of organizational analysis. However, the account of organizational construction would indeed be 'stagnant' and 'freedomless' without a companion tentative theory of individual initiative to join the structural exposition of categorization, vertical problem complexity, and authority.

In chapter 14 a case study based on research in this area is included for those who wish to examine one research base of the contentions that appear in this chapter.

I intend now to expand on several conclusions reached about administrative capacity in the case study, recasting them in the light of the ideas presented so far, and to examine the implications for the construction of welfare bureaucracies. The implications will be discussed under four headings:

- the first section considers the consequences of personal equilibrium between organizational role and administrative capacity;
- the second section looks at social policy changes and the link with adminis-

trative capacity, and some of the measures taken to overcome deficits in the supply of capacity;
- the third section explores the relationship between recruitment and organizational models and how this can go wrong;
- the final section discusses the possibilities and limitations of training.

Individual administrative capacity and level of work

Near the walls of London's Swiss Cottage post office someone had sprayed in red paint 'All roles are cages'. He, or she, had a point. So did the respondent who painted underneath in equally vivid colours: 'Some roles are cagier than others.'

Undoubtedly, bureaucratic roles can feel cage-like, bringing the concept and practice of bureaucracy into disrepute. In moving in this chapter from theories of structure to theories of capacity, the practice of bureaucratic life becomes a more central theme. Organizational roles represent the expected work to be done and the accompanying authority, and their essence is in fact to set boundaries. But even if the role construction is well done – if boundaries are explicit and defensible, and authority matches accountability – we are still left with the need to match the individual and the designated role.

Since it has been argued in the preceding chapters of Part II that there are at least three dimensions to roles (categorization, complexity, and authority), potential mismatch could occur with respect to any or all of them. However, in the introduction to this part we have already noted that administrative capacity will be defined only in terms of *the ability to handle different levels of work*. Therefore I shall discuss only the balance in this (complexity) dimension of role.[2] This view of individual capacity is a dynamic one and there will always be the need not only to match capacity to role, but also to watch and possibly change the equation. (In the illustration of these issues, roles will continue to be represented by circles and specific individuals will be represented by triangles.) At any given moment there could be three possible situations illustrated in Figure 9.1.[3]

Situation A represents a state of equilibrium between an individual's capacity and level of work in role. Mr X is 'on top of the job'. There is an absence of what Jaques describes as 'pathological stress' as distinct from the 'ordinary feelings, worry and concern that we all experience in our work and which from time to time can be very severe' (1970: chapter 9, p. 147: see also van Sell, Brief and Schuler 1981: 43–71). The experienced outsider working with organizations will be familiar with what appears to an absence of extreme tension and anxiety in individual or group discussions involving X. A genuine, open, and strenuous struggle for explicit formulations takes place. There is an added quality to the collaboration between X and

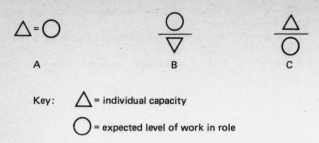

Key: △ = individual capacity

        ◯ = expected level of work in role

Figure 9.1   Individual capacity and level of work

the outsider stemming from the former's feeling of being 'in control'. Sometimes the analysis has an almost 'disembodied' feel, since person and role are clearly in harmony. There is a sense of objectivity to the discussion; of firmness and confidence. The general feeling of balance can exist above and beyond the personal interaction between outsider and X.[4] It pervades all the contexts within which interaction with X takes place, be they meetings with X and his superiors, or with colleagues, or with subordinate staff.

In case B, X does not seem capable of fulfilling his role. His collaboration with outsiders may be characterized by attitudes of extreme defensiveness, caution and anxiety. Collaboration can be genuine but guarded. X may be anxious to protect the imbalance – that the role is really too much for him – from the outsider's questions. If he has subordinates, he may not wish them to participate in the research project and can be suspicious of their opinions of him. In turn, group discussion with X and his subordinates are fraught with 'hidden agendas' and unspoken opinions. Low trust abounds.[5]

In situation B, if X has a central role in the collaborative research, the project itself can be endangered. Meetings with X and his superiors can be embarrassingly empty of content. In private, the superior may confidentially explain why nothing has been done. When the superiors are themselves trained social workers, their explanations are often full of understanding for X's personal situation and predicament. In one example X had risen over a period of twenty years, through the various organizations of local government, to a senior management post. Neither his boss (the director) colleagues, or staff, believed that X could do the job. With three years left to X's retirement, nothing was done. Managerial unwillingness to act resulted in high staff frustration. The subordinates 'did their own thing', some left for other posts. X was bypassed and ignored. He stuck it out. The director refused to act, and work was left undone. The impact of all this on the community cannot be evaluated.

In situation C, the insider-outsider collaboration may be characterized by disinterest. X has left the role behind. He is looking elsewhere for the possibilities of alternative employment or more challenging endeavours. Or the collaborative project might come just in time – as in the case of the intermediate treatment officer illustrated in chapter 13. There, analysis of the work to be done and the identification of a 'high flier' in role, led to a realignment of role and individual.

These snapshots of personal equations must be seen against the backcloth of the development of administrative capacity over time. Thus, equilibrium and disequilibrium can arise from the differential development of capacity illustrated in Figure 9.2. This diagram will be particularly important in the later discussion on recruitment.

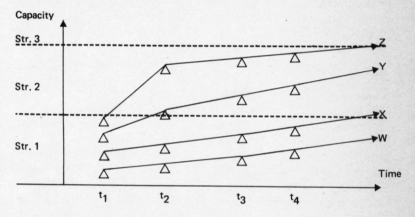

Figure 9.2 The development of capacity over time

Capacity is represented by the vertical axis, and time along the horizontal axis. Four snapshots at three-year intervals (t_1, t_2, t_3, and t_4) are presented. At the beginning of their careers, at point t_1, all four individuals possess Level 1 capacity and are coping with Level 1 work; but Z is already showing signs of moving through the boundary. Three years later he could be launched into Level 2 work, and is about to be joined by his colleague Y who is also just ready for a Level 2 role. Meanwhile X and W demonstrate solid Level 1 ability. At point t_3, Z could be a fully-fledged professional in mid-Stratum 2, and Y is still in the early stages of Stratum 2 development. X is moving to the top of Stratum 1 capacity, perhaps taking on foreman or supervisor duties. W's position is little changed.

The final snapshot, at time t_4, indicates two of our group poised to make another significant career leap, provided that – it must be emphasized – a suitable role is available. Z may be moving away from direct client-impact work, displaying an ability to participate in developmental and policy matters. Y is now an experienced professional and may be content to perform situational response work for a large part of his career. Meanwhile X is about to take probably his most important step. After a lengthy period in prescribed output work, possibly in a variety of 'supervisory' posts, he is almost ready to take on Level 2 work. This, in view of the relatively slower development of capacity, may entail the control of subordinate staff, rather than Stratum 2 client-impact work. Our final snapshot shows W still in mid-Stratum 1.

The introduction of a theory of the differential rate of development of administrative capacity immediately indicates how difficult it is to avoid bureaucratic mismatch of role and person. At the very least, this contention reinforces the case for strong personnel functions in complex organizations. These may be part of the managerial role, but can also in larger organizations be quite distinct. Someone, somewhere, must be aware of both role structure and individual development.

Social policy changes and administrative capacity
Changes in social policy often entail the reshuffling and reshaping of bureaucratic boundaries. This can be the case even in more modest proposals than the sweeping Seebohm reorganization. Central government legislation may increase or diminish the statutory obligations of local government service agencies. Thus, the horizontal dimension can be altered by increasing an agency's responsibilities with regard to a client group. Sometimes legislation can entail the wholesale transfer of workers from one agency to another as with the medical social workers. Major changes will – as in the case of the legislation following the Seebohm Report – probably require alteration of both horizontal and vertical dimensions. In England and Wales the internal construction of SSDs is in the hands of each local authority. No two authorities have precisely the same organizational structure. And each structure will in turn have its own demand for administrative capacity. An SSD with three assistant directors will need a supply of three Stratum 4 capacity people. The neighbouring SSD which has decided to organize itself on the basis of eight divisional directors will need a supply of eight Stratum 4 people. The latter structure may not only cost more in senior management salaries, it also has a larger demand for administrative capacity.

Total organizational supply and demand of administrative capacity are rarely taken into account in social policy proposals requiring organizational change. It seems to be assumed that the supply of additional administrative capacity will somehow materialize!

The severe effect of imbalance between the supply and demand of administrative capacity is illustrated from the experience of kibbutz bureaucracy (Billis 1977). The somewhat pessimistic conclusions that can be drawn are that whilst governing bodies can decree expected responses to problems, the supply of administrative capacity can be 'inelastic'. It takes time to respond to new demands. From where, for example, were the new higher level people expected to emerge post-Seebohm? Possibly, there were a number of Level 5 capacity people under-employed in the commanding heights of the former children's, welfare, and mental health departments. But it would be unrealistic to expect that at the time of reorganization sufficient Level 4, and possibly Level 5, administrative capacity was immediately available. Research projects since then suggest that lack of administrative capacity continues to plague departments. Thus, 'development' officer posts are sometimes created to bolster-up gaps; that is to say, to deal with situations illustrated in Figure 9.1B (Billis *et al.* 1980: chapter 10). In like fashion my research into the role of deputies shows that they too are sometimes used to take over and fill gaps caused by lower level incapacity (Billis 1981c). Probably there are additional means by which departments could compensate for insufficient administrative capacity.

The concept of the supply of administrative capacity has implications for (i) the 'decentralization/centralization' debate, and (ii) the relationship between central and local government.

The move to some of the types of 'patch' organization is intended to raise the level of decision-making at the grassroots (Hadley and McGrath 1980). In their review of existing patch schemes, Hadley and McGrath suggest that 'the role of individual workers seems to have been extended . . . and it is also claimed that workers have more individual responsibility . . . (p.10)'. It may be questioned whether changes of this kind could be introduced nationally without drastic steps in recruitment and training policies to alter the front-line organization (DHSS 1976; see also Cooper 1981). Here and there, higher level patch responses may be practicable. As a national policy, a sudden and dramatic change is improbable. *All that may result is a further gap between community expectations and organizational response.*

Social policy changes, such as the establishment of SSDs with a higher expected societal-impact, have implications for the relationship between central and local government. Many directors are now. influential figures moving amongst the political structures in a manner previously unknown or rare. The balance of power has changed, both at the local and in the central-local relationship. SSDs are in most cases more powerful and interact with other agencies on a more equal, and a more than equal, basis.

Central government advisers can no longer always obtain the same quick access that they may have been accustomed to with the directors' (less harrassed) predecessors in the 'old days'. The imbalance between central and local government may develop in an unexpected fashion. Directors and their senior staff may be thinking in broader, more theoretical, and innovatory terms than the central department advisers. Unless central government changes its own approach, the impact of its 'advisers' is likely to be treated with less and less significance. The real experts might be found in the locality. Adrian Webb (1977) has suggested that an important role of central government policy will be in 'facilitating the intellectual exploration of problems, causal explanations, philosophies of intervention, models of care and evaluation criteria'. But if this is to be 'the heart of central planning activity', are there not important implications for the level of work of central government staff?

Recruitment

Recruitment policies help fashion the shape and size of occupational groups, professions, or organizations. Elitist groups jealously maintain control over entry in order to ensure purity of membership. Questions of professional calibre and standards may not be the only real consideration. Control over entry restricts the supply of labour and can protect jobs and salaries. *Poor or incorrect recruitment policies can jeopardize the entire organizational venture.*

The early potential kibbutz members, preparing for their 'ascent' to the land of Palestine, often developed intensive and comprehensive recruitment strategies. Those intending to become members of the struggling kibbutz movement prepared for their new lives by working in training farms which, as far as possible, replicated the social and work conditions they could expect to meet when they were eventually permitted to enter Palestine. The future kibbutz member would have passed through a series of 'trials' where commitment to the organization would have been demonstrated in real sacrifices. Comfortable, middle-class family homes would be left, higher education and good jobs abandoned. Many of the trainee kibbutz members never left the shores of their birthplaces. Even greater numbers joined and then left the settlements when faced with the harsh reality of pre-State kibbutz life. It was little wonder that those who remained represented a core elite force in most areas of national life (see Amir 1969).

In paying great attention to recruitment, the kibbutz was not unique. It was an explicit policy, justified by reference to the failure of previous cooperative ventures of Owen and Fourier. It was – or rather is, since much of the basic approach still remains – also not unique, in that many work-doing groups, the professions in particular, also insist on their own stringent barriers to entry. Of these, examinations and qualifications are the most common, although a distinctive uniform and a private language are often part of the formal entry conditions. The kibbutz experience is far from unusual. Recruitment policies are an essential part in the control and maintenance of organizational boundaries.

Recruitment poses a particular problem for most types of welfare bureaucracies. They often have difficulty in answering the key question: recruitment for what? For example in England and Wales energetic attempts continue to be made by government departments, quangos, professional associations, academics and an array of working parties, to answer fundamental questions about the 'social work task'. Despite the many training schemes and the thought given to qualifications, the broad issue (as the Birch Report pointed out) remains obscure. It may continue to remain obscure without a theory of work. I suggest that the type of analysis discussed here could provide a useful approach. To support this contention, examples will be drawn from educational welfare and housing associations.

The link between recruitment policies and the work to be done, and the utility of the levels of work theory, emerged during a research project based in the Education and Social Services Departments of a large northern county (Billis 1974). The purpose of the project was to develop alternative models for the future of the county's educational welfare service, at that time part of the Education Department. Key figures from both departments, including the directors, participated in the project. The following comments are extracted from the 'cleared' individual reports of some of the participants.[6]

Mr H, one of the educational welfare officers (EWO), was a qualified social worker and was not satisfied with the present position whereby many EWOs were appointed after retiring from another job. For example, about one-third of the EWOs were ex-policemen: 'they are not necessarily the best for the service and tend to be authoritarian'. Such entrants, he felt, were not likely to be concerned about developing the service in the same way as other career-minded people. He wanted to see younger people appointed with a career structure and training parallel to the SSD. The duties of the EWO were not laid down and there was no uniformity in the country or county. Therefore, 'considerable discretion is left with the individual whether the emphasis is placed on welfare or attendance'. He believed that 'welfare' was not just getting a child to school but involved becoming accepted by the family and showing them that the officer had the long-term interests of the child at heart. The specific specialism of the EWO was in 'selling' the idea of education to families in order to break the cycle of deprivation. Mr H felt that a lot of the effort of EWOs would be wasted 'until Headteachers are re-educated into seeing the role as a welfare role on behalf of the family rather than getting a body back to school. Heads in general, don't look at the underlying principles.' A relevant point was considered by Mr H to be the pressures placed on the EWOs, each of whom was dealing with from 6 to 7000 school children. Even if a small percentage of these had problems, the EWO was overwhelmed. In consequence, work was undertaken only with questions of attendance.

Mr B, the headmaster of a primary school, did not consider that there was much work for an EWO in his or similar schools. 'In the main, the children want to be in school and parents want their children to be in school. There are no attendance problems and the EWO would be seen only when sent for, or when families require material assistance.' Despite this Mr B was very much aware, through his participation in working parties etc., of the doubts and worries expressed by colleagues who did require educational welfare services. Secondary schools in particular had real problems of getting children to school, and Mr B appreciated the position of some of his colleagues 'who continue in what is generally called the "school bobby" or "kid-catcher" approach to the EWO'. Mr B linked the issues of work and recruitment to career development. He pointed out that the SSD offered opportunities for promotion that the Education Department couldn't provide at that time. He felt that a system should be found to enable EWOs to be paid at comparable rates and which would permit them to be eligible for promotion. Whilst the present system threw up many good people, the possibility needed to be explored of attracting the right sort of candidates with greater academic ability who, if necessary, might be promoted 'sideways' into the SSD. 'In this day and age, properly trained people will be necessary for the service, and it is probably unrealistic to expect a continuation of the former traditional sources for recruitment to the Education Welfare Service.'

Mr M, the Assistant Director of the SSD, succinctly summed up the difference between the two levels of work in a manner generally accepted by all the participants. He considered that the work was (or could be) carried out at two levels. The first level might be described as the 'school bobby' approach which many headteacher and divisional education staff saw as right and proper. A lot of the 'policeman' work was bound up with attendance and truancy, school meals and clothing allowance enquiries, access to resources, e.g. community homes seeking help, etc. The second wider (Level 2) work he referred to as 'real social welfare work'. Level 1 work was seen to be primarily characterized by routine jobs, form filling and routine enquiry work. Level 2 had wider implications and would include group work in secondary schools, etc.

The final joint recommendations of both departments absorbed and utilized the distinctions illustrated above. Level 1 and Level 2 work was defined and brought into the executive recommendations for the work, recruitment, and career patterns of the proposed service.

Housing associations are excellent social institutions in which to examine the meeting between individual initiative and bureaucratic structure. For they have traditionally recruited staff with a wealth of personal dynamism and ability, attracted by the apparent range and level of discretion of the front-line tasks. It is an image which those directors of associations who may have themselves been young 'high-fliers', not many years previously, actively encourage. I shall describe relevant aspects of a case study of 'Dynamo' housing association in order to illustrate the relationship between recruitment and task.

Recruitment was in the image of the director, and a director's baton the aspiration of the young and enthusiastic graduates. (I hasten to add that this research was undertaken at the end of 1979, when such aspirations did not seem quite as far-fetched.) That most housing associations at that time could fairly be described as 'bureaucracies' was unpalatable, but accepted by many directors. With sizeable and growing numbers of staff, varying levels of responsibility and titles, and substantial absolute and differential salaries, the association had entered the bureaucratic family. The widespread introduction of the company car for senior staff was merely a last finishing touch.

New recruits to Dynamo were given the impressive title of 'area management officers' (AMO). At first sight their expected work might appear to be at least at Level 2. As the manager of the AMOs, one of the district officers, put it: 'The basic organizational concept is of patch responsibility for all that happens in the patch.' His colleague district officer had a similar view of the front-line role and wanted '. . . the patch to be a self-determining area'. Discussions with these managers of the AMOs revealed considerable tension at the front-line. This tension was confirmed in the interviews with the AMOs themselves. Simplifying the issues, the strain was between a view of the work that was called 'day-to-day estate management functions', such as straightforward rent collection; and a higher level expectation of the role whereby an AMO would be expected, for example in the case of rent arrears, 'to go in and assess the situation, make a decision about the payment, and a course of action'.

The levels of work theory was utilized by the participants in the Dynamo project, and the alternatives of either a Stratum 1 or Stratum 2 front-line were discussed in explicit fashion. One district manager 'wondered whether the second level of work is actually being performed'. He noted:

the difference in approach between the older staff who are good at the day-to-day estate management functions and the younger, newer, idealistic staff who do not need to be motivated to become involved in the community, but who do need to be supervised in order to ensure that they perform basic, bottom-level functions. (PORTVAC 1979b).

The Head of Development, responsible for Dynamo's acquisition and improvement of property, felt that they were 'recruiting young graduates who . . . can exploit the situation. . . . People should not be appointed without experience of collecting rents, accounts, etc.' In individual and group discussions with the AMOs, the general view was that there was a large mass of highly skilled, prescribed output work which they saw as the core of their work.

The dilemma was that the organization had probably 'over-recruited' and had a number of AMOs whose ability and expectations moved well beyond such a role. The director himself accepted the utility of the analysis and recounted an example of the sort of recruitment problems that he faced. Two candidates had appeared for interview for a vacant post of AMO. One, a middle-aged lady with few academic qualifications but a wealth of practical experience and maturity; the other was a lively young graduate of the type identified by the Director of Development. The graduate got the job – a decision the Director now regretted. For 'with hindsight' he realized that the organization needed a Level 1 client-impact – albeit of considerable sensitivity – and that the unsuccessful candidate would have been a more suitable choice. Furthermore, the Director linked the organization's problem of a rapid turnover of AMOs with the recruitment policy. In the language of Figure 9.2, he had been recruiting too many Ys and Zs, when what was really required for the post of AMO was W or X.

Training

It is not my intention to discuss the detailed history and present state of training for work in social services departments. Anthea Hey has analysed both 'social work' and 'basic services work' utilizing the work strata theory in relation to various courses (Billis *et al.* 1980: chapter 3). I will pursue, in accordance with the wider theme of this book, several broad topics that might be relevant to welfare bureaucracies in general.

That training – as distinct perhaps from 'education' – must be linked to the expected work to be done, is hardly a controversial statement. The problem, which often appears insoluble, is the unresolved dilemma of the client-impact level and the fragile state of the horizontal dimension in many sections of social welfare provision. It is difficult to establish training schemes without explicit and societally-backed tentative theories of the two dimensions. Nevertheless, without embarking on a detailed analysis, it is possible to put the broad proposition that *training responses will need to be different depending on whether the expected client-impact is at Level 1 or Level 2*.

Figure 9.3 depends on the assumption that the categorization of work (horizontal boundary) is explicit. I have done no more than take a first pot-shy at possible patterns of training, in response to the proposition that the two different client-impact levels will require different training schemes.

Expected Work		
Str. 3	Advanced management courses	Advanced management courses Post-professional courses
Str. 2	Basic management courses Refresher courses	Basic professional ▽ qualification
Str. 1	Basic occupational ▽ training	Apprenticeship schemes

Key: ▽ = client impact level

Figure 9.3   Training and client-impact levels

It can be argued that where a *pot-pourri* of courses exists, this will reinforce a pot-luck response. The proposition is, thus, that all concerned with training need to know not only the content but also the level of the response. If these models are linked to the development of individual capacity, it is possible to begin model building related to training, type and complexity of work, and individual development. It is not central to my argument that, for example, 'advanced management courses' are at Level 3, or that any *particular* course ought to be linked to a given level. The point is more general. The wide variety in level of courses (currently existing in the UK) which, for example, provide the basic professional qualification for social workers, is not conducive to clarity of client-impact level.

Summary
This chapter has focused on the place of individual initiative in bureaucracies. In the first section we discussed the *differential development* of administrative capacity and the consequent difficulty of matching person to role.

The second section examined the implications of social policy changes for the total *supply* and *demand* of *administative capacity*. Whilst major social policy changes usually require changes in both the horizontal and vertical dimensions of organizations, the implications for administrative capacity are rarely considered.

The link between *recruitment*, capacity, and level of work was the concern of the next section. The Education Welfare Service and Housing Associations provided examples of the utility of having a conceptual language to distinguish between Level 1 and Level 2 client-impact levels when recruiting staff.

We concluded with comments on the relevance of the theory for *training*, being content to make a few general observations.

Notes

1. For an account of the development of 'tentative theory' and the work of Karl Popper, see chapter 2.
2. In the description that follows immediately there may be some overlap in cases where other dimensions are out of balance. More precise examples are to be found in the case studies in Part III.
3. For Elliott Jaques' definition of capacity and its link with pay, see *A General Theory of Bureaucracy* (1976) chapter 14.
4. For a more detailed explanation of 'outsider' and 'insider' see chapter 2.
5. For 'high' and 'low' trust, see chapter 2.
6. For an explanation of 'cleared' reports and the research methodology employed, see chapter 2.

PART III

The Generation and Utilization of Usable Theory

The studies in this part are included in order to illustrate how some of the usable theory presented in Part II has been generated and utilized. In other words, they attempt to demonstrate how the gap between theory and practice might perhaps be narrowed.

Chapter 10 is a historical note which shows how a body on inherited 'initial conceptions' left unresolved a further series of problems and how this provided an important impetus for the development of the levels of work theory.

Chapter 11 indicates both how existing theory may prove usable and how further ideas might develop. In particular this study of day care was instrumental in raising questions about the meaning of 'social distress', 'prevention', and 'at risk'.

Chapter 12 discusses levels of decision-making in the 'Entry Into Residential Care'. It is included primarily in order to provide another strand in the history of the levels of work theory. However, we might just note that, more than a decade later, many of the substantive issues discussed would repay further examination.

If Chapter 11 focuses on the *categorization* dimension of organizations, and chapter 12 on the *vertical* level of work dimension; then chapter 13 may be said to illustrate the *authority* links. This case study of an intermediate treatment officer demonstrates quite clearly how theory can prove usable, and by all accounts useful.

Finally, chapter 14 is a rather different sort of case study and discusses only the development of theory about administrative *capacity*, the fourth dimension of organization.

The Generation of Usable
Theory: a Historical Note

This chapter provides some personal observations on the general development of a theory which has steadily been applied well past its original substantive area – SSDs – to welfare bureaucracies, and beyond. This short history also illustrates, at the level of a research 'enterprise', the relevance of the Popperian schema for the development of theory, discussed previously.

From categorization to level
In tracing briefly the history of the development of the levels of work theory from earlier work on categorization, we might be guided by the suggestion that:

A theory is comprehensible and reasonable only in its relation to a given *problem-situation*, and it can be rationally discussed only by discussing this relation. (Popper 1974a:199; emphasis original).

Early analysis of the categorization dimension in SSDs led to the contention that most of the operational work with individuals and families could be represented as in Table 10.1. The full list of the activities of the department also included operational work at the community level, research and evaluation, strategic planning, public relations work, logistics, financial and secretarial work. Several of the specific problems leading to the compilation of the list were noted at that time. (Earlier in the same book we presented a more comprehensive list of the main problems encountered in the research: Brunel Institute of Organisation and Social Studies Social Services Organisation Research Unit 1974: 8–10) We stated that:

there can be no completely satisfactory answer to any specific questions of organization or procedure without preliminary understanding of what the department as a whole is trying to do – *what it is in business for*.

For example, such an understanding is needed when studying general departmental structure. (What sorts of activities are implied when terms like 'field work', 'residential work', and 'domiciliary and day care' are used to identify various main divisions; and what activities, if any, are in danger of being overlooked when employing such terms?) It is needed when considering the role of the trained social worker and how this is differentiated from the role of the social work assistant or the occupational therapist or home help. (Does the term 'social work' encompass all that SSDs have to do; and if so what activities are carried out by those other kinds of staff?) (ibid., p. 35).

Table 10.1   Operational work with individuals and families

Work with individuals, singly or in groups, aimed directly at prevention or relief of social distress

---

Basic social work (the basic or central core of social work with individuals)
    making assessments of need and of appropriate response
    providing information and advice
    monitoring and supervision
    helping to maintain and develop personal capacity for adequate social
      functioning
    arranging provision of other appropriate services

Basic services
    providing money and goods
    providing meals
    providing accommodation
    providing transport
    providing help in daily living
    providing recreation, social, and cultural life

Supplementary services
    providing aids and adaptations
    providing communication and mobility training
    providing occupational training and sheltered accommodation
    providing management of clients' property
    providing an adoption agency service
    providing medical and paramedical treatment*
    providing formal education*

---

* in some degree

Source: Brunel Institute of Organisation and Social Services, Social Services Organisation Research Unit (1974)

So here was an attempt to develop a theory of departmental activities (the categorization dimension) which, it was claimed, would help resolve these (and probably other) issues. What in fact happened? Well, it is always difficult in the social sciences to trace the impact of new ideas, but in at least one of the problem areas (residential work) it is possible to demonstrate how the analysis of functions was actually utilized.

In 1973 the Central Council for Education and Training (CCETSW) produced its discussion document *Training for Residential Work* in which considerable use was made of that analysis. An intensive national discussion took place around the relationship between the work to be done and the nature of residential workers' training and careers. It can reasonably be claimed that, in this vital area of social welfare provision, problem-driven research led to the generation of tentative theory which was found useful. Exploration of the activities carried out by field and residential workers indicated a common core. The analysis of the horizontal dimensions of the work of the two groups did not produce an explanation that would justify separate occupational existences. The logic of the argument at that time seemed to point to the need for a common base for training. Significantly, the next important report from the CCETSW was entitled *Residential Work is Part of Social Work* (1979).

The debate on occupational boundaries continues, and may be expected to form a continuing theme in the years to come. Although often painful for the members of occupational groups, these debates represent the continuous and changing nature of perceptions and explanations of social problems. The least persuasive theories will lead to the more tentative organizational and occupational structures (see chapter 1). And these least persuasive theories in turn stem from the failure to explicate the distinctive characteristics of the problems under consideration.

The early analysis of the horizontal dimension of SSDs proved to be a valuable tool, not only in the analysis of the 'problem-situation' of residential work, but also in an examination of the problems of emerging professional groups in SSDs (see Hey 1980).

However, as might be expected from the Popperian schema of the development of tentative theory, critical discussion of the theory of the horizontal dimension left unsolved a series of further problems. These can be summarized as the 'felt absence' of a satisfactory explanation of the complexity of different sorts of work.

One problem that was of particular concern was the nature of *case accountability*. All the evidence from practitioners was that there was a felt distinct, qualitative, difference between case accountability and a 'lower' level of work. From hundreds of discussions in many SSDs, it seemed that certain social workers spoke of 'their' caseload; whereas many other workers (assistants, trainees, etc.) did not carry full case accountability and talked in a different fashion. Furthermore, there were groups of more senior staff (area officers, advisers, etc.) who often regretted no longer being able to carry a personal caseload, and were more concerned with general systems and procedures. But how could this and the other differences be developed into a theory that could be critically discussed and tested in the light of good sense and practical experience?

The development of the work strata theory
A full reconstruction of the background to the final paper 'The Stratification of Work and Organisational Design' would demand a major investment of time, and would also raise the question as to

whether it would be worthwhile (Rowbottom and Billis 1977). (Although in passing we might note the general failure of the field of social administration to develop a critical debate about the *way* in which its theories are generated and tested.[1]) But leaving aside this question, I shall be content to describe some personal recollections of a few of the main threads in the production of ideas which, whatever their eventual fate, have at least sparked off discussion of a wide range of welfare problems.[2]

This brief description is provided in keeping with the propositions put earlier regarding the development of theory. Whilst a historical reconstruction is impractical, the earlier theories are well documented. Their utilization in the health and welfare fields can be seen in two books published in the early 1970s – *Hospital Organization* and *Social Services Departments*. Both books owed a substantial debt to the work that had emerged from the Glacier Project. The main texts referred to were Wilfred Brown's *Exploration in Management and Organization* (1960); Elliott Jaques' *The Changing Culture of a Factory* (1951), *Measurement of Responsibility* (1956), and *Equitable Payment* (1967); and their joint book *Glacier Project Papers* (1965).

Both *Hospital Organization* and *Social Services Departments* utilized the social analytic strategy and applied the inherited conceptual analysis to a formidable agenda of 'problem-situations'. Here, we might usefully distinguish what Rowbottom, in tracing a similar process, calls 'fundamental theories' of social analysis, from its 'middle-level generalizations and propositions, the former acting as a "seed bed" for the latter' (1977: 117). Both books emerged from the same 'seed bed', and in so doing, developed a sizeable body of middle-level theories. It is not these, however, which are our present concern, but the deeper areas which can be seen as the immediate precursors of the work strata theory. These theories are succinctly summarized and described as 'initial conceptions' in an early chapter of *Hospital Organization*. Thus:

The initial conception then, sees hospitals (like other organizations) as groups of people working within a structure of interrelated roles. Each role is describable in terms of:

(a) the functions or duties to be performed, broken if desired into the kinds of task to which they give rise;
(b) the authority of the occupant, i.e. his right to act at his own discretion, within limits;
(c) the accountability of the occupant for his performance. (Rowbottom *et al*. 1973: 31).

The key terms in the initial conception are in turn explained and defined in both books. Of paramount importance was the 'managerial role', where the definition that had evolved in the Glacier Project was

taken as a starting point and amended to meet the specific conditions
of the hospital service.

(A)

(B)

In a *superior-subordinate* (or *managerial*) relationship, where a superior A is accountable for ensuring that certain work is carried out and
has a subordinate B to assist him in this work, it is requisite that:
(1) A may prescribe B's work and assign tasks to him;
(2) A may veto the appointment of B to the role;
(3) A may apply sanctions to B (the chief sanction in the Hospital
Service being the recording of assessments of performance in
such a way as to affect B's future career);
(4) A may initiate the tranfer of B from the particular role he
carries, where he judges his performance not to reach an adequate standard. (ibid.: 43).[3]

The two dimensions of role structure were (a) the functions or
duties, and (b) the twin concepts of accountability and authority. The
importance of the managerial role, in addition to its more straightforward utilization in specific organizational problem-solving, was in its
contribution to an understanding of the authority component of the
structure of organizations (see chapter 8). You either were or were not
a 'manager'. And if not, a battery of alternative roles was available,
often referred to by social analysts as the 'organizational tool kit'. By
identifying the strong managerial roles in any organization it was
possible – in most cases – to lower the height of the pyramid, to
'strip-down' the bureaucracy. This proved the case even in compara-
tively small sections of the new welfare bureaucracies established
following the Seebohm Report. Thus, in an early project based in a
home for the elderly, the initial organization of the home was depicted
by the matron, as in Figure 10.1.

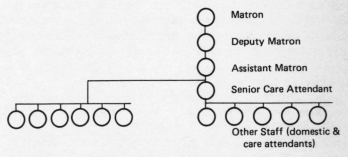

Matron

Deputy Matron

Assistant Matron

Senior Care Attendant

Other Staff (domestic &
care attendants)

Figure 10.1   The manifest organization of a home for the elderly

According to this initial 'official' or 'manifest' view the home had a
maximum 'chain' of five. Following discussions with the staff and
using the notion of managerial (and other) roles, a rather different
picture of the internal relationships emerged. It became clear that the

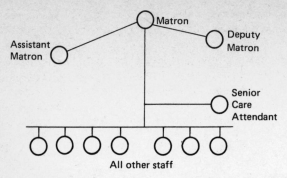

Figure 10.2   The organization of a home for the elderly – after clarification

matron was the only manager (as defined); all other staff were directly managed by her, albeit assisted by a wide variety of supporting roles.[4] Figure 10.2 presents the role structure of the home as finally clarified with the four senior members (matron, deputy matron, assistant matron, and senior care attendants). It shows the matron managing all other staff, with the deputy and assistant acting as 'staff officers', and the senior care attendant as a 'supervisor'.[5] In the official organizational structure of the home, the four senior staff are understood to be on *different grades* (levels of payment), but there is only one managerial line between the staff and the matron. In other words, there is only one *managerial rank* or managerial level in the hierarchy, within which there may be many grades reflecting different salaries.

The tendency for grades to be regarded *as* the organizational structure is a well-known organizational phenomenon. Since grades appear to represent the organization's desire to reward differential experience, training, qualifications, responsibility or other factors, there are few limits to the number of grades that can be introduced. (I am reminded here of the story related by a senior civil servant to explain how his Department had succeeded in squeezing an additional grade 'between' two existing grades in the already formidable system. In desperation, since all the standard titles and their permutations had been exhausted, the newcomers were widely referred to as 'the tweenies'.) It can easily be demonstrated that in most large-scale organizations there are more grades than ranks; replacement of the latter by the former must inevitably lead to elongated and unrealistic hierarchical chains.

The inherited 'initial conceptions', with the definition of the 'accountable manager' appearing prominently, also draw on the earlier works of Jaques in his examination of the spacing of managerial tiers in terms of 'time span' measurement (see also Evans 1979). The approach to organizational structures was a discontinuous one (Jaques with Gibson and Isaac 1978). Organizations could be analysed into structures of roles with clear-cut boundaries between the various managerial ranks. It was possible at that time to transform grading hierarchies into organizational structures of precise 'heights' based on analysis of the genuine managerial roles. A typical area fieldwork team in an SSD was depicted as in Figure 10.3 (Brunel Institute of Organsation and Social Studies, Social Services Organisation Research Unit 1974).

Thus, we can see the way in which 'distinct' numbers started to be attached to the different 'levels' or organization. In *Social Services Departments* the first faltering steps were taken towards the idea that distinct types of work could be attached to different levels of worker. At that point there was no generalized theory but, rather, isolated statements that related to fieldworkers or residential workers.

Another piece of work, partially reproduced here as chapter 12, indicates the search in the same direction. That paper, amongst other things, produced models of the organizational *levels* at which the key *decisions* that appear to have the most influence in the entry of clients into residential care could be taken, if certain criteria were to be met.

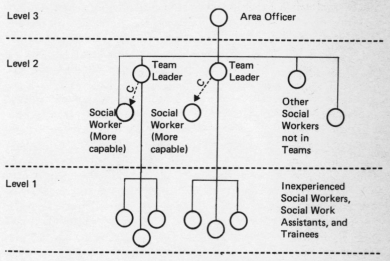

C = Coordinative relationship

Figure 10.3   An early analysis of an area fieldwork team

In short, the scene was now set for the explication of another dimensions of organizational structure based on a discontinuous approach to the decisions, or complexity of work undertaken at different levels of the hierarchy.

Summary

Early research in the health and welfare fields utilized a body of inherited 'initial conceptions', which focused on the *categorization* and *authority* dimensions of organizational structure. Together with this, 'time span' measurement had provided the thesis of a spacing of managerial tiers based on qualitatively different individual capacities.

However, the 'problem-situations' in which the inherited theories were used revealed a further series of unresolved problems. One of these was the specific characteristics of 'case accountability' and the nature of the work required. Using these, together with a number of other strands, a general theory of *qualitatively different work* in organizations was developed alongside the thesis of managerial tiers.

Notes

1. This in turn would take us into the entire area of the organization of research, and the place of 'private' research (based on the individual researcher, often a teacher) and 'public' research (based on an institute, with a declared area of concern).
2. In addition to the works emanating from the Brunel researchers, there is a growing body of literature utilizing, to a greater or lesser extent, the levels of work theory. For example, Kings Fund Working Party (1979); Hayton (1980); Thomas, Kat, and McPherson (1980); Piper (1980); and Cooper (1981).
3. A discussion of the meaning of 'requisite', as used in social analytic research, is contained in chapter 2. See also Rowbottom (1977), especially chapter 8.
4. A pertinent example of what can happen if the 'official' view of organizations is taken as in the research by Tannenbaum and his colleagues (1974).
5. The precise definitions are not necessary for the present argument. They may be found in Appendix A of Brunel Institute of Organisation and Social Studies, Social Services Organisation Research Unit (1974).

11 Day Care: the Case of the (Almost) Disappearing Category

This chapter traces the changing structure of a department as it struggled over a seven-year period to resolve chronic problems of 'day care'. During these seven years two research projects took place, one in 1973 and the second in 1976/7. We shall see how the phrase 'day care' disappeared as a useful organizational description. Or almost disappeared. For it remained in the title of the assistant director, and individual centres also retained the title. However, the notion of a set of activities that could be regarded as 'day care' and treated as an identifiable and distinct categorization disappeared. In its place this local authority G, or LAG as we shall call it, began to introduce a client-group focus.

But in 1973 day care in LAG was regarded as a group of activities and units for which a day care manager, supported by four advisers, could be held accountable. The list of their responsibilities comprised: luncheon clubs, social and veterans clubs, meals-on-wheels, workrooms, entertainments for the elderly, holidays and outings for the handicapped, orange badge schemes, providing incontinence pads, welfare foods, transport, adult training centres, day nurseries, sheltered workshops, occupational therapy units, special units for the elderly, work centres, aids and adaptations, monitoring and supervision of private playgroups and nurseries, coach escorts . . . .

We can sympathize with the difficulties faced by the Central Council for Education and Training in Social Work in its endeavours to make proposals about training for day care since the activities embraced in LAG seem a reasonable example of the national position. After much deliberation the Council could only conclude that 'day care' is:

a heterogeneous field of social services and it is hard to describe the many different services that are provided under this umbrella description. (CCETSW 1975).

All that need be said is that 'heterogeneous fields' and 'umbrella descriptions' are not readily compatible with explicit and systematic policy-making.

1973 – problems but no action
In May 1973 I received a somewhat hesitant invitation to meet the day

care advisers in order to discuss their role and the organization of day care within the department.[1] The advisers appeared to feel the problems of day care most severely and they put forward a weighty list of problems, revealing considerable discontent. As they expressed it:

- 'I have a nice manager of a Centre, but he has problems with two of his workers who do what they want. I tried to do social work with the three people concerned. As a consequence a note was sent to the director asking – what is a day care adviser?'

- 'The response of one Head of Centre – who had 'soldiered on alone for many years' – was seen to be typical. I've never had an adviser – what do you do?'

- 'One Head comes sometimes to me, sometimes to the Head of Day Care, or the Assistant Director, or even the Director.'

- 'Our appointment is described as fourth tier management, but we are in a position of giving advice to people who are often on a higher grade.'

- 'The job description is ambiguous. One of the misnomers is "advice" – to give advice someone has to ask for it. If we see something wrong what do we do about it?'

- 'At present I feel like a social worker in the role of a spy.'

- 'We seem to be an anomaly in the eyes of the area teams. They do not know where to put us. The seniors look at us rather queerly.'

- 'The area teams turn to us for an enormous range of advice and information. The symptoms of the general confusion about our role can be seen by the fact that the area teams think that we can be much more flexible than we are and social workers keep asking us why can't we change things.'

These few extracts illustrate the general confusion surrounding the major group of staff having 'day care' in their title. In the face of this and other evidence it might at first sight seem odd that LAG was unwilling to embark on a more enthusiastic collaborative analysis of its day care situation.

My initial report which tentatively raised what appeared to be already at that stage a fundamental question, 'What is day care?', was returned with the comment that although I might have difficulty in knowing what day care was, they (the advisers) 'did not have this difficulty'! Quite the reverse. I was informed that 'the present organizational structure makes sense and that it possesses an internal cohesiveness and logic'. I thought then that this sounded unconvincing. However in 1973, the department decided that it had more urgent problems in other sections and attention was focused on these. An important reorganization of the central management of residential care was still being digested. The middle managers had been given client-group accountability (see Figure 11.1).

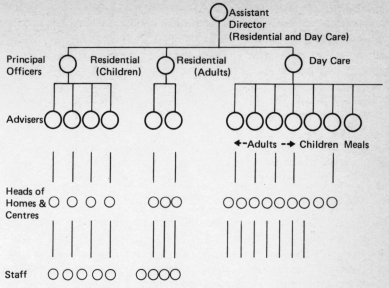

Figure 11.1   Partial representation of manifest organizational chart LAG 1975

It was only four years later that a really convincing invitation was extended to re-examine the day care situation.

1976–77
Different people, higher grades, new titles, but the same (or almost the same) core problems. This summarizes the apparent main changes in the condition of day care and its advisers after four turbulent post-Seebohm years.

In the intervening period there had taken place a departmental regrading exercise which had, as a consequence, led to the retitling of the advisers' posts.[2]

It can be helpful if the title of the job reflects the essence of the work performed; in particular in new areas of activity where there has not been time to demonstrate the range and effectiveness of the work. So a change from the misleading 1973 title of 'adviser', which all considered a misnomer, would have been useful if it had demystified rather than, as had happened in 1974 in LAG, further compounded the existing confusion. (Still, my main theme is not 'mistitling'. Neither am I primarily stalking idiosyncratic grading structures – the abominable snowmen of the bureaucratic wastelands.)

The regrading exercise may well have made sense if it had been underpinned by an explicit and logical explanation of the expected work. Without this it merely exacerbated feelings of resentment and injustice from other sections of staff.

My renewed involvement with day care was a direct consequence of the continuing conflicts in the day care section. This time, unlike the more modest exercise in 1973, everyone who was in any significant way involved in the supervision or management of day care staff, or the provision of services, was invited to collaborate in the exercise. Nineteen people joined in the project. The manifest organizational structure is illustrated in Figure 11.1. In the figure only the headquarters organization is ullustrated in full. In addition to the assistant director and the day care manager, the participants consisted of all the five advisers then in post, six heads of various day care units, the manager and two senior staff from the adult training centre, an adaptations officer and two representative occupational therapists. The individual interviews centred around discussions of the areas of work and the main problems as seen by each person.[3]

Each participant was fed back a draft of the discussion and asked whether any changes were needed. This was a sensitive and crucial step in the research since the participants were faced with the realization that the 'cleared' (amended) documents would be circulated to other members of the project. In this particular project this step was moved through in a relaxed fashion.[4] The length of the discussions, the need for amendments, and the extent of detail in the final documents, varied from person to person. So too did the extent to which it was felt appropriate to introduce concepts. In some instances staff were already familiar with the work strata idea (from workshops and other sources), and these were a natural part of the discussion. Indeed in one or two cases, the joint effort of researcher and insider to understand the problems resulted in further theory development. It was this project – as I shall shortly indicate – which was an important stage in the development and testing of the notion of BEW.

With all the cleared reports available, I had a unique 'cross-perceptual' view of the issues. I then prepared what I call a 'covering report', attached this to the individual documents, and circulated the total package to all the members of the group. It is difficult for the outsider to know precisely what the impact of receiving this sort of material is on insiders.[5] I regard the 'covering report' as 'my' document, which attempts to tap into the main issues and to propose tentative alternatives to these problems. If care has been taken, this stage should be reached with a general sense of buoyancy and optimism. If participants know that every effort will be made to take their standpoint into consideration, and that efforts will be made to take executive action, then this is an exciting moment. In LAG previous experience had indicated that matters would be thrashed out, opinions listened to, and action taken.

The analysis consisted of three sections, each of them brief : (i) the problems raised, (ii) misconceptions and the conditions for change, and (iii) day care and its organization.[6]

Many of the comments and criticisms had a familiar ring. One adviser felt that he had 'an ill-defined role'. Consequently he was 'losing enthusiasm and opting out'. He saw himself as a 'messenger boy bogged down in itsy-bitsy running about.' He was, he thought, expected to monitor the work of the work centre, but although he was treated 'courteously' by the manager of the centre, he had to 'tread warily'. Another participant saw himself as 'the meat in the sandwich'. One slice of bread being senior management, and the other the heads of centres.

LAG's day care heads of units were no less unhappy.

● 'Most of their ('advisers') functions are not real and they appear to be superimposed upon the general structure.'

● 'The main problem is the superfluous role of the advisers.'

● 'They are a frustration rather than a help.'

I divided the problems into two main categories. There were those that related to the internal organization of various units such as the Adult Training Centre (ATC) and other day centres, and those that focused on client groups. The former (internal) problems were left, at this stage, to one side. The latter were listed as they related to each group.

The department was providing resources to a group known as the 'able elderly' who were sharing resources with the house-bound and physically handicapped elderly brought to the day centres by coach. The manager of a centre felt that the actual situation was that good facilities were being provided for the able elderly, whilst the less-able elderly were not being provided with any significant resource, and were just becoming less and less able.

The state of affairs was elaborated on by the head of a unit working with a group of the elderly confused. She described the poor relationships existing between her clients and the members of the senior citizens and luncheon clubs (the able elderly) who came to the same centre. Members of the senior citizens' club wouldn't speak to clients of the unit, and things were little better with regard to relationships with members of the luncheon club – members wouldn't move from their set places and didn't talk to clients.

Not far from this large day centre was a work-room, urban aid funded, and once again catering mainly for the elderly. Whilst a small amount of money was paid, it was mainly for social purposes. The manager of the work-room felt isolated, rarely being visited by headquarters staff.

The physically handicapped received services from a number of units. The manager of the work centre, catering for 80 clients, saw the focus of his role as 'responsibility for the quality of products provided by the centre'. Both he and the manager of a new sheltered workshop wondered whether, in view of the contract nature of the work, they were misplaced in an SSD. One occupational therapist (OT) regarded the profession as split between those working with psychiatric and those with physical problems. This OT was in fact based in a field-work area team and raised many issues of lines of accountability with the residential and day care division. But a group of questions centred around the boundaries of OT work and other workers such as technical officers; and she asked whether an OT should be dealing with everything that comes through and 'looks like OT work'? Here are echoes of a wider professional debate with this participant suggesting that an 'OT aide' could be used for a proportion of basic work (see Jaques 1978: chapter 9).

Staff working with the mentally handicapped in the ATC felt there was an absence of policy and management principles at headquarters. The manager of the ATC considered himself a professional 'in contrast to the advisers'. (This project led to a series of national workshops with managers and staff from ATCs.)

Staff responsible for mentally ill clients were unclear where and whether policy was defined for their clients. Thus, the head OT of a unit working with what she described as psychiatric 'patients' saw the role of the SSD as co-ordinating the services and providing the building equipment and materials. As far as she was concerned her 'manager' was the doctor of the referred patient. 'The doctors would be the people who would know if substantial work was really being performed.' The visiting psychiatrist was also seen to have an important part to play in the general supervision which took place once a week. It was this participant who felt that the advisers were 'superfluous'.

The adviser working with the under-fives felt there were 'massive problems in the LA which are not being tackled systematically'. She pointed to 'poor co-ordination between the various sections of the department concerned with the under-fives. Those concerned with day nurseries, playgroups, child-minders, private nurseries, all work on their own in isolated pockets.' This adviser was in a rather different position in that she was clearly managing the 15 nursery matrons who, in turn, were absolutely accountable for work in the nurseries. Here the superfluous post was seen to be of the day care manager 'who does not know much about the day-to-day running of nurseries and is not seen to have a valid role'. This adviser reported 'where necessary' to the assistant director.

The general picture that emerged was one of confusion in the units as to whether there was a policy, and if so, who was accountable for the formualtion of that policy in all the heterogeneous collection of activities and services called 'day care'.

In the final part of the report a start was made on model building. The concept of Basic Expected Work was introduced and the existing provision of 'day care' services was analysed as where BEW is either:

Specialist situational
to assess the needs of clients belonging to one of the specific categories (physically handicapped, mentally handicapped, under-fives). In this model the BEW is that of a Stratum 2 professional working with Stratum 1 instructors, supervisors, technicians, ancillary staff;

or

General demand
giving services 'on demand', on condition that resources are available and clients fit *general* categories of eligibility (much of the work for the able elderly, outings, entertainments). Here the BEW with clients is Stratum 1 and the question then arises whether the managers of such units need be 'professional' social workers, or could they be 'professional' administrators.

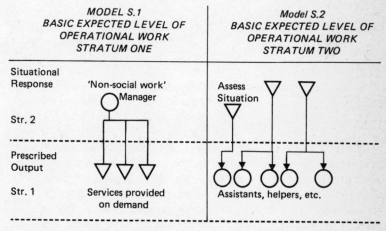

Key: ▽ = Basic Expected Work (BEW)

Figure 11.2   Two models of basic operational work (partial representation)

Figure 11.2 was included to illustrate the two different models.

The entire covering report was a few thousand words; and the final section was equally terse. Apart from the two models of operational work I was content to raise questions and present a few alternatives. I thought that a lengthy analysis might run the danger of obscuring the most burning issues. (I do not under-estimate the significance for LAG, and for social policy analysis, of other problems raised by participants; it was just that my experience was that the equivalent of organizational toothache tends to preclude giving attention to less-pressing ailments.)

The starting question to the group was: what organizational structure could best serve client needs? (I did not wish to fall into the trap of helping in the design of welfare organizations primarily for the benefit of the staff.) One possible alternative form or organization might be based on 'occupation'; that is to say, for example, grouping all the OTs in one section and the managers of work units in another section. If this approach were to be explored, obvious questions that came to mind were the coherence of the occupational groups and the organizational base of those services that did not fall neatly into occupational categories.

Another possibility raised for discussion was to continue the move towards client group organization with a third tier of 'systematic service' managers for the mentally handicapped, mentally ill, and physically handicapped. Whatever the chosen model, four questions were raised.

Should the 'general demand' services be based in another division?

What should be the boundaries of departmental work with the 'able elderly'?

What is the most appropriate organizational base for the under-fives' services?

Could some headquarters and unit management roles be combined?

This last question was in response to the increased number of genuine Level 3 managers that would be needed to handle any new organization. For two things were clear from the analysis so far. First, the department *could* improve its organizational structure – so some change was highly likely. Second, any change would need to take into account an important lesson from the present troubles – the untenability of Level 2 advisers 'managing' Level 2 heads of unit – (not to speak of what to do with the Level 3 unit heads!)[7] The manifest chart of Figure 11.1 didn't reflect the work to be done – and the levels of work theory could at least provide an explanation for the widespread feeling of being squeezed.

The covering report and individual documents were discussed at a number of meetings of the full group. During the following three years I was to be invited on many occasions to discuss various aspects of the reorganization that was consequently set in train, but essentially the initiative was in departmental hands.

Executive action

During 1977–8 intensive departmental activity took place around the possibility of reorganization. From the documents sent to me, and from my own discussion with staff, it was evident that the project was being treated very seriously. Finally in March and April 1978, the assistant director had a detailed discussion with the director explaining the way in which his division was approaching reorganization, and quoting large chunks of the covering report in the various memoranda that moved to and fro.

Towards the end of the year a report was prepared for the social services committee proposing a restructuring ('after considering a number of alternatives') based on four client groups: (i) children under 5; (ii) children 5–18; (iii) the elderly; and (iv) the disabled. Detailed job descriptions had been prepared for all key staff in the new structure, the 'advisory' role was to be strengthened and given managerial responsibilities, and the principal officers were to become 'co-ordinators' (see Figure 11.3).[8]

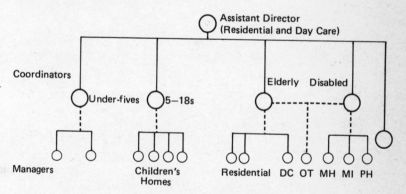

Key: DC = Day Care; OT = Occupational Therapist; MH = Mental Handicap;
MI = Mental Illness; PH = Physical Handicap

Figure 11.3   LAG proposal 1978

The full cycle of this reorganization was not completed until 1980, and I have in my files about a dozen variations of the basic client group approach; but for the purposes of this case study it is a suitable point to pause.

At the end of the year the assistant director prepared, for his staff, a resumé of how he saw the events and the reasoning behind the proposals. I include below extracts from that document as an 'insider's' view of the collaborative exercise. =

In 1973 a review of the management structure of our residential services was undertaken which resulted in their being divided into two sections, Children and Adults. So far as the day care services were concerned, it appeared at the time that the same degree of restructuring was not necessary; this opinion being based on the concept that the day care service was an entity and that the day care management should operate as a team . . . .

We began again from the principle that the task of management was to serve the clients' needs. The clients seemed most easily to fall into four groups:

(1) Pre-school children
(2) Children of school age and over
(3) The elderly
(4) The disabled

At this stage the reorganisation of the whole of the residential and day care facilities into sections for each of these client groups appeared to have a number of advantages:

(a) Principal Officers would have responsibility for co-ordinating, controlling, planning and evaluating a wide range of services for their client group, thus giving greater flexibility and better co-ordination and effectiveness of resource;

(b) Advisers would be able to provide specialised support for sub-groups of clients, and be given a more vital professional role and responsibility over a wider range of resource;

(c) Within the structure, there could be built logistic support for services such as transport, meals, holidays, aids and adaptations; some of these might be centralised while others could continue to function under the most appropriate manager. The decision here would rest mainly on whether the content of their task would be primarily 'professional' or 'administrative'.

(d) Opportunity could also be taken to see how overlapping services with the Fieldwork Division could be better aligned. This would particularly relate to services for children such as fostering, child-minding, nursery centres, and Intermediate Treatment.

In practice, the degree of interaction which takes place between residential and day care establishments varies within each group. Within the children's services, with the continuing trend to reduce residential nursery provision, and with the demands for specialist expertise in residential care for older children, the staff involved could continue to specialise on day care for pre-school children or residential care for older children. Whilst there was a need to co-ordinate the full range of services for the elderly, the increasing fragility of residents in old persons' homes meant that their interaction with day centres was not a priority, and it was possible for two Advisers to continue to specialise in residential care of the elderly and to draft into this section one officer to develop and supervise the day care services. Within the field of the disabled (the physically handicapped, the mentally handicapped, and the mentally ill) the contacts between residential and day care provision was seen to be particularly important, so that in this section each Adviser would have a vital co-ordinating role at operation level as well as a management role for both residential and day care establishments . . .

The question of overlap of services had to be given close attention, particularly in relation to mentally handicapped children with mentally handicapped adults, and the elderly with the physically disabled. The allocation of establishments to Advisers did not in practice present any great problems, although in one or two cases there would be need for further review as services developed and changed.

Apart from the chore of preparing the detailed job descriptions for some 20 posts, two more basic reviews were required.

Although the structure is not yet in operation, in retrospect the old separation into residential and day care sections already appears to have restricted our moving towards a more co-ordinated approach with other services, in measuring the effectiveness of existing resources and in filling the gaps in services for people in the various client groups.

Summary

This case study illustrates both the implementation of existing theory and the generation of new ideas.

Covering as it does a period of seven years, it has been possible to provide only an outline of several of the key stages. The well-tested concepts of managerial and other roles were found useful by participants and comfortably absorbed into the vocabulary of departmental discussion. The theory of different levels of work also, it appears, proved helpful in illuminating the reasons for tension in the relationships between middle managers and heads of operational units. This project also contributed to the concept of Basic Expected Work discussed in Part II.

More importantly, the work in day care was instrumental in the development of ideas about the *horizontal dimension* of SSDs. The existence in LAG of a client group called the 'able elderly' set in motion a train of thought which was explored in other departments. Should SSDs be in the business of 'preventing' social distress? What did this really mean? What were the consequences for clients, staff, and the community, of providing so-called 'preventive' services? These questions, underpinned by a developing philosophical approach to organizations (discussed in Part I), led to the publication of several critical papers questioning the concepts of 'at risk', 'prevention', and 'social distress' (see chapter 4; Billis 1981a and 1981b).

Notes

1. See chapter 2 for an account of 'social analysis' as a research approach, including a definition of *strategy*. There are implications here for the *strategy* of collaborative research. I have suggested that the issue has to be

'burning' for this form of research to succeed. In 1973 it became evident after the initial explorations, that the total pressures were insufficient to drive the research forward. The assistant director was still involved in the residential reorganization and the presence of a day care manager (strong and unenthusiastic) precluded a full-scale project. All these factors were to change in the next few years and the structural factor re-emerged as a major issue.

2. To preserve anonymity, the new titles will not be given.

3. This follows the process of explication outlined in chapter 2 in which the available concepts are utilized in situational analysis in order to bring forward issues for critical discussion.

4. This need not necessarily be the case. In 'low trust' organizations it is not unusual to find some participants rather more apprehensive about the clearance of documents. In such cases it is the researcher's duty to protect the position of participants and to have ensured in the research *strategy* that anyone could back out of the project without harm being done to themselves (see chapter 2).

5. For a discussion of the research methodology and the idea of 'outsider' and 'insider', see chapter 2.

6. I can note here only several key points in the analysis.

7. I am here, of course, referring to the expected work in the role, and not the personal capacity of the advisers and heads.

8. There was still a certain 'fudging' of the issues and the detailed job descriptions were not totally convincing on the issues of the relationship between co-ordinators and managers. However, the reorganization was sufficient to resolve many questions and the 'burning' problems were now elsewhere.

Levels of Decision-Making and 'Entry Into Residential Care'

This chapter includes the second half of a case study based in the London Borough of Brent and published in 1973 (Billis 1973c). The section that has been omitted dealt with the specific conditions of the Borough, and with a particular method of placement into residential care which functioned within a particular organizational structure.

The omitted section traced the history of a project which began in 1971 and which was one important strand in the development of a theory of levels of work. That section gathered the perceptions of key people in the Brent placement process in order to arrive at a list of desirable qualities as seen by the participants in the research project. It was seen how the structure existing at that time met few of these desirable qualities or preconditions. The departmental decision-making process 'resembled a web of interwoven decisions, not beginning from one point and progressing steadily towards an end result but taken simultaneously in a number of different corners of the Department' (ibid).

It seemed that one way forward might be to isolate the key decisions which appeared to have most influence in shaping the nature of the final output – the physical movement of the client into care. Thus, a large number of decisions which were taken primarily by area and headquarters administrative staff were not included. Not that it was felt unimportant for the Department to know which staff were accountable for the notification of vacancies, for the passing on of case details, and so on; but that the assignment of accountability for these decisions must occupy a secondary and supporting role where the fundamental decisions remained to be clarified.

Eight decisions were isolated in the project which appeared to lie at the heart of the placement system. These decisions provided the material for wider national testing in workshops, seminars and other research projects (see the discussion on the 'extended strategy' in chapter 2). It is this wider analysis (Part II of the original paper) which is reported here.

The decisions and requisite answers – (Part II of 'entry into residential care')[1]
In view of the impossibility of examining in detail the vast number of

organizational structures that are to be found in social services departments, two skeletal archetypes have been chosen for illustrative purposes. For ease of description these may be described as 'centralized'
(or functional) and 'decentralized' (or geographic) departments or
simply Model A and Model B (Rowbottom and Hey 1973). The
former resembles many structures to be found at the moment and is
close to the position in Brent. Typically, it consists of the director and
a number of assistant directors, one of whom is accountable for the
work of field staff organized into geographical areas; and another who,
for the purpose of this analysis, can be considered to be accountable
for the work of all residential staff. Part of this structure (Model A) is
depicted in Figure 12.1.

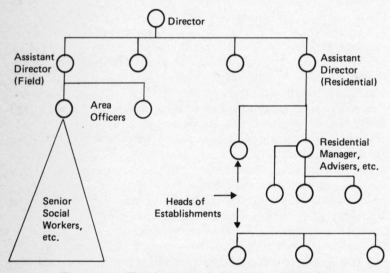

Figure 12.1   The 'decentralized' department – Model A

In Figure 12.2 (Model B) an outline of the 'decentralized' department is illustrated. The key feature for the present discussion is the
fact that the heads of residential establishments are (in the main) seen
to be subordinates of the heads of the 'mini-departments'. In Figure
12.2 these heads have been called area officers, although other titles
abound. The use of the word 'division' as an equivalent for the
mini-departments appears to be gaining favour, but to avoid confusion we have in this paper restricted its usage to the functional
divisions of Model A.

In Part I of this report it was observed how a series of key questions

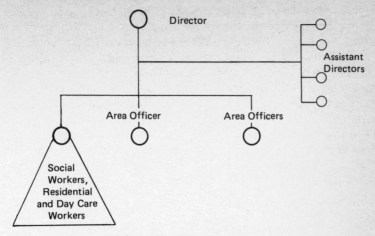

Figure 12.2   The 'decentralized' department – Model B

and decisions were isolated and considered to be crucial in establishing the framework within which clients entered residential care. We shall pose these same questions to the two archetypal departments – Models A and B. Drawing on conference experience, we shall endeavour to reach a greater degree of specificity than was described in the project work in Brent. In other words, whereas in Part I answers to the key questions related to the functional divisions, here we shall attempt in addition to suggest which level (social worker, team leader, area officer, etc.) of worker shall requisitely take the decision.

Decision 1 — Whether residential care is needed
There has been almost unanimous agreement concerning a requisite answer to the first question in Table 12.1. Field and residential staff concur that a preliminary evaluation of whether residential care is needed or not can only be made by fieldworkers. It is they who know, or ought to know, the comprehensive background to the client's case. Where the client is a child, this is a longstanding professional viewpoint. Winnicott, in a persuasive article (1970), refers to the 'integrative functions of the child care officer' who 'is in a position to know so much about the child'. The position of the elderly has been very different. This has already been mentioned in this study and will be returned to shortly. The structure of the department is not seen to affect the issue. In both instances the evaluation will be made at area level either by the social worker or senior carrying accountability for the particular case.

Table 12.1   Placements

Decision	Model A Department		Model B Department	
	Which division	At what level	Where	At what level
1. Whether residential care is needed	Field	Social worker/ senior	in area	Social worker/ senior
2. Classification of case	Field	Senior/area officer	in area	Senior/area officer
3. Priority of case in area	Field	Area officer	in area	Area officer
4. Priority in department	Field	Assistant director	*	
5. Matching clients to vacancies	Placement Bureau (probably residential division)	Clerical staff under supervision of Homes or manager	in area	Homes adviser or residential manager
6. Suitability of Home for client	Field	Social worker	in area	Social worker
7. Suitability of client for Home	Residential	Head of establishment	in area	Head of establishment
8. Final resolution. Possibly in two stages	Residential	Residential manager, assistant director	in area	Residential manager, area officer

* This decision might not apply; but in the case of scarce resources, or inter-area resources, the decision would have to be taken centrally by a designated subordinate of the director.

Decision 2 – Classification of case

Given that the client is thought to be in need of residential care, limitations imposed by inadequate resources impose their own logic on the answers to the second decision – in particular, with regard to the top priority classification, by whatever name this is known in the department. For simplicity, this top priority stream has been called an 'emergency'. Apart from statutory obligations there is little evidence to suggest that departments have as yet been able to come to grips with policy guidelines as to what ought to enter into this category. It may be, as some staff have suggested to us, that it is not really possible to define an 'emergency'. Whether this is true or not, and to date research work has been able to touch only the periphery of this question, it is likely that classification will be primarily relevant for specific departments; but even if a definition of 'emergency' is not available, positive steps can still be taken. It seems dysfunctional for example, to leave the decision to the discretion of the individual caseworker.

There would seem to be a strong argument for moving this decision to someone in the division who is not so directly involved in the case, but who has as part of his duties, the possibility of seeing a broader cross-section of clients, and who is able to bring a wider range of experience into the decision. This would remain within the area and could be taken either by the team leader (senior social worker) or the area officer. In a decentralized department, where residential establishments are accountable to the area officer (or his subordinates), this might be one of the duties of a specific post.

Decision 3 – The relative priority of the case in the area

The third decision can be dealt with rapidly. It follows from what has been said so far. Who else but the area officer can decide the relative priority of cases if he is truly accountable for that area? In both Model A and Model B, whilst the area officer remains accountable for the final decision, he might decide to utilize one or more of his subordinates to assist with special categories of clients.

Decision 4 – The relative priority of the case in the department

The fourth decision, certainly in the case of the centralized department, is probably the most important. Yet it is precisely at this point that logic comes into conflict with some current practices. Assuming that resources are inadequate, and that the assistant director (field services) is accountable for the work of the area officers, it would appear almost self-evident that the person fulfilling that role be held accountable also for deciding on the relative priority of cases throughout the department. But there are departments where this critical allocation of priorities is apparently not distinguished from, or confused with, decision 5 – the matching of clients to vacancies. In other words, in these departments requests for entry into care bypass the assistant director (field services) and arrive directly at some other destination at headquarters.

This break in the logical flow of decision-making seems particularly widespread when systems for placing the elderly into residential care are examined. There are historical reasons for the different attitudes towards children and the elderly. With the creation of a united department it is now difficult to find any moral, professional, or 'objective' reasons for the failure to exploit maximum professional discretion at the pinnacle of the process.

Ideally, resources and assessment procedures may be so organized that the decision will be taken as close to the client as possible.

Nevertheless, if someone *has* to decide on inter-area priorities, this cannot be a decision that is abrogated, or goes by default to someone other than the assistant director (field services) or one of his staff officers. In the decentralized department this decision might not arise – at least not on a regular basis. Resources will presumably have been allocated according to the diversity of area needs. There will, despite this, remain the necessity to allocate scarce resources, and the further requirement to 'iron out' emergent differences in need between areas. These would seem to be decisions appropriately made by a designated officer at assistant director level, or as a last resort by the director.

Decision 5 – Matching clients to vacancies

The fifth decision has already been touched upon. Chronologically, this might have been entered later in Table 12.1. The reason for its inclusion here is to draw a sharp distinction between this and the previous decisions, which were concerned with establishing priorities.

When the complete placements table has been analysed it will be seen that what remains to be done in the centralized department is to match potential residents with available vacancies. The administrative staff of the placement bureau, or its equivalent, will need to provide data concerning the supply of, and the demand for, places to the operational sections of the department. We may distinguish between this service-giving function and another important activity – making suggestions with regard to specific clients and homes. This later activity necessitates the exercise of professional discretion, and departments will presumably wish to staff the bureau accordingly. In Model A there appears to be logic in placing the bureau within the orbit of the assistant director (residential) since we shall see the considerable authority possessed by the head of the home with regard to potential residents.

In the decentralized deparments these problems may, in view of the lower level at which decisions will be taken, be less intense. Area placements might then be undertaken by some designated member of staff attached to the area office.

Decision 6 – Suitability of home for client

Earlier, it was contended that the decision concerning the relative priority of the case in the department was the most important decision to be taken. This might incorrectly be interpreted to assume that the vital views and interests of the client and the residential staff were being ignored. This is not so. The intention was to indicate that their views will be of little relevance if the client is destined to remain on a low-priority waiting list and never in fact reaches a residential establishment. The point is now reached where a vacancy is available, the client has top priority, and a particular home is proposed. Winnicott and others have demonstrated, and the research clearly supports the view, that field and residential staff operate within different contexts.

We suggest that the experienced area social worker is the appropriate departmental worker to pronounce on the suitability of the home for his or her client. Here, once again, the divergences of practice found between the different categories of client cannot be avoided. Whereas fieldwork involvement in residential placements for children is generally seen to be an integral part of any decision-making, such involvement with regard to the elderly is sometimes conspicuous by its absence.

The placements table brings a number of questions out into the open. Are the present variations in practice between categories of client the consequence of deliberate departmental policy? In this situation a separate procedure might be required for each category. Or are they the result of historical chance and departmental intertia? Without social worker involvement in this decision, will there not continue to be clients in residential care who would be more beneficially receiving some other form of assistance? Without adequate client consultation and social worker involvement, will there not continue to be a chronic problem of long 'transfer' lists of residents wishing to move to other establishments? The answers to these questions would appear to be the same whatever departmental structure is considered.

Decision 7 – Suitability of client for the home
It is in the search for answers to the seventh question – suitability of the client for the proposed home – that due importance is given to the participation of residential staff. They are the people who are accountable for what happens in the establishment 24 hours a day, 7 days a week. Opinions differ as to the extent to which they may pass judgement concerning the suitability of the client for their establishment.

A general consensus appears to be however that the head of establishment should possess what might be crudely described as an 'initial right of veto'. If the head feels that a proposed client will upset the social composition of the establishment, will not find it easy to integrate into the home, or simply that the home does not possess the necessary physical requirements for the client, departmental staff consider it appropriate that the matter be referred back and another attempt be made to find more suitable accommodation. Should this prove impossible – and there are (as has been noted) pressures caused by resource limitations on clients, heads and social workers to accept suggested vacancies – the issue must move up to a higher level for resolution. No significant differences between the two structures are seen in this respect.

Decision 8 – The final resolution, possibly in two stages
In practice, this final decision may affect only a small minority of cases; but a few incidents can cause great unpleasantness and an undesirable atmosphere in the department.

In Table 12.1 it has been assumed that both centralized and decentralized departments are neatly and clearly organized. The decision-making table compels us to come to grips with the real structural composition of the department. What is the real role of the residential division? Is it really accountable for all work carried on in the establishment? Or is it what is sometimes called a 'bricks and mortar' division? These issues go beyond the brief of this paper but they must be borne in mind if satisfactory answers are to be found to the questions raised in decision 8.

For the purpose of this article it has been postulated that the residential division has total accountability for the establishments. Given this, and on the assumption that the fieldwork division agrees to the suggested placement, decision 8 can be seen as an extension of the previous decision, with the residential manager, or even the assistant director (residential) making the final decision. But in the last resort, in Model A the only person who can resolve issues of disagreement between the two assistant directors is the director.

In Model B both field and residential workers are accountable to a common manager in control of a defined geographical area. It would be this manager, or a specified member of his staff, who would have authority to make decisions binding on the two sides.

Conclusions
According to a recent estimate nearly 400,000 clients live in 11,000 residential centres in the United Kingdom (CCETSW 1973). From the same source we learn that 6000 of these establishments are run by statutory, and 5000 by voluntary bodies; together there are 'nearly 65,000 care staff currently in post'. It has not been our intent to discuss the desirability (or otherwise) of residential care, standards of social work assessment, or the adequacy (or inadequacy) of resources. On these and other associated issues we may hold strong opinions. I have concentrated on what might appear to be less exciting but, I would claim, a critical aspect of the vast residential scene – the interaction between placement procedures and the organizational structure of the social service department.

There are, it is suggested, appropriate procedures to ensure that policy regarding entry into care can be implemented. By drawing on research experience tested in conference and other discussions, a placement table (Table 12.1) has been proposed which contains the key operational decisions taken in the move from client to resident. For each division the question has been asked as to who is the logical person to make that decision in two situations, the functional Model A and the 'decentralized' Model B; 'logical', that is to say, in order that departmental criteria may be met.

It is contended that if the professional expertise of both field and residential social workers is to be effectively harnessed, their judgement must be brought to bear at specific places in the process. If the authority's clients are to be assured of a fair deal, priorities cannot be arranged in isolation from those staff who are most closely aware of the real nature of the problems. Likewise, the chronic problem of 'emergencies' must be faced. If an emergency cannot be defined (and this remains an open question), can the decision be left solely to the grassroots social worker? What is the role of the placement bureau (if it exists)? Who makes the final decision for admission to care? To these and other questions, answers have been sought.

No analysis and no table is valid for all time and for all places. A more reasonable expectation is that the analysis might point the way to a clearer understanding of what is by all accounts, a murky area of social service organization.

Summary

This analysis of decision-making as it affected the entry of clients into residential care contained important pointers to the later development of a theory of the vertical dimension.[2] For in considering the 'classification' of cases, I noted that there was a 'strong argument for moving this decision to someone in the division who is not so directly involved in the case but who has, as part of his duties, the possibility of seeing a broader cross-section of clients'. And in considering the priority for the department and the allocation of resources, it was up to the assistant director who it appeared was the appropriate decision-maker. Thus, the links began to be made between theories of managerial level and the identification of distinct levels of decision-making (see also chapter 10). Area officers, the second distinct *managerial* level, were expected to cope with ranges of cases (what eventually became 'Systematic Service Delivery') and assistant directors with scarce resources and unmet need (what was later to become 'comprehensive service provision').

Both the testing of the specific table of decision-making in entering residential care and the development of the work strata theory took time. Usable theories must be tested against the problems they are intended to resolve – a theme discussed in Part I.

Notes

1. For stylistic reasons I have not altered the original text which, it must be

emphasized, relates to the period following the Seebohm Report.

2. This was, of course, not the only strand in the development of the theory which was the product of a joint effort by Ralph Rowbottom and myself. Both of us acknowledge the contribution made by our colleagues in BIOSS.

13 The Intermediate Treatment Officer

I shall, in this chapter, present a case study from local authority S – or LAS. The key subject of the research project was the 'Intermediate Treatment Officer', or ITO. 'Intermediate treatment' – the area of work for which this officer was to be held responsible – has been referred to as 'a mongrel of somewhat mixed parentage and doubtful history (DHSS 1974a). So, it is the nature of the authority relationship between 'mongrel' and 'master' that is our main concern, and to carry the metaphor just a little further, an exploration of the possible causes for the difference between sturdy, fun-loving, socially-useful creatures and those mongrels that are frail and oppressed nuisances.

I shall shortly trace the clarifications which took place in LAS from the original problems through to the executive action which was based on an analysis which in turn pointed to possible future problem areas.[1] The project led to a number of national research conferences and raised issues which have been published elsewhere (Billis 1976).

But first a few background comments on the 'doubtful history' of Intermediate Treatment (IT). Joan Cooper, speaking in 1974 as the Director of DHSS Social Work Service, saw IT as 'in part no more than a systematized extension of many resources used by social workers to supplement relationship therapy' (DHSS 1974a).[2] She traced its origins back to the 1927 Departmental Committee on the Treatment of Offenders which proposed various alternative penalties to custodial measures, and she pointed out that the Home Office Advisory Council (1962) on the treatment of the offender made suggestions for non-residential treatment of offenders up to the age of 21. The White Paper 'Children in Trouble' was followed a year later in 1969 by the Children's and Young Person's Act. As the DHSS' own Development Group noted in 1973, the term 'intermediate treatment' is not used in the Act but has been adopted since the White Paper to describe:

new forms of treatment for children and young persons found to be in need of care or control by juvenile courts. It . . . can only be provided by a requirement . . . added to a supervision order. It is 'intermediate' . . . between [placement] in the care of the local authority, or . . . the care of his parents. It . . . may be exercised at the discretion of the supervisor [who] will have a range of facilities at his disposal, both residential and non-residential, set out under a scheme prepared by the Children's Regional Planning Committee . . . facilities . . . in the main already being used by [others] not subject to supervision orders. It is intended to enable a child to develop new and beneficial attitudes and activities . . . (DHSS 1973).

In 1976 a further attempt was made by the relevant Secretaries of State to impose some order. It seems that there are 'narrow' and 'broad' breeds of mongrel. The Secretaries declare that Intermediate Treatment can:

be used narrowly to describe the treatment undertaken by a supervised person under a supervisor's directions as provided for under Section 12(2) of the 1969 [Children and Young Persons] Act;

or

more broadly, to describe arrangements for helping children in trouble or 'at risk' as envisaged by Section 1 of the Children and Young Persons Act 1963. (Home Office 1976).

This, and other formal statements, indicates considerable confusion over the categorization of IT. Thus, the Ministerial Guide states that 'given this wide range of possibilities, it is difficult to offer guidance in general terms' (DHSS 1972). This, it is sometimes suggested approvingly, indicates the virtues of a 'flexible approach' (Home Office 1975: para 117). Those who have to implement this flexible approach tend to look upon it with a rather more jaundiced eye. The 1974 Birmingham Conference indicated wide discord, and my own research conferences at Brunel echoed that confusion. One ITO saw himself as 'Her Majesty's Loyal Opposition'. Recent comments have been even more damning:

The blanket approach whereby IT subsumes a multitude of activities under its umbrella has not only rendered it meaningless (since it is anything one can do with kids) but has also allowed workers to avoid tackling the real problems of young offenders . . . (Salzedo 1981, see also Hume 1982).

The following study took place in one of the first departments to come to grips with IT and its organization. Whilst all the dimensions of the ITO's role required clarification, the nature of the *authority* in his role certainly occupied an important and probably predominant position.

LAS 1973–4[3]

At the end of 1973 and during the opening months of 1974, a number of meetings were held with senior departmental staff responsible for intermediate treatment; the purpose: to clarify the initial terms of reference and the precise nature of my involvement following an initial request for help from the Intermediate Treatment Officer. It was agreed that the terms of reference would be:

to examine the problems that are arising or that may arise in the Department's implementation of the intermediate treatment programme.

Two years later we concluded the project. In the intervening period the examination ebbed and flowed in response to the urgency of the situation. The management consultant's more rapid appraisal is very different from the collaborative, analytical, long-term bases of this action-research method. So, neither this nor indeed the previous day care study are accounts of lightening remedies brought forth with dazzling panache from academic shirt-sleeves. Any genuine movement from problems to tentative theories and critical discussion is bound to be – and was – an operose process.

As things stood in January 1974, a number of facilities were included in LAS's IT plans. The most significant as far as the role of the officer was concerned were: (i) a day centre for children truanting from school; (ii) a warehouse which it was intended to use as a centre for a range of activities such as art and craft work, remedial drama, work training, etc.; (iii) camping and allied activities; and (iv) a work centre for training in carpentry and joinery.

At that time (January 1974) the ITO felt that his official job description expected him to be accountable for 'the continuing development of a programme of intermediate and intermediate-type treatment'. This included:

● having ideas and getting information to the local authority;
● studying alternative provisions inside and outside the authority, and maintaining nationwide contacts;
● formulating proposals;
● 'selling' proposals across the department;
● the detailed operational planning of the new proposal (after sanctioning by the Department and Council) including costing and finding sites, 'finding' personnel, and seeking suitable resources;
● clarifying the boundaries of what is and is not included in intermediate treatment;
● evaluating the existing IT facilities.

The job description also placed an expectation on the ITO to 'liaise with and foster the involvement of all appropriate statutory and voluntary agencies and individuals by all available means, including publications'. More precisely, the ITO saw that as having authority to:

● inform and educate other people and institutions about the nature of IT;
● actively promote co-operation with other agencies;
● publicize the Department's plans, for example by articles in *Social Work Today* and *New Society*. (However, he felt that articles must be based on actual experience and that this was a 'sleeping duty for the time being'.)

The ITO was further expected to 'help initiate a system of assessment to measure the effectiveness and appropriateness of initiatives taken under the Children and Young Persons Act 1969'. The ITO saw his role as 'helping to initiate' assessments, the actual assessment being done by research teams inside or outside the Department. Whilst the ITO did some research work himself, this was a 'when-time-allows type of activity'. Finally, not the least of the expected duties was the supervision and management of IT facilities. The ITO considered that not until facilities were in operation would he know what was involved but, as a basic minimum, he would be responsible for the supervision of social workers, as is any other senior. He was also responsible for all the logistical support for IT facilities. But as a senior he was only allowed to authorize expenditure up to £10 without the sanction of the Assistant Director (Fieldwork), although he had wider discretion with regard to advance ordering from accredited suppliers.

In the light of all this, it is perhaps not surprising that the officer thought that he was 'seen as all things to all men', and that he felt that unless his role was defined there will be 'interesting discussions but little in the way of intermediate treatment'. The most burning problem at that time surrounded *sanctioning*.

A number of examples were given to illustrate the lack of clarity regarding the sanctioning of actions taken by the ITO. Disputes had occurred when it was unclear to disputants whose sanction was required for future action. The unclarity was reflected by the fact that the ITO and the Principal Officer in the Fieldwork Division (the ITO's official 'boss') saw the Director once a month to discuss general trends. Furthermore, the ITO found it necessary to write lengthy memos to various members of staff, with copies to different people.

The work strata theory provided some help in understanding the ITO's position. Judging by the job description, the supposition would be that the Department was unclear whether (in our terms) it wanted a Stratum 2 or Stratum 3 post. To judge by salary and status alone, it would seem that the lower level of work was envisaged. The ITO was appointed on a par with senior social workers whose work would generally fall within Stratum 2. (This, it will be recalled, demands a situational response to each specific concrete situation.) However, looking at the range of expected work, there were phrases such as 'the continuing development of a programme' which clearly indicated an anticipated Stratum 3 response. All in all, it is probably accurate to state that, at that stage of the research project, the Department did not differentiate between the two levels of response.

In clarifying the sanctioning of his actions, the tool kit of organizational roles proved invaluable. In particular the difference between *managerial, co-ordinating* and *monitoring* relationships.

Eventually, senior management became heavily involved in the project. This took place after it became clear that the initial analysis with the ITO in 1974, pointing to the need for role clarification, stood up to the test of the continuing experience during the following year.

Theory in the test of experience
At the end of 1974 further meetings took place which led to a briefer and more urgent restatement. What, it was asked, was the essence of the officer's role? By this time the broad alternatives and possible choices had begun to emerge. The intervening year had demonstrated that there were many strands with varying authority, not all of which were mutually compatible. Amongst this mixture it was now evident that the ITO was expected to act as:

- an operational *manager* of a number of 'day care' type projects;
- a specialist *co-ordinator* of something called intermediate treatment – at that time regarded as a specialist in group work methods, supervising other social workers;
- a specialist *practitioner* working with individual children;
- a *liaison* officer;
- a *new project* officer.

The work of the ITO in this period could be regarded as being suspended organizationally in mid-air. The officer himself noting the recent collapse of one project, described his work as attempting to 'keep twenty plates in the air'. In order to avoid additional crashes the Department instigated a period of intense clarification regarding intermediate treatment and its implementation.

The research had entered a new phase with senior management participating actively in the discussion, in contrast to their previous position of acting primarily as a sanctioning body for the project. Eventually, two documents were produced by the Department: the first was concerned with 'policy' guidelines, and the second, the organizational implications of these guidelines. Another way of looking at this might be to say that the policy document revolved around clarification of the horizontal dimension of work, whereas the second document concentrates on the authority and level of work dimensions.

Guidelines for a departmental policy
The final analysis of departmental policy guidelines concluded with the statement that intermediate treatment could be seen as:

A number of activities and projects, some experimental, which depend on interdepartmental collaboration for success and which, by the utilization of primarily group work methods in a non-residential setting, aims to provide an appropriate alternative to residential care for children at risk, in at risk areas, or on supervision or care orders.

This represented the Department's effort to clarify realistic boundaries in response to the 'flexible' or 'broad and narrow' approach of central government. The above one-sentence policy summary represents the end-product of a phase of lengthy, critical discussion. What is the target group of intermediate treatment? To what extent are the activities to be performed by specific methods and in characteristic settings? These and other questions were posed.[4]

Definition of the target group – the clientele – coming within the intermediate treatment programme was not easy. Discussions in early stages of the project had produced theories that referred to intermediate treatment containing joint work with 'normal' children. Was this still realistic? Deeper investigation indicated that some boundaries have to be, and were in practice, delineated. So, despite what was seen as 'the spirit of the 1969 Children and Young Persons Act', it was possible to identify four groups of children in the age group 10–18 (the determination of an age group was in itself a not insignificant boundary). The groups were:

(1) normal children in non-risk areas;
(2) normal children in at-risk areas;
(3) children who are considered to be, or feel themselves, at risk;
(4) children under supervision or care orders.

This initial classification appeared to be helpful in the light of the actual work of the Department.[5] For example, the last group had to be seen as a distinct category since there are defined statutory responsibilities in relation to the child and defined relations with the Juvenile Court. In this area of work the guidelines declared that the Department has to function 'in public' within a finite period of time. In reality, and in partial answer to the earlier question, the Department was not working with 'normal' children in non-risk areas.

Alternative organizational implications of these guidelines were outlined in a separate research document.

Organizational implications of policy guidelines

The policy guidelines settled a number of outstanding issues. Intermediate treatment, as defined, did not fit neatly into the functional divisions, and the new role would require authority to work across the board inside and outside the Department. There was also a clear-cut commitment to the need for someone who would be making a systematic (Stratum 3) response. A number of organizational models vied for

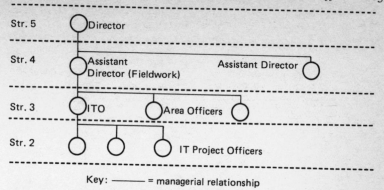

Key: ———— = managerial relationship

Figure 13.1 The intermediate treatment officer as a manager in the fieldwork division

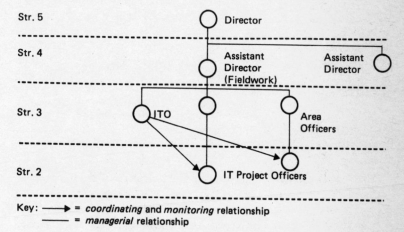

Key: ——▶ = *coordinating* and *monitoring* relationship
———— = *managerial* relationship

Figure 13.2 The ITO as a co-ordinator in the fieldwork division

consideration. Three of these are illustrated in Figures 13.1–13.3. (For some characteristics of *managerial co-ordinating*, and *monitoring* roles, see chapter 8.)

At the end of the day the Department decided that since it was organized on functional lines, and since a Stratum 3 operational manager was desired, the fieldwork division was the best organizational 'home'. So after considerable deliberation, the first model depicted was chosen. The main advantages were seen to be that:

● the ITO would be firmly established as an operational *manager* in Stratum 3, working with area officers as *collateral* colleagues, with the assistant director (fieldwork) as *his* manager;

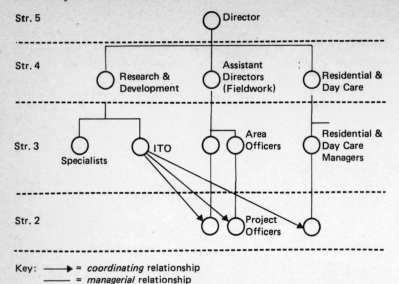

Figure 13.3   The ITO as co-ordinator in research and development division

- the ITO would participate in divisional management team meetings where policy *vis-à-vis* intermediate treatment could be agreed and made binding on all concerned;
- an appropriate percentage of social work resources could be guaranteed to intermediate treatment which would thus not be dependent on 'goodwill or overtime'.

The organizational implications documents pointed out that the change in role of the ITO would involve reconsideration of the primary job description and presumably necessitate a withdrawal from activities that ought to be pursued by project and group leaders (Stratum 2), and careful examination of activities appropriately performed in the research and development division. A number of potential problems were also noted for further attention – and this will be the reality of any analysis.

Summary

This extract from the research in LAS demonstrates the utility of clarifying the dimensions of organizational roles. Because of the unique position of the ITO as the main 'provider' of a particular type of service, the analysis naturally moved into a discussion of the activity (intermediate treatment).

During the project the Department had little difficulty in identifying that it really wanted the ITO to focus on a Stratum 3 response. It was also confident in the officer's capacity to handle the work. What proved more complicated was the teasing-out of the various authority links. Finally, decisions were taken which established the ITO as a definite manager in the fieldwork division, a position which gave him the necessary authority to make a significant contribution to the work of the Department.

The ITO, who at the time of the original invitation to collaborate had been very unhappy and considered leaving, stayed in the new post for five years, to the considerable satisfaction – so I understand – of all concerned.

Notes

1. Thus providing an example of the generation and implementation of theory. For a broader 'philosophical' explanation, see chapters 1 and 2.
2. There is now a substantial body of literature devoted to the theory and practice of intermediate treatment. The Youth Social Work Unit of the National Youth Bureau publishes an excellent series of booklets containing references to most of the literature. The results of a DHSS-funded research project are to be found in Vincent (1980). See also Paley and Thorpe (1974); Personal Social Services Council (1977); and Leissner, Powley and Evans (1977).
3. This is an abbreviated account, although I have attempted to ensure that the main issues are retained.
4. This analysis was to lead to the identification of key variables reported in Billis (1976). I would now see clarification of the target group as a major element in the clarification of the horizontal deminsion of organizations.
5. I have since cast doubts on the concepts of 'at risk' and 'prevention' in Billis (1981a).

14   Differential Administrative Capacity: the Kibbutz Experience

Unlike the previous three case studies this chapter deals only with the development of theory. It differs also in that it draws on twenty years' experience and association with the kibbutz movement, including ten years membership in one kibbutz. At first glance this may seem a far cry from 'welfare' and its 'bureaucracies', but the distance is less than it appears.

The origins and ethos of the kibbutzim are rooted in a deep concern for needs and problems that are social. They are, after all, 'total' societies. How can each person have a satisfying place of work? What is the best way to educate the younger generation? How should the unsatisfactory position of women in the kibbutz society be improved? How to respond to the increasing number of the elderly? How can the standard of housing be improved? How to handle problems of bereavement? These are but a few of the social issues which are basic to kibbutz life.

As for 'bureaucracy', few would dispute the existence of an explicit hierarchic system of decision-making (Tannenbaum *et al.* 1974). And whilst there is no employment system (the other element of the earlier definition of bureaucracy), members are *dependent for their livelihood* on membership of the settlement. It can be argued that despite the many differences the concept of 'bureaucracy' is one that can usefully be explored in the kibbutz context.

Most important of all, the lack of any payment system, the absence of economic classes, and the total nature of the community, furnish almost laboratory-like conditions for a discussion of 'administrative capacity'. It is difficult to think of any other social phenomenon that could compete with the kibbutz in this respect.

I have, in the following sections, abstracted those elements of a more detailed case study based in a settlement called 'Degem' which illustrate the career progressions of a number of kibbutz managers (Billis 1977). This was done in order to support the contention (in chapter 9) that the rate of development of administrative capacity varies.

The nature of administrative capacity

What then do we mean by administrative capacity? In an analysis of the problems of the post-1948 kibbutzim, the conclusion was reached that one of the chronic limitations facing a young settlement – called 'Degem' in the case study – was the inadequacy of available 'administrative talent' to meet the needs of the settlement, which had been modelled on veteran settlements (Billis 1971). The notion of administrative talent was understood in a pragmatic and generalized way. It referred to the ability of individuals to 'handle' the activities of a branch of the economy or to act as chairmen of important committees. Members of the kibbutz knew who had this ability. At the least it was clear that administrative capacity did not necessarily equal intelligence. In a small, closely-knit community the difference between intelligence and administrative capacity was obvious; confusion between the two attributes could only be temporary. In those instances where the mistake was made, adverse consequences followed swiftly. I have in mind one particular example of a gifted intellectual (Mr Z) elected to the post of farm manager, who later proved unable to carry the burden of that office.

The voluntary and total nature of the community results in a 'face-to-face' and continuous administrative task that is probably unparalleled in any other organizational form. There is literally no hiding place for those managers and chairmen who have what we might roughly call administrative duties. The symptoms of Mr Z's stress could not be concealed. The increase in conflict and the deterioration in personal relationships come under the microscope of the community's collective judgement. The kibbutz can be a tough and harsh society in the sphere of interpersonal relationships (a contention that will surprise only those who have not lived in it). There is no possibility of 'carrying' key office-holders, no 'Buggins' turn', no nepotism, and no security of tenure for such personnel. The end result can be unpleasant for the unfortunate role incumbent. As one kibbutz secretary announced at the end of his term of office: 'My feeling is that before I accepted the task I was an honoured member of the kibbutz. Today there are members who don't want to look me in the face.' (Billis 1971: 283).

The kibbutz member cannot be dismissed from the organization if found unsuitable for managerial posts. Every effort must be made to find appropriate work. The optimum that is expected is that members perform to the best of their abilities. The kibbutz basic value of 'self-labour' does not permit the employment of hired workers. In a number of settlements no more than lip service is paid to this part of the ideology of the founding fathers; but even where outside workers are hired these are in the main at the basic or operative levels. The kibbutz movement as a whole is unwilling to relinquish control of any of its key administrative positions to non-members.

Some further refinements are necessary to the notion of administrative capacity if we are to use it for a study of career development. In the 'work-doing' sphere the basic unit of the kibbutz is the branch. Each branch has a clearly defined 'centralizer' or 'co-ordinator' (a literal translation from the Hebrew). The role of the branch co-ordinator has many of the attributes of the managerial role defined earlier. Although a full comparative role study would indicate distinctions, the branch co-ordinator is undoubtedly held accountable (by the community) for the work of his team. If something goes amiss, if mistakes are made, the kibbutz branch co-ordinator is expected to appear before the relevant committee and explain the action. The similarities between the kibbutz branch co-ordinator and first-level managers are such that the former will also be referred to as managers. This will be done despite the fact that the Hebrew word *meracez* is a deliberate attempt to find a softer, more culturally acceptable, term in the light of the radical anti-managerial attitude of the kibbutz. But, as Diamond (1957) pointed out, while 'to call a man a manager is a kind of blasphemy – this merely masks a situation that has become, in reality, increasingly managerial'. The ease with which branch co-ordinators, if they leave the kibbutz, transfer into the role of 'capitalist' managers, and the eagerness that outside organizations display in snapping up ex-co-ordinators, is persuasive supporting evidence.

The kibbutz also has a wide-ranging system of committees covering all aspects of community life. The more important committees require abilities not dissimilar to the branch manager's. It is interesting to note the correlation between success (measured by whether the member was asked to do a similar job again) in the two positions. I can recall few cases where an ordinary member not considered suitable for branch manager was elected to co-ordinate the activities of a key committee.

These first-level managerial jobs will be referred to as necessitating administrative capacity of AC2. But a stage of kibbutz development is eventually reached that requires a higher level of administrative capacity. Haphazard methods of co-ordinating the total farm economy are inadequate. What is required is a farm manager needing what will be referred to as AC3. As living standards and expectations rise, the work of other functionaries, in particular that of the kibbutz secretary, becomes more complex. The secretary is expected to act as chairman of the weekly general assembly and of the powerful secretariat composed of the key office-holders. He must act as arbiter between competing internal interests and demands and as representative of the settlement *vis-à-vis* many outside bodies. Thus, the kibbutz community has a demand for administrative capacity in both its economic and its social life. In addition it will be suggested that the 'industrial revolution' of the kibbutz movement has witnessed the emergence of a demand for AC4 administrators inside the kibbutz.

The following sections do, I believe, express intuitively held evaluations of members in the case-study kibbutz. The particular value may well lie in this attempt to place on paper a collective judgement about differential capacity which may be possible only by those who have been an integral part of that total judgement over a long period of time.

The argument so far may be summed up by stating that for the purpose of this chapter administrative capacity will be regarded as being of three levels: AC2, AC3 and AC4.[1] Administrative capacity is defined in terms of the ability to cope with the duties of strata of specific organizational posts.

The development of administrative capacity

To what extent can administrative capacity be developed? In large part the answer depends on whether we consider AC2, AC3 and AC4 to be part of a gradual continuum, or steps in a ladder, the higher rungs of which not everybody might reach. Some interesting facts about selection for office may aid in answering this question. In the first place the kibbutz stresses experience in the job. While it was necessary to participate in courses to gain knowledge and skill, this alone could not transform a branch member into a branch manager. Training would seem to have taken place with two objectives: to make members and managers more effective as members and managers; and to groom members and managers for higher administrative capacity posts.

In the latter case the collective judgement of the community, which had by the very nature of the total society been observing and evaluating the candidate, perhaps from birth, will have decided that a particular member is 'ripe' and can probably almost handle the next step. Training is seen as part of a normal path of administrative development for that individual. If the judgement has been inaccurate, training alone could not lift members from one level to the next. Members are not equal in height, weight or colour of eyes; neither are they expected to be equal in administrative capacity. The influence of training might be depicted as in Figure 14.1.

Training could influence the effectiveness and progression from o to x but could not itself cause the jump to v. Most branch managers and top committee chairmen (AC2) were never chosen as farm managers (AC3) despite ample opportunity and pressures to 'increase the number of backs' carrying administrative burdens.

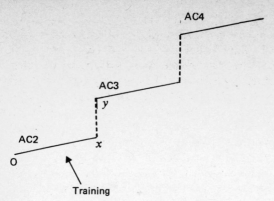

Figure 14.1   Training and administrative capacity

The contention that differential capacity exists and that training alone cannot lift a member through the critical boundaries might not be disputed by serious commentators from inside or outside the kibbutz movement. For the former, differential capacity is not in question. For the latter, its existence is used as yet another 'conclusive' proof of the dominance of 'specialists and elected managerial functionaries' (Eisenstadt 1967: 168). The tautological manner in which stratification is sometimes analysed is discussed elsewhere (Billis 1973a); it was not a problem in the case study. As far as the spectre of 'managerial domination' is concerned, this is marginally more relevant, though not a totally convincing image. Holders of the higher-level administrative posts were certainly influential and their comments would be granted additional weight, but this is a far cry from domination. There was little evidence of the development of a permanent managerial class, although pressure groups certainly existed. (Billis 1973b).

Degem, our case-study settlement, was founded in 1948. By that time the basic model of a kibbutz was already well established. No futile attempt was made to establish the settlement without a minimum organizational framework. National agriculture was more developed, many regional and national institutions for mutual support existed, loans from a variety of agencies were available; in short, the organizational environment of Degem in 1948 was more complex than the pioneering period at the beginning of the twentieth century (see Kanovsky 1966; Shatil 1968). Organizational roles such as farm manager, kibbutz secretary, and treasurer had to be filled. Etzioni (1957) has also described how 'as the kibbutz grows and becomes more complex . . . a formally organized heirarchy is established'.

True, the economy of Degem was modest. Living standards were low. Nevertheless, the demand for AC2 was an absolute necessity. Until 1954/5 economic and social development was steady if unspectacular. The settlement had survived a number of political crises, many of the founding members had left, but sufficient talented founders remained to cope with an economy based solely on agriculture, and with the limited social ambitions of the community.

In 1954–57 a massive (in proportional terms) influx of new members began. The 120 remaining founders were swamped by a new group of reinforcements from the Israeli Youth Movement. Over 100 young, vigorous members arrived in Degem. Farm economies cannot be rapidly expanded. The physical manpower at the operative level could be absorbed in a variety of ways. More labour-intensive crops were planted, in some cases muscle power replaced machines, and members of the new group were sent to work outside the settlement. But among the new members were army officers and others already used to occupying positions that can be assumed to demand AC2. A struggle developed for domination of the economic branches. There are numerous examples of the bitter exchanges between the veterans and the newcomers that took place both inside and outside the kibbutz institutions. Perhaps the most dramatic 'takeover' was in the dairy, which was transformed in ten years from an ailing failure to an outstanding success. Some of the new talent found its outlet in organizing more complex and new social activities.

Degem 1959–67
This situation lasted until about 1959 when a number of new and interesting processes began to develop. In keeping with the national economic trends, prosperity began to reach even the smaller settlements. Agriculture became profitable, national institutions began to inject substantial sums for investment into the settlement, and the consumer boom began.

Degem's agricultural branches became larger and more sophisticated. Increasing demands were made of the social organization of the community. The number of children grew steadily. The public service branches (dining room, laundry, clothing store, etc.) faced rising community expectations. The manager of the combined dining room and kitchen had one of the most onerous tasks in Degem; planning supply to meet a continuously changing demand, arranging menus, supervising a wide variety of unskilled staff, planning special diets, and arranging the daily work rota (sometimes not knowing until the very last moment whether workers would be taken from kitchen duty to more urgent jobs). In organizing the services for the rising child population, Degem, in common with other kibbutzim, faced its most sensitive community expectations and demands. Children, livestock, members – this was the traditional kibbutz order of priorities. With the increase in the number of children's nurses it became evident that another organizational role was required. Someone was needed to co-ordinate the activities of the greater number of nurses, to supervise their activities, and to suggest the implementation of common standards. Yet another higher-level administrative post was demanded.

Doubtless there were individual members of the settlement who already in the earlier period possessed the administrative capacity to deal with higher levels of work (AC3 or higher). We can note that before the crises of the mid-1950s, when the community had no demand for AC3, some of its branch managers had left to take up work in large outside organizations. In those instances in which I have been able to trace their movements it seems that their new employment was significantly higher in terms of administrative capacity.

It was only in the 1960s that Degem began to demand occupants for roles that were felt by the community to be qualitatively different. Mr Y, the new farm manager appointed in 1960, exemplified the changing conditions. Young, well-educated, highly intelligent, and prepared to take risks, he had already served as work organizer, arranging the daily work schedule. To prepare him for his new job the kibbutz sent him to the newly established combined kibbutz movement course for farm managers. This course, which lasted for a year, covered a wide range of subjects thought necessary for the future administrator: natural sciences, agriculture, irrigation, economics, planning, administration, and the structure of the kibbutz branches. In order to exploit fully this course it was felt that candidates should have experience at branch manager level, together with a solid educational basis. To translate this to a different context, this was the sort of course in which the inputs were, broadly speaking, at first-degree level, where the participants would be expected to be capable of absorbing material at that level and to have had substantial experience of kibbutz life and branch management. The curriculum has the feel of a course designed for middle-managers and enables us to grasp more precisely the nature of AC3.

Degem's first participant in the farm managers' course, Mr Y, was probably not the most typical of participants in that, as a result of the chaos caused by the departure of veteran branch managers, the settlement had been unable to release an incumbent branch manager. More precisely, and more importantly, the *experienced* branch managers were not felt by the community to be suitable candidates. So we are now provided with yet another clue to an understanding of administrative capacity. Certainly, intelligence was a factor in selection. But were it the sole factor there would have been no lack of possible participants, since many of Y's colleagues had as good, if not better, academic records. Nor, as we have noted, could it just be experience. Finally, even experience plus intelligence cannot define administrative capacity. This might have been difficult to discern in 1960 when Y was chosen for the course. But we are now able to observe a distinct pattern of community evaluation concerning the filling of the farm manager and other AC3 posts. As we have noted, there were colleagues of Y who were as intelligent and who also had some branch management experience. Yet the struggle was for AC2 posts; none of Y's colleagues were seriously considered to be groomed for the new 'felt higher' role. Relentless community pressure was placed on an unwilling Y to join the course. Respected national kibbutz figures from outside Degem were brought in to persuade him where 'his duty' lay.

We shall return to the career path of Y shortly, but as further evidence to support the contention that intelligence plus experience do not equal administrative capacity, we may cite once again the case of another farm manager, Mr Z, mentioned at the beginning of this chapter. That unfortunate farm manger, as was stated, was of demonstrable intelligence, yet failed in the judgement of the community. What can now be added is that he had also previously been a branch manager for at least five years.

Degem after 1967
Is age a valid variable in our understanding of differential administrative capacity? In a crude attempt to illustrate this contention and at the same time to hint at the emergence of an even higher level of administrative capacity, charts have been constructed to demonstrate the 'career' progression of five managers over a period of approximately twenty years.

We have already discussed two of these managers in this paper, Mr Y and Mr Z. It will be remembered that Y was the reluctant first participant from Degem in the farm managers' course. Mr Z, on the other hand, was the gifted intellectual, a branch manager who proved unable to stand the additional stresses of the farm manager post. Before mentioning briefly how managers W, U and V fit into the general thesis, a few explanatory comments are required. The use of the word *career* can be justified; but even so the notion does not rest easily within the kibbutz ideological framework. In order to consider the career progression of a kibbutz member, we first have to recollect that no additional monetary rewards are received by accepting higher-level posts. Our figures, therefore, do not plot salary, but job progressions. This is probably a strength rather than a weakness of the analysis, since it forces attention to the essential administrative capacity demands of the work. The second point to be made is that part of

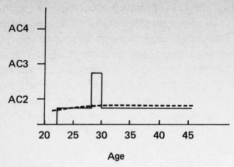

Figure 14.2   *Mr U: career progression*

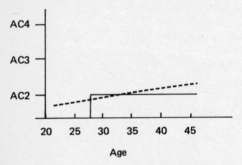

Figure 14.3   *Mr V: career progression*

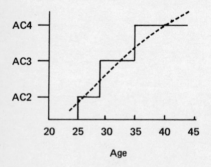

Figure 14.4   *Mr W: career progression*

the democratic ideology of the kibbutz movement is reflected in the practice of job rotation. Not all jobs are rotated; only those that are considered to be administrative. This system is not applied with equal persistence in all the roles that we have designated as having AC2 AC3 and AC4 qualities. In Degem, rotation was strictly implemented in the farm manager, treasurer, secretary, and committee chairmen roles. Branch managers were rotated more casually in contrast to the regular election every two or three years for the farm manager. These factors are relevant to an appreciation of the figures. For example, compelled by its ideology to elect a new farm manager, the settlement may at that precise moment not have an available candidate. There may be strong reasons why the ideal candidate cannot accept the post at once. So a stop-gap farm manager is elected, a borderline man who can hold things together until the new person is available.

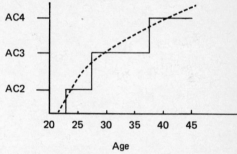

Figure 14.5   Mr Y: career progression

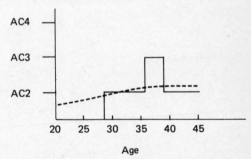

Figure 14.6   Mr Z: career progression

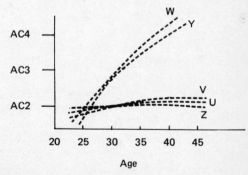

Figure 14.7   Combined progression curve U, V, W, Y and Z

Unlike the situation of full rotation the expectations on the temporary incumbent are less. More work is done in committee; outside experts from national kibbutz and state organizations are more frequent visitors to the settlement. This explains the jump from AC2 to AC3 and back in the case of U in Figure 14.2. After a brief spell as farm manager, U returned to a lower-level post, where he has remained for the past fifteen years. Mr V illustrates a somewhat different development, entering an administrative post rather late in life and remaining in AC2 posts until the time of writing. It must be stressed that we shall observe shortly how in the early 1970s AC3 posts were available. Therefore, I do not think that in the case of either Mr U or Mr V it could be claimed that capacity was in any way being suppressed. Mangers W and Y are our 'high fliers', progressing steadily from post to post. At the end of 1974 we find one acting as farm manager and the other in charge of a factory that after only two years is well on the way to dominating the whole of Degem's economy. It does not appear that the farm manager has any real authority over the factory manager.

What is AC4? Here the ground is more tentative, since it is difficult to depend just on the case study. If we compare Degem with a typical veteran settlement we may obtain insight into the more complex functions that need to be administered. This must be treated as a shorthand list that indicates some important differences.

The veteran settlement need not be more profitable, but it would have a far more substantial economic base. With one or more factories, industry rather than agriculture is the major contributor to income. The top industrial staff are already seasoned world travellers. It would be both older and larger than Degem and could already be facing the problems of the generation gap, and the elderly in its midst. Its most successful members would be influential in the national scene, perhaps even cabinet ministers. The veteran settlement might well have its own high school, resident doctor and nurses, museum, theatre, printing press, library, and so on. Degem, on the other hand, sent its children to a neighbouring kibbutz high school, had a visiting general practitioner, and a modest library. A sufficient list perhaps, to indicate that the management of a veteran community can be postulated to demand a qualitatively higher level of administrative capacity – AC4 (or higher, but this is not central to this paper).

There were signs in the early 1970s that potential AC4 members were available in Degem. Demands began to appear from national and regional institutions for Degem's most successful farm manager to fill important roles. The kibbutz, unwilling to release its most talented members, began to explore new fields of endeavour. Its emergent AC4 members concentrated their attention on the settlement's major agriculture branch, the dairy, and built it into a national showpiece. Large sums of money were invested and, in a country of considerable agricultural achievements, Degem built its dairy on a scale and with equipment to outshine even the largest of veteran settlements. With the dairy, a factory in everything but name, Degem turns its talents to the genuine article. I suggest that at this point the settlement is beginning to break the AC3 barrier, and AC4 becomes a definite factor.

Postscript

At the end of 1974 I was able to return to Degem to study the development of the settlement's factory and the interaction between the manifest concepts of democracy and participation amidst the growing industrialization.[2] This visit made possible the completion of the individual career progressions outlined in Figures 14.2–14.7 and a retesting of the equations of administrative capacity. An interesting picture emerges.

The kibbutz can now be seen facing the demands and expectations of a veteran settlement but without as yet having integrated its second generation, who are still too young. The majority of members are in the 38–45 age bracket. They seem to have settled comfortably in AC2 roles or, in the case of many women, have bowed to the 'needs' of the situation, and work often grudgingly with the children or in other service branches. There is a strong impression that the supply and demand of administrative capacity at AC2 is at least in equilibrium. Indeed, members from the 38–45 age group are released for study or other external duties without great difficulty. But above and below this broad body of AC2 the situation appears very different.

Despite continuing mechanization there is still high demand for the non-managerial, manual, or operative labour. The introduction of a self-service in the dining room, for example, has only marginally reduced the demand for unskilled labour. The fruit still have to be picked, the lawns watered. Temporary labour is utilized to the fullest extent. A whole colony of students and volunteers is a permanent feature of the landscape. But these are temporary residents, rarely remaining sufficiently long to acquire the skills of an expect tractor driver or dedicated herdsman. The kibbutz rests on a shaky foundation of transient labour. Mechanization of the agricultural branches has been counter-balanced by the establishment of a factory and an increase in the scale of agricultural production. Such reliable labour as does exist has been drawn, in the face of loud complaints from the agricultural managers, into the fast-growing plant.

Above AC2, things are rather different. A few outstanding members appear to have dragged Degem into a leading position in the national kibbutz profitability league. At this stage it is difficult to enumerate more than two posts requiring AC4 (farm manager and factory manager), and we have noted in the previous section the rise of members with AC4 in Degem. At the level of AC3, however, supply is still not keeping pace with demand. The poor state of the combined kitchen and dining room, which with some thirty workers probably requires AC3, is acknowledged to be a consequence of the lack of suitable managerial manpower. The idea has been mooted, but not implemented, of moving a high-level agricultural manager into this post. The magnificent cultural centre stands empty, a reminder of Degem's inability to release the sort of member with the drive, talent, and imagination to co-ordinate the communal activities that such a centre could and, in other settlements, does embrace.

The work of Tannenbaum *et al.* (1974) suggests that the managerial chain in kibbutz factories is between 2 and 5. However, their hierarchical chain is loosely defined and is described as 'the number of persons intervening' between the top and the bottom of the official organization chart. Taking into account that the authors in their study of ten kibbutz factories use a more generous definition of hierarchical level than the notion of managerial strata used here, the suggestion here that Degem's factory requires AC4 would match the national picture. This supports the general contention that Degem's AC3 members work in the factory or the major agricultural branches.

Conclusions and implications[3]

It has been claimed that the kibbutz provides laboratory-like conditions for this and other social investigations. Nevertheless, the kibbutz should not be mistaken for a utopian endeavour divorced from any wider societal setting. The entire history of the kibbutz movement is concerned with communities that are an integral part of national life. Kibbutz members are to be found everywhere, whether it be in the Cabinet or in the television studios! Thus, the analysis of kibbutz experience, provided it is sufficiently extensive and intensive, may perhaps justifiably claim to have more than local implications.

This study of Degem has claimed that the growth in size and complexity of the community gave rise to qualitatively different levels of demand for administrative capacity. These strata have been defined as broadly equivalent to the concept of managerial rank precisely analysed by Jaques (1976), or in more general management parlance, 'lower, middle, and senior management'.

Recent work by the author and colleagues is concerned with testing an emerging theory of stratification of work in organizations (Rowbottom and Billis 1977; Billis1975a). However, despite intriguing possibilities, this paper has not attempted to utilize the work-stratum theory to analyse the kibbutz demand for administrative capacity. It is felt that such a project would require additional research. Administrative capacity as an individual attribute has not been tightly conceptualized. The best that we have achieved are statements declaring what it is not. It is not merely intelligence, nor just experience or knowledge. These and other factors enter the concept. But even this modest proposition, if it is accurate, may be considered an advance on those approaches that identify managerial ability with just one or other of the factors. It is additionally suggested that administrative capacity varies between individuals and that its rate of development is different. Training is not seen as a panacea capable of solving short-falls in the supply.

Notes

1. The original paper uses different titles (AC1, AC2 and AC3); I have amended that paper for uniformity of presentation in this book. The argument is unaffected.
2. This visit was made possible by a research grant from the Nuffield Foundation.
3. These relate to the original paper.

PART IV

Conclusions

The final chapter of the book highlights some of the more important arguments, and speculates on the relevance of usable theory for model-building in the discipline of social administration.

Having argued for a tentative approach, it would be inconsistent to produce 'conclusions' in a final chapter. This would have a ring of misleading finality out of keeping with what I hope is the general spirit of the book. Admittedly, the 'usable theories' presented in Part II may appear rather emphatic; if so, this is perhaps the appropriate place to reiterate that they too are tentative. They represent the 'best' ideas that I can muster at this time in order to respond to a given range of problems.

Actually, researchers who adopt this stance, and hope to develop usable theory, face a rather tough dilemma. To put it bluntly, they have to 'stick their necks out' vigorously and sometimes painfully, in a manner which belies the basic tentative context. Thus, the Levels of Work theory will not be superseded by 'better' or alternative ideas unless it is subjected to widespread and determined critical evaluation. And even then, when the cracks begin to appear, as they surely must, and the next round of problems emerges, we may still have no alternative but to utilize our existing theories – unless, and until, we have the wit to devise more persuasive explanations.

But although 'conclusions' as such might be out of place, it is nevertheless useful to recollect and highlight briefly some of the major and more controversial arguments. We might also speculate on one or two topics that have received less than their due in this book. I refer here to the relevance and implications of usable theory for those broader models generated in the disciplines of public, and more importantly, social administration.

The context of usable theory for the middle-ground
It will be recalled that our opening task was the central social policy one of attempting to answer the question: how can we make a systematic response to social problems? Whilst acknowledging the important place of the informal sector and other mediating groupings in the provision of care, I have assumed that a significant position will continue to be occupied by agencies (public, voluntary, or private) that employ staff – the 'bureaucracies' of our title. Naturally, given the key role of the state in the provision of welfare, and the concentration of research resources in this area, governmental agencies have provided much of the material for this study. However, I have also

drawn on material which is slowly but steadily becoming available from our work with voluntary agencies. In Part I we attempted to set the scene for tackling our opening task by exploring what was called the 'context' of usable theory along three main paths: the philosophic, the methodological, and the disciplinary.

From the early discussion, we might highlight the prominent place reserved for 'problems' – very different from the usual aims-orientated approach. Thus, the problem-solving bureaucracy, with its structure of roles, was regarded as a major mediating agency standing in the middle-ground between political statements of intent; and the citizen with problems. As such it can both implement *and* generate explanations for the resolutions of those problems. We noted that with all its faults, societies with varied political ideologies, have found few alternatives to bureaucracy in their search to make a systematic response to social problems. We further drew attention to the fact that the notion of 'social policy' would look pretty empty without its organizational, and mainly bureaucratic, structures.

The 'methodological' path took the problem-orientated stance a step further. If it is worthwhile to examine organizations as problem-solving, might it also be worthwhile to adopt a similar attitude to research and the development of theory? The essay on the social-analytic approach was presented to illustrate one way in which usable theory might be generated. We need not repeat that discussion, but we might highlight the importance of *explication* and *critical discussion*.

The organization that agrees to embark on a collaborative exploration of its problems has taken a step along what could be a very radical path. Explication, it was argued, can threaten frameworks. For the informal and inexplicit cannot easily, if at all, be controlled and changed. Whilst explication, by itself, is no guarantee *of* change, it can be regarded as an essential precondition *for* change. Problems that are not made explicit cannot be subjected to mutual rational control by critical discussion. If 'informality' implies an unwillingness to engage in a search for explicit formulations, then it should be regarded with caution. Indeed, the bureaucracy that does not periodically and naturally open itself up to this sort of exercise justifiably attracts public suspicion. Measured against this criterion, social services departments, for example, come out not too badly. Many of them have actively sought opportunities to examine and make their problems explicit.

The role of critical discussion, it was suggested, is not only vital for the control and change of bureaucracies, it is also undervalued as a component of social science. Any research approach that aspires to develop usable models must be subjected to that self-same process. We attempted in chapter 2 to demonstrate how strategies for the extension of critical discussion might be incorporated into a research approach.

The final contextual chapter was described as 'disciplinary'. We need say little here since several implications will be discussed in a later section. We might just note once more the prominence of 'problems': that at the core of social administration as a discipline is a concern for the difficulties of everyday life.

The presentation of usable theory for the middle-ground

In Part II we returned towards a more direct confrontation with the opening problem of constructing a systematic response to social problems. I have posed this question, and joined in the search for an answer, with many students, practitioners, managers and policy-makers, during the past decade. Suppose we were given this task, how might we set about tackling it? Undoubtedly, there are other starting points and other approaches to those presented here. Nevertheless, it has often appeared to be helpful, and I would contend usually essential, to clarify the four 'dimensions' of *categorization, level, authority*, and *capacity*. Again, in these recollections, we might take the opportunity to highlight several significant and more controversial points.

Part II opened with an analysis of the categorization boundary of SSDs. What 'business' do they appear to be in, and what might serve as a more cohesive statement of that work? This discussion enters controversial territory and rarely fails to cause an initial rise in the collective blood pressure of social services staff presented with these ideas in courses and workshops. To consider the possibility, for example, that 'prevention' might not perhaps be regarded as part of the business of SSDs requires a radical shift in entrenched beliefs. The contention that it might even not be in the best interests of the community, clients, and staff must always be made with an eye to a quick exit from the room. Still, as we slowly pursue the argument, blood pressures decline and the case can be discussed on its merits. We discover that the word 'prevention' is a sloppy idea and that it might have damaging, unanticipated, consequences. At the end of the day, the word can be stretched to describe intervention in unbounded 'problem-situations' – or the prevention of almost everything. All work, no matter how mundane and straightforward it might appear, can be described as 'preventing' something. Feeding an elderly person 'prevents' them becoming hungry; cleaning the room 'prevents' it becoming dirty; giving information to potential clients 'prevents' them going to the wrong department; and so on. Of course, the word is usually employed at the other extreme to describe work in more intangible situations in an attempt to give it an aura of extra significance and priority. I have argued the case against prevention in detail elsewhere and suggested that the creation of a false dichotomy between 'work' and 'preventive work' within the boundaries of the same department contributes to an unfair deal for clients and those who ought to be receiving services, confusion and status differentials for departmental staff, and problems for the community as a whole (Billis 1981a).

As part of the analysis in chapter 4 it was suggested that *social breakdown* – the actual or imminent loss of independence – might replace current definitions of the work of SSDs. We also presented the concept of *social discomfort* – the need for 'love, affection, and belongingness' – as a separate category deserving attention in its own right. Here, we touched upon the issue of the boundary between governmental and non-governmental provision of welfare, and raised doubts about the former's entering into the social discomfort (loneliness) arena.

If we follow this general line of argument, there may be implications for current trends which we have not necessarily pursued in earlier chapters. Thus, the increasing privatization of residential care, perhaps accelerated by the 1983 residential workers' strike, raises fundamental social policy questions. If residential care and other 'breakdown' services are hived off to small-scale entrepreneurs in the private sector, who then is accountable for the systematic resolution of these problems? It has been difficult enough to develop policies for residential care in the public and voluntary sectors; but how will these higher level responses be implemented if residential care is taken over by thousands of small hotels, hostels, and boarding houses?

Unless we are moving into an era of massive social indifference towards those no longer, for whatever reason, capable of living independent lives, then government (either central or local) will have to continue its broad accountability for systematic and comprehensive provision, and employ staff to do that work. (In other words, in the language of later chapters, Level 3 and above roles will need to be established somewhere.)

Paradoxically, privatization may well be accompanied, in due course, by the development of a growing governmental bureaucracy of 'monitors', 'evaluaters' and 'controllers'. I cannot help feeling that we have become caught in a cycle of events with unforeseen and painful results for many of the actors. The undue emphasis on prevention and the consequent primacy given to 'preventive work' in social work education may have contributed to the tendency to undervalue the work of residential staff, their low status, salaries, and poor training facilities; this in turn contributes to dissatisfaction, strikes, and the possibility of increased privatization – a crude and partial characterization of the cycle of events, but probably worth considering.

The central chapters (5 6 and 7) of this Part presented a theory of the second 'dimension'. Clarification of the *level of response* that is to be made to social need is as critical for social policy as clarification of the first (categorization) dimension. In these chapters the concepts of *client* and *societal impact* were introduced, and these in turn were used to develop a typology of alternative organizational responses to social problems. From this discussion we might highlight the contention that the desired response is a matter of *choice and explicit decision*. I believe that the typology extends the possibility of critical discussion about real social policy alternatives. I shall in a following section attempt to demonstrate how my own models relate to the different sort of models developed in the discipline of social administration. For the moment I would only emphasize that the reluctance of the discipline to enter middle-ground research, and the absence of usable theories and models, has left us open to invasion by every insubstantial whim and fad.

The latest mishmash, or 'hoola-hoop', as one SSD Director disparagingly described it, is 'decentralization' (Townsend 1983). There is little doubt that thorough confusion reigns. We might not quite reach the famous number of varieties claimed by that well-known food manufacturer, but we shall not be far short. It is clear that in attempting to implement the concept, departments have not succeeded in clarifying *either* the categorization *or* the level questions. It seems that with regard to the first dimension, 'decentralization' is being used to describe a number of different combinations of activities.[1] Sometimes it is taken to mean integration of field and residential services, or field and domiciliary services, or a variety of permutations of existing services. In at least one local authority it is being used to describe an extension into front-line co-operation with allied departments such as housing. Equally unclear is what level of client impact is desired, or what level of integration of functions is being sought. One agency is attempting to implement a Level 1 front-line; another appears to wish its impact to be at Level 3.

All this is not a question of academic jargon. We have used the concepts presented in Part II in work with staff in social services departments, without strain or embarrassment. (I might note here my reservations about the long-term political feasibility of a high, Level 3, response at the front-line – as some of the 'patch' models appear to be advocating.)

Our third dimension, it will be recalled, dealt with the question of the *authority* to be given to those in the bureaucratic middle-ground. In chapter 8 we not only presented a table of 'pluralistic' authority, *we moved on to challenge the concept of delegated authority itself*. In its place we explored the notions of *control* and *assistance*. Perhaps the structural model of bureaucracy, presented in that chapter, might provide better answers to the continued dilemma of pinpointing accountability when 'things go wrong'. Clearly, the prevalent 'directorial' models, which see all authority as delegated from the top, do not answer the needs of democratic control and large-scale bureaucratic problem-solving.

The final chapter of this part introduced ideas about *administrative capacity*. Have we the people for the job? We claimed that this question is rarely taken into account when considering social policy changes. All too often 'a magic wand' theory of individual ability appears to underpin suggested institutional change. We can use the same example of decentralization to illustrate this point. If high level responses are demanded at the front-line, where are they to come from? How are they to be recruited and trained? Can we just wave our wands and hope that people will automatically be capable of doing the new work? It is perhaps fitting that in closing this section which has highlighted some of the more controversial aspects of usable theory, we emphasize the dynamic and differential view of the growth of individual development which is outlined in chapter 9.

Action in the middle-ground

In Part III we attempted to demonstrate how usable theory might be generated *and* utilized, and how these two processes must proceed hand in hand. Although these essays represent only a small proportion of the projects that might have been chosen, I hope that they are sufficient to indicate the way in which this objective – of closing the gap between theory and practice – might be pursued.

With two exceptions these essays recount 'action' taken in the middle-ground. The exceptions are the brief historical note (chapter 10) and the kibbutz case study (chapter 14). The former was primarily included to illustrate the development of theory at the level of a research enterprise, and the latter provided an opportunity to understand a little more about individual capacity. The remaining three central chapters are all accounts of messy encounters of theory and practice, and I shall concentrate mainly on these.

Let us return immediately to the issues of the development of theory, research enterprises and appropriate methodologies. Glennerster reminds us that:

American experience suggests that you cannot build up good inter-disciplinary research teams unless there is a fairly continuous supply of work and grant aid to support the administrative infra-structure. It is no use expecting methodologies to appear except as a result of a lot of trial, error and failure. (1975:244).

All the studies in Part III demonstrate one important feature about research of this sort: it takes time. This is not the place to take serious issue with research funding policies, but the movement towards shorter-term research contracts, the abysmal plight of many contract researchers, taken together with the current unfashionability of 'applied' research (a point which Glennerster also makes) do not bode well for sustained research efforts by groups of workers over long periods of time (Kogan and Henkel 1983). This policy would lead to a proliferation of studies based on limited excursions into the field which hardly gives us time to test out ideas, learn from our mistakes, and develop better theory and methodology.

In addition to the implications for the research process, these accounts of action in the middle-ground, can tell us something about the nature of this field of study which lies between statements of political intent and the citizen in need. Such studies are sometimes criticized for failing to take into account the adjacent territories – the political process and the 'clients voice'. I am not sure why it should be thought inappropriate to focus on one of these areas, providing that the terms of reference of the endeavour, its range of problems and tentative theories are all spelt out. After all, there are many useful studies of the political process which show only a modest understanding of – or interest in – the mediating structures. Given the present state of the various disciplinary arts involved in these areas, this would not appear to be unreasonable. Nevertheless, whilst I do not claim to have studied the political (social policy) process, or the views of clients, I do think that the case studies 'absorb' these other two facets in a manner not always fully appreciated.

In the first place, every significant collaborative research project which has appeared in one form or another in this book has received political sanctioning from the governing bodies of the agencies, be they governmental or non-governmental. Furthermore, those who collaborate in the projects are acutely aware of the political boundaries. Reports have to be made and suggestions justified. One example of this process was provided in the day care study with the lengthy extract of a report from the assistant director of residential and day care. Similarly, in the study of intermediate treatment, the senior staff had to be constantly aware of, and sensitive to, the political pressures and realities. Central government policy statements had to be hammered into realistic operational policies by paid officers interacting with local politicians. The political process is 'absorbed' into the bureaucratic (and vice versa) constantly and subtly in innumerable formal and informal exchanges. In like fashion, tentative theories of the middle-ground, if they are to be usable, must naturally absorb and take that political boundary into account.

The clients' voice is absorbed in no less an intensive and subtle fashion. Unless we are to assume that on entering town and county halls, normal human beings become uncaring bureaucrats, we might accept that social welfare workers, in the main, act in the interest of their clients. There will be exceptions at both the individual and group level, but I doubt that it could seriously be questioned that, in the main, staff work hard and conscientiously. Naturally they are interested in their own salaries, positions, and prospects; and we might need to remind them that organizations are set up to resolve social problems, not just to provide careers. Still, my main point does, I believe, hold good. There is a fund of commitment that organizations must nurture and foster. The effective bureaucracy, amongst other things, must always be sensitive to the needs of those it is serving, especially if they are vulnerable and dependent. The studies of day care, entry into residential care, and intermediate treatment, all demonstrate this absorption of clients' needs into model-building and executive action.[2] We could have included many more examples to illustrate how welfare bureaucrats attempt to keep the clients' interests in mind when developing proposals for organizational change.

As I noted earlier (in chapter 3) I do not understand how those academics who castigate bureaucracy *per se* can explain its capacity for innovatory practices (such as 'patch'). Even less can I understand why those same members for the Bureauphobic Tendency should be prepared to expend energy to help a fundamentally flawed organizational form (SSDs) in the implementation of those new 'radical' approaches. Can it be that there is, after all, hope for bureaucracy? Might we be capable of understanding and controlling it?

And this, I suppose, is the most suitable point to conclude these recollections and turn towards the possible links between the models presented in this book – which have as their objective the design and control of welfare bureaucracies – and those models developed elsewhere.

We shall first briefly consider some of the models with a public administration focus, and then look in somewhat more detail at model-building in the discipline of social administration. This exercise represents a modest speculative attempt to push out the boundaries from the middle-ground as a possible prelude to the development of broader models.

Usable theory and model-building in public administration

We noted in Part I that a key interest of public administrators, and a natural focus for model-building, has been the challenge to representative democracy posed by the necessity to 'delegate' decision-making to officers. However, it seems that this relationship between politicians and officers is difficult to study academically: 'The participants are bound by mutual interdependencies and they are loath to reveal the unclothed realities which exist behind the show of conventional dress.' (Hampton 1980). Hampton identifies five characteristics affecting the relationship: the extent of service provision; of officer professionalism; of party political organization; of sensitivity to public opinion; and of central government interest or influence. Using different mixes of these characteristics, he develops six possible models as a contribution to forwarding our understanding regarding their reality and significance.

Goldsmith expresses the problems as follows:

No longer do national and local elected representatives debate the issues of the day at their leisure: rather, they are often caught in a situation where they appear to be responding to a bewildering series of complex events. In doing so, they are dependent on the preliminary work and expertise of highly paid civil servants and local government professionals (1980: 18).

Later, the same author suggests that 'of all the changes in twentieth-century urban politics, the rise of the paid official is perhaps the most important' (p.173). He argues that in many areas of local authority work such as planning, education, transport and highways, social work and environmental health, officers will dominate decision-making. In other policy arenas like housing or leisure, there is more likely to be heavier councillor involvement because 'the professionalization of the officer-class is relatively under-developed' (ibid.).

Interestingly, planning is taken as the focus for study by Regan (1978) who takes a different view to Goldsmith's, and groups it together with education as activities 'where laymen often feel able to make judgements'. Planners are 'in trouble'; they are 'the butt of public contempt. In the last couple of years they seem to have been joined in the doghouse by educationists.' (He might have added social workers as companions in the kennels.) Theoretically, planning could be 'professional' (based on *technicality* and *rationality*); 'judicial' (characterized by the existence of a body of *rules* and the determination of disputes by *reference* to them); or 'political' (characterized by the attempt to discover the wishes of the public at every stage). Regan argues that professional planners have been given their head, and that this has produced unsatisfactory results. According to this analysis the 'pathology' of planning might be remedied by reducing the professional element and replacing it by political factors, which must be accepted as the mainspring of the system.

In both the Goldsmith and Regan studies the political dimension is analysed in relation to whole 'areas', or what I have called *categories*, of work such as 'planning', 'education' 'housing', etc. In this book we have presented an analysis of bureaucracy which also takes into account the expected *societal* and *client level* of work. I believe that the alternative models of organizational response, together with the analysis of work and authority, and capacity, may provide the basis for treating welfare and other bureaucracies, such as those discussed by Regan and Goldsmith, as complex systems which interact with a politically dominated environment. The definition of alternative client-impact level is, I shall suggest, of particular relevance in understanding the possible links between democratic control and bureaucratic discretion – a central concern of public administration.

In previous chapters it was argued that the concept of one 'front-line' is itself inadequate, and that there are at least two qualitatively different front-lines. In the first instance there is a client-impact provided by staff whose output is prescribed. Client problems are treated as if they were demands to be met and work consists of activities that are fairly straightforward and routine. Typically, the allocation of council houses based on waiting lists falls within this mode of provision (see Norman 1975). Supplementary benefits, bus passes and luncheon clubs are additional examples of the many services that are often (but not necessarily) provided in this fashion. There are major advantages to this model relevant to our theme of political control. The end-product (the service) is provided in a more or less demonstrable and equal fashion between recipients. When in doubt, appeals can be made to the rule book. This manifest (numerical) equality of the prescribed output model has the considerable political attraction that its end-product can be clearly understood by the layman. The model is readily susceptible to political control. Intervention in specific cases can be easily undertaken by councillors.

A competing model has a 'professional' front-line, and staff are expected to make a Stratum 2 client-impact. In contrast to the prescribed output bureaucracies, we do *not* know beforehand what the end-product of the work is going to look like. The problems are regarded as situations which are allocated and have to be dealt with one by one, and whose 'real needs' are to be investigated, appraised and judged. In this model, services are apportioned according to 'professionally' diagnosed needs. It follows therefore, that cases are less susceptible to political control.

It must be stressed that any category of work can be provided at different levels of response. Thus, although I have used bus passes and luncheon clubs as examples of typical Level 1 client-impact services, they could just as well be provided at Level 2. There would then be an evaluation of the 'real' need for the bus passes based on an assessment of the wider situation of the applicant (not merely age), taking into account, for example, psychological and social factors. Front-lines can also be at Level 3 (and higher). Indeed, if it were the case that Regan's planners had ambitions of a Level 3 client-impact – not only replying to individual situations but developing plans for ranges of situations – then this might lead to an alternative explanation for the issues he analyses.

I do not pretend that this four-dimensional analysis 'solves' the dilemma we have been discussing: of political control and bureaucracy. However, I would claim that usable theories of the middle-ground must play an important part in the development of 'better' models of the interaction between the political system, bureaucracy, and client need.

In the following section we shall consider what the state of model-building is in social administration (which we have already suggested has not paid much attention to organizational theory) and how our models of the middle-ground might be seen in that context.

Usable theory and model-building in social administration

In the study of social administration we are dependent on models produced by that handful of writers who have found model-building a worthwhile enterprise. This general absence of models, or at least those that have succeeded in engendering debate, is puzzling. Perhaps it is part of that atheoretical approach which has troubled sociological social administrators, and which has led several authors to attempt to stake rather indigestible theoretical flags over the discipline.[3]

Reading some of the recent examples of 'grand theorizing' in social policy, it is tempting to echo Wright-Mills and ask whether this theorizing is 'merely a confused verbiage or is there, after all, also something there?' (1971: 35). It may well be, as Wright-Mills himself acknowledged in his 'translation' of Parsons' *The Social System*, that 'something is being said'. Whilst we await translations, we are more or less forced back, in the search for models, to the work of Wilensky and Lebeaux, and Titmuss.

Titmuss outlined three models of welfare: (i) residual welfare; (ii) industrial achievement; and (iii) institutional redistributive. He preceded his brief presentation (a course of lectures published after his death) by explaining that for him:

The purpose of model building is not to admire the architecture of the building, but to help us to see some order in all the disorder and confusion of facts, systems and choices concerning certain areas of our economic and social life. (1974: 30).

The residual-welfare model was based on the premise that social welfare institutions should come into play only when the private market and family breakdown. The industrial-achievement model regards social welfare institutions as adjuncts of the economy, meeting needs on the basis of merit, work performance and productivity. The institutional-redistributive model sees welfare as a major integrating institution in society, providing universalist services outside the market on the principle of need. Wilensky and Lebeaux had also earlier described two 'conceptions' of social welfare in the United States: the 'residual' and the 'institutional'.

The first holds that social institutions should come into play only when the normal structures of supply, family and the market, break down. The second, in contrast, sees the welfare services as normal, 'front-line' functions of modern industrial society. These are the concepts around which drives for more or less welfare service tend to focus. (1965: 138).

These models emerged from the social conscience thesis, and these and others developed by Pinker, Butterworth and Holman, and Mishra, are regarded as 'caricatures to some extent' by Higgins (1981: 41 –6). Despite these comments it is still worthwhile asking whether the models do in fact help to 'see some order', as Titmuss put it. And if they do, is this sufficient?

The answer to the first question is probably 'yes' since they have provided the basis for further debate and the development of more elaborate models. For example, Mishra has attempted to describe the main characteristics of the residual and institutional models (1977: chapter 6). Thus, according to Mishra, in the residual model the range of statutory services is 'limited', covering a 'minority' of the 'population', giving 'low benefits' to the 'poor', who have a 'low' status in relation to a 'coercive' service. In contrast, in the institutional model, services are 'extensive' to a 'majority' of the population, giving 'medium' benefits to 'citizens' who have a 'medium' status in relation to a utilitarian agency where State responsibility is 'optimal'. These general descriptive accounts serve to indicate a range of value stances and of attachment to a particular ideological 'team'.

In answer to the second question, as they stand, a further set of usable models will be needed if organizations are to be constructed. These models will have to define both the *categories* of the problem to be encompassed, *and* the *level* of response.

'Institutional', 'residual' and other descriptions, whilst they help to see 'some order', in Titmuss's phrase, do not provide a sufficient basis upon which to construct organizations. Thus, 'universalists' might find themselves sympathetic towards models of governmental direct service agencies set up with high level responses (Level 4 or 5). They would presumably be less happy with a categorization boundary of *social breakdown*, preferring more open-ended terms of reference which include what I have called *social discomfort*. Selectivists, on the other hand, might at most tolerate a Level 4 response, preferably non-governmental. For a Level 5 comprehensive field response will open too many possibilities of searching out and requesting additional services. Side by side with this, a selectivist approach might be happier with a narrower categorization boundary – social breakdown – as the proper role for governmental welfare bureaucracies.

But in general, the models produced in this book do not sit tidily *within* social administration's descriptions. I believe they *extend* the range of choices beyond those arising from within the social conscience tradition, or indeed from the newly established social policy arm of the Institute of Economic Affairs (for example Anderson 1980). Let us pursue that contention a little further.

The presentation of 'social breakdown' as a response to safety needs is not that distant from an approach expressed in Titmuss's essay 'The Social Division of Labour' (1958:chapter 2). He referred to the 'states of dependency' which 'arise for the vast majority of the population whenever they are not in a position to "earn life" for themselves and their families; they are then dependent people'. Titmuss argued that there are 'natural' dependencies (childhood, extreme old age, etc.); and 'man-made' dependencies (caused by social and cultural factors), which now constitute the major source of instability in the satisfaction of basic needs. However, his major concern was with what he called 'systems' of social service striving to attain aims such as the 'search for equity', rather than with th lower level of organizations with their own explanations attempting to resolve problems. But, as Sinfield points out, 'Titmuss was more concerned to establish the similarity of the different systems to a generally unreceptive audience than to reflect on their differences.' (Sinfield:1978).

If we turn away from Titmuss's 'systems' of social institutions, and return to the lower level of organizations such as welfare bureaucracies, then organizational model-building is feasible. Thus, I have suggested that 'universality' and 'selectivity' do not fit easily into the more extended range of models developed in earlier chapters.[4] The permutations are many. I shall therefore take just a few examples drawn from the analysis in Part II.

These examples that I have chosen are what we might call the 'comprehensive breakdown' models of government intervention. *Social breakdown* is taken as the *categorization boundary* and social discomfort needs are left to fall elsewhere. This upsets the universalists. However, *societal-impact* is designed at Level 5 and the director of this governmental agency is expected to search out, plan, and meet, social breakdown needs of a designated social territory. Many questions then follow. Why are some breakdown groups not being catered for? Why are some dependent groups outside current provision? Why are some social breakdown groups being catered for by other government agencies? Why do some people get a raw deal? Consequently, requests may be made to provide significant additional services. This upsets the selectivists.

And of course, we have not yet decided what is the appropriate *client-impact* of our comprehensive breakdown model. A level 1 front-line will further mathematical equality of treatment for recipients, and make political control easier (see earlier argument). It upsets professional aspirations. On the other hand, a Level 2 front-line accords with the professional aspirations of occupational groups, but makes political control over individual cases more difficult. Universality and selectivity begin to retreat as helpful concepts in the face of the need for real organizational construction.

We have not yet finished with the comprehensive breakdown model. Putting aside social discomfort as needs that are outside the province of our welfare bureaucracies, still leaves unanswered the question as to *who, if anyone, should resolve those needs?*

I have already indicated my doubts as to the feasibility of widespread government intervention in responding to the need for love and affection. Nevertheless governments could, at least in theory, attempt to organize direct service 'comprehensive social discomfort bureaucracies' – despite the shiver that might go down the backs of even the most enthusiastic social conscience universalists.

Alternatively, governments may abandon all interest in this field, or perhaps restrict their intervention to 'conceptual' inputs by setting-up $(\frac{5}{4})$ (see chapter 7) agencies to guide and advise the approaches taken by private and voluntary agencies, families, neighbourhood and other groups: a role in fact rather like that taken by those quangos that exhort us to abstain from drinking or smoking, or to take more exercise or whatever.

Finally

To be consistent with our general approach, a final chapter ought perhaps to have been titled 'further problems'. If I have balked at being quite that consistent, it is mainly because the agenda of problems is so large. For example, although I hope that readers from the voluntary sector will find the ideas reported here of use, there are undoubtedly many distinctive problems that await better tentative theories (Billis 1984).

So, I have preferred to highlight several of the issues that may be more controversial, and to point only to further problems in the specific area of linking usable theory to broader ideas and models in social administration. Furthermore, to have laid out a lengthy list of new problems, although valid, would inevitably have appeared as the traditional stock-in-trade of the researcher – the call for 'further research'.

In this last matter I confess to being rather an optimist, despite the occasional painful blows dealt by funders and sponsors. Theory, if it is genuinely usable and useful, ought to be able to 'pay its way' in a very literal sense. For if such theory cannot find support, what grounds are there for optimism in social policy; for believing that tomorrow's solutions may be better than today's?

Notes

1. These statements are primarily based on discussions with participants in a special workshop devoted to the subject of decentralization.
2. Once again we can turn to the statement of the Assistant Director (Residential and Day Care) for supporting evidence (see chapter 11).
3. I have in mind, for example, the following example: 'The Foucauldian pun of subjection to the subject provides a precise account of the re-entrant trajectory of social administration's theoretic liberation from its atheoretic heritage.' (Taylor-Gooby 1981a).
4. These concepts have, in any case, been thoroughly explored and dissected in Reddin (1970). In an important paper Kogan (1973) suggests that these terms are 'instrumental concepts' which are 'concerned with the advancement of basic "oughts" or "value axioms" '.

Bibliography

Abrams, P. (1978) *Neighbourhood Care and Social Policy: A Research Perspective*, Occasional Paper, London: Volunteer Centre.

Adler, M. and Aquith, S. (1981) *Discretion and Welfare*, London: Heinemann.

Alaszewski, Andy (1977) 'Occupational therapy – case study of a professional strategy', *Health and Social Services Journal*, Centre Pages B5–8, 14 October.

Alexander, A. (1982) *Local Government in Britain Since Reorganisation*, London: Allen and Unwin.

Amir, Y. (1969) 'The effectiveness of the kibbutz-born soldier in the Israel defence forces', *Human Relations*, XXII, April.

Anderson, D.C. (ed.) (1980) *The Ignorance of Social Intervention*, London: Croom Helm.

Argyris, C. (1958) 'Creating effective research relationships in organisations', *Human Organisation*, 17, 1.

Argyris, C. (1980) 'Making the undiscussable and its undiscussability discussable', *Public Administration Review*, May/June.

Baker, J. (1979) 'Social conscience and social policy', *Journal of Social Policy*, 8, 2, April.

Baker, R.J.S. (1975) 'Systems theory and local government', *Local Government Studies*, 1, 1, January.

Barnes, J. and Connelly, N. (eds.) (1978) *Social Care Research*, London: Bedford Square Press.

Bartlett, Harriett, M. (1970) *The Common Base of Social Work Practice*, National Association of Social Workers, Inc. New York.

Bebbington, A.C. and Davies, B. (1980) 'Territorial need indicators: a new approach', *Journal of Social Policy*, Part One, 9, 2, April; Part Two, 9, 4, October.

Becker, Howard, S. (ed.) (1966) *Social Problems: A Modern Approach*, New York: Wiley.

Bell, C. and Newby, H. (1971) *Community Studies*, London: Allen and Unwin.

Bennis, W.G. (1972) 'Changing organisations' in M.J. Thomas and W.G. Bennis (eds.) *Management of Change and Conflict*, Harmondsworth: Penguin.

Berger, P.L. and Luckman, T. (1975, first published 1967) *The Social Construction of Reality*, Harmondsworth: Penguin.

Berlin, I. (1980) *Concepts and Categories*, London: Oxford University Press.

Billis, D. (1971) 'The process of planning in the kibbutz', PhD Thesis, London University.

Billis, D. (1973a) 'Living with equality', *New Humanist*, May.

Billis, D. (1973b) 'Community planning and group interests', *Community Development Journal*, 8, 1, January.

Billis, D. (1973c) 'Entry into residential care', *British Journal of Social Work*, 3, 4.

Billis, D. (1974) *The Social Services and Education Interaction Project — Final Report*, Doc.2365, mimeo, Social Services Unit, Brunel University.

Billis, D. (1975a) 'Managing to care', *Social Work Today*, 6, 2.

Billis, D. (1975b) *Volunteers, the community and the department*, Doc.2463A, mimeo, Social Services Unit, Brunel University.

Billis, D. (1976) 'Intermediate treatment – in search of a policy', *Social Work Service*, 11.

Billis, D. (1977) 'Differential administrative capacity and organisational development: a kibbutz case study', *Human Relations*,30, 2.

Billis, D. (1979) *Voluntary Organisations: Management Issues, I*, A report from the first PORTVAC Workshop, mimeo, Brunel Institute of Organisation and Social Studies, Brunel University.

Billis, D. (1981a) 'At risk of prevention', *Journal of Social Policy*,10, 3, July.

Billis, D. (1981b) 'Reforming welfare bureaucracies: the Seebohm Report outcome' in G. Caiden (ed.) *Policy Studies Journal (Special Issue)*,9, 8.

Billis, D. (1981c) 'Delegation and control: the experience of social services department directors and their deputies', mimeo Brunel Institute of Organisation and Social Studies, Brunel University.

Billis, D. (1982) 'The hole in the middle', *Social Work Today*, 13, 25.

Billis, D. (1984) 'The missing link', in B. Knight (ed.) *Mangement in Voluntary Organisations*, ARVAC Occasional Paper No. 6.

Billis, D., Bromley, G., Hey, A. and Rowbottom, R. (1980) *Organising Social Services Departments*, London: Heinemann.

Birch. A.H. (1971) *Representation*, London: Macmillan.

Blau, P.M. (1963) *The Dynamics of Bureaucracy*, revised edn., University of Chicago Press.

Blau, P.M. and Scott, W.R. (1963) *Formal Organizations*, London: Routledge and Kegan Paul.

Borger, Robert and Cioffi, Frank (eds.) (1970) *Explanation in the Behavioural Sciences*, London: Cambridge University Press.

Bottomore, T.H. (1975) *Sociology as Social Criticism*, London: Allen and Unwin.

Bottomore, T. and Nisbet, R. (eds.) (1979) *A History of Sociological Analysis*, London: Heinemann.

Boudon, R. (1971) *The Uses of Structuralism*, London: Heinemann.

Bradshaw, J. (1972) 'The concept of social need', *New Society*, 19.

British Association of Social Workers (1977) *The Social Work Task*, London: BASW Publications.

Brown, A. and Heller, F. (1981) 'Usefulness of group feedback analysis as a research method: its application to a questionnaire study', *Human Relations*, 34, 2.

Brown, R.G.S. (1971) *The Administrative Process in Britain*, London: Methuen.

Brown, W. (1960) *Exploration in Management and Organization*, London: Heinemann.

Brown, W. (1971) *Organization*, London: Heinemann.

Brown, W. and Jaques, E. (eds.) (1965) *Glacier Project Papers*, London: Heinemann.

Bruce, I. and Darville, G. (1976) *Over the Defences: The Volunteer in the Area Team*, London: Volunteer Centre.

Brunel Institute of Organisation and Social Studies, Social Services Organisation Research Unit (1974) *Social Services Departments: Developing Patterns of Work and Organisation*, London: Heinemann.

Bulmer, M. (1982) 'The merits and demerits of covert participant observation' in M. Bulmer (ed.) *Social Research Ethics*, London: Macmillan.

Burgess, R.G. and Bulmer, M.(1981) 'Research methodology teaching: trends and developments', *Journal of Sociology*, 15, 4, November.

Burns, T. and Stalker, G.M. (1961) *The Management of Innovation*, London: Tavistock Publications.

Carrier, J. and Kendall, I. (1977) 'The development of welfare states: the production of plausible accounts', *Journal of Social Policy*,6, 3.

Central Council for Education and Training in Social Work (1973) *Training for Residential Work* (Discussion Document).

Central Council for Education and Training in Social Work (1975) *Day Services: An Action Plan for Training*, November.

Central Council for Education and Training in Social Work (1979) *Residential Work is Part of Social Work*.

Central Housing Advisory Committee (1969) *Council Housing: Purposes, Procedures and Priorities*, Ninth Report of the Management Sub-Committee, London: HMSO.

Cherns, A. (1971) 'Social research and its diffusion', in F.G. Caro, *Readings in Evaluative Research,*New York.

Child, J. (1977) *Organisation: A Guide to Problems and Practice*, London: Harper and Row.

Clark, Peter, A. (1972) *Action Research and Organizational Change*, London: Harper and Row.

Cloward, R.A. and Piven, F.F. (1969) in R.M. Kramer and H. Specht, *Readings in Community Organization Practice*, London: Prentice Hall.

Cohen, J.L. (1978) 'Is Popper more relevant than Bacon for scientists?' *Times Higher Educational Supplement*, 14 July.

Cohen, S. (1979) 'Community control – a new utopia', *New Society*, 15 March.

Cooper, D. (1981) 'A wasted opportunity', *Community Care*, 2 November.

Culler, J. (1976) *Saussure*, London: Fontana.

Curran, J. and Stanworth, J. (1981) 'A new look at job satisfaction in the small firm', *Human Relations*, 34, 5.

Curzon, L.B. (1979) *A Dictionary of Law*, London: Macdonald and Evans.

Cypher, J.R. (1980) 'Specialisation by stealth and design' in T. Booth, D. Martin, and C. Melotte, (eds.) *Specialisation* London: BASW Publications.

Dahrendorf, R. (1972) *Class and Class Conflict in an Industrial Society*, London: Routledge and Kegan Paul.

Darville, G. (1975) *Bargain or Barricade*, London: Volunteer Centre.

Dean, Sir Maurice (1969) 'Accountable management in the civil service', *Public Administration*, 47, 1, Spring.

Department of Health and Social Security (1972) *Intermediate Treatment,*London: HMSO.

Department of Health and Social Security Development Group, Social Work Service (1973) *Intermediate Treatment Project*, London: HMSO.

Department of Health and Social Security Development Group, Social Work Service (1974a) *Intermediate Treatment*, Report of a Residential Conference, London: HMSO.

Department of Health and Social Security (1974b) *Report of the Committee of Enquiry into the Care and Supervision Provided in Relation to Maria Colwell*, London: HMSO.

Department of Health and Social Security (1976) *Manpower and Training for the*

Social Services (The Birch Report), Report of the Working Party, London: HMSO.

Department of Health and Social Security, Social Work Service (1979) *Residential Care for the Elderly in London*, London: HMSO.

De Saussure, F. (1974) *Course in General Linguistics*, London: Fontana.

Diamond, S. (1957) 'Kibbutz and shtetl', *Social Problems*, 5, 2.

Donnison, D.V. (1974) 'Training for social work', *Social Work Today*, 10, 24, 13 February.

Donnison, D. (1979) 'Social policy since Titmuss', *Journal of Social Policy*, 8, 2.

Donnison, D. (1980) 'The quality of public service', *New Society*, 53, 28 August.

Donnison, D.V. and Chapman, V. (1965) *Social Policy and Administration*, London: Allen and Unwin.

Durkheim, E. and Mauss, M. (1973) 'The social genesis of logical operations' in Mary Douglas (ed.) *Rules and Meanings*, Harmondsworth: Penguin.

Eisenstadt, S.N. (1967) *Israeli Society*, London: Weidenfeld and Nicolson.

Etzioni, A. (1957) 'Solidaric work-groups in collective settlements (kibbutzim)', *Human Organization*, Fall.

Etzioni, A. (1968) *The Active Society*, New York: Free Press.

Evans, J.S. (1979) *The Management of Human Capacity*, MCB Publications.

Follett, Mary, Parker (1973; first published 1926) 'Pluralistic Authority' in E.M. Fox and L. Urwick (eds) *Dynamic Administration*, London: Pitman.

Ford, P. (1968) *Social Theory and Social Practice*, London: Shannon.

Fox, A. (1974) *Beyond Contract: Work, Power, and Trust Relations*, London: Faber.

Fox, E.M. and Urwick, L. (eds.) (1973) *Dynamic Administration*, London: Pitman.

French, W.L. and Bell, C.H. Jr. (1973) *Organisation Development*, New Jersey: Prentice Hall.

Friedrich, C.J. (1972) *Tradition and Authority*, London: Macmillan.

Friedrich, C.J. (1976) 'Reflections on democracy and bureaucracy' in J.A.G. Griffith (ed.) *From Policy to Administration*, London: Allen and Unwin.

Gerard, David (1983) *Charities in Britain*, London: Bedford Square Press.

Gerth, Hans and Wright Mills, C. (1970) *Character and Social Structure*, London: Routledge and Kegan Paul.

Gerth, H. and Wright Mills, C. (1974, first published 1970) *From Max Weber*, London: Routledge and Kegan Paul.

Giddens, A. (1979) *Central Problems in Social Theory*, London: Macmillan.

Gladstone, F.J. (1979) *Voluntary Action in a Changing World*. London: Bedford Square Press.

Glaser, B.G. and Strauss, A.L. (1973) *The Discovery of Grounded Theory: Strategies for Qualitative Research*, Chicago: Aldine.

Glennerster, H. (1975) *Social Service Budgets and Social Policy: British and American Experience*, New York: Barnes and Noble.

Glennerster, H. (1981) 'From containment to conflict?: social planning in the seventies', *Journal of Social Policy*, 10, 10 January.

Goldsmith, M. (1980) *Politics, Planning and the City*, London: Hutchinson.

Goodlove, C., Richard, R. and Rodwell, G. (1981) *Time for Action*, Joint Unit for Social Services Research, University of Sheffield.

Gouldner, A.W. (1970) 'Anti-minotaur: the myth of a value-free sociology', in

Bennis Benne and Chin (eds.) *The Planning of Change*, London: Holt, Rinehart and Winston.

Greenwood, R. Norton, A.L. and Stewart, J.D. (1969) 'Recent changes in the internal organisation of county boroughs', *Public Administration*, Autumn.

Greenwood, R., Walsh, K., Hinnings, C.R. and Ranson, S. (1980) *Patterns in Management in Local Government*, London: Martin Robertson.

Griffith, J.A.G. (ed.) (1976) *From Policy to Administration*, London: Allen and Unwin.

Hadley, R. and Hatch, S. (1981) *Social Welfare and the Failure of the State*, London: Allen and Unwin.

Hadley, R. and McGrath, M. (1979) 'Patch-based social services', *Community Care*, 11 October.

Hadley, R. and McGrath, M. (eds.) (1980) *Going Local — Neighbourhood Social Services*, National Council of Voluntary Organisations Occasional Paper No. 1.

Hadley, R., Webb, A. and Farrell, C. (1975) *Across The Generations*, London: Allen and Unwin.

Hall, A.S. (1971) 'Client reception in a social service agency', *Public Administration*, Spring.

Hall, A.S. (1975) *Point of Entry*, London: Allen and Unwin.

Hall, Phoebe (1976) *Reforming the Welfare*, London: Heinemann.

Hall, P. L., and H., Parker, R. and Webb, A. (1975) *Change, Choice and Conflict in Social Policy*, London: Heinemann.

Hall, R.H. (1967) 'Some organisational considerations in the professional-organizational relationship', *Administrative Science Quarterly*, 12.

Hampton, W.A. (1980) 'Local administration and politics: political science and the realities', in Research Institute of Public Administration and Policy Studies Unit (1980) *Party Politics in Local Government: Officers and Members*, Syposium Report.

Hanson, A.H. (1969) *Planning and the Politicians*, London: Routledge and Kegan Paul.

Haraway, Dona Jean (1976) *Crystals, Fabrics and Fields: Metaphors of Organicism in Twentieth Century Developmental Biology*, Yale University Press.

Harris, M. (1983) *Governing Bodies and Voluntary Agencies: A Study of Local Management Committees in the Citizens Advice Bureaux Service*, MA Thesis, Department of Government, Brunel University.

Hatch, S. (1980) *Outside the State: Voluntary Organisations In Three English Towns*, London: Croom Helm.

Hayek, F.A. (1967) *Studies in Philosophy, Politics and Economics*, London: Routledge and Kegan Paul.

Hayton, C.R. (1980) 'Management arrangements below district level', *Hospital and Social Services Review*, May.

Herbst, P.G. (1981) 'Non-hierarchical organizations' in F.E. Emery (ed.) *Systems Thinking*, Volume 2, Harmondsworth: Penguin.

Hesse, Mary (1980) *Revolutions and Reconstructions in the Philosophy of Science*, London: Harvester Press.

Hey, A.M. (1980) 'Providing basic services at home' in Billis *et al.*, *Organising Social Services Departments*, London: Heinemann.

Higgins, J. (1981) *State of Welfare*, Oxford: Basil Blackwell and Martin Robertson.

Hill, M.J. (1972) *The Sociology of Public Administration*, London: Weidenfeld and Nicolson.

Hill, M. (1981) 'Front-line administrators: policy implementers or the real policy-makers?', mimeo, paper produced for the Research Institute of Public Administration Conference, 10 November.

Holman, R. (1980) 'Growth without roots', *Community Care*, 3 January.

Holme, A. and Maizels, J. (1978) *Social Workers and Volunteers*, London: Allen and Unwin.

Home Office (1932) *Committee on Ministers' Powers*, London: HMSO.

Home Office (1963) *The Children and Young Person's Act*, London: HMSO.

Home Office *et al.* (1968) *Report of the Committee on Local Authority and Allied Personal Social Services (Seebohm)* Cmnd 3703, London: HMSO.

Home Office (1972) *The New Local Authority – Management and Structure (The Bains Report)*, London: HMSO.

Home Office (1975) *Eleventh Report from the Expenditure Committee*, Session 74 –75, Vol 1, London: HMSO.

Home Office (1976) *Social Services for Children in England and Wales* 1973–75, December, London: HMSO.

Hume, S. (1982) 'Resources without policy is no solution', *Intermediate Treatment*, National Youth Bureau, 12 November.

Illich, I. (1976) *Limits to Medicine*, London: Marion Boyars.

Institute of Housing Managers (1972) *The Comprehensive Housing Service – Organisation and Functions*, London.

Jaques, E. (1951) *The Changing Culture of a Factory*, London: Tavistock.

Jaques, E. (1956) *Measurement of Responsibility*, London: Tavistock.

Jaques, E. (1965) *Glacier Project Papers*, London: Heinemann.

Jaques, E. (1967) *Equitable Payment*, 2nd edn., London: Penguin.

Jaques, E. (1970) *Work, Creativity and Social Justice*, London: Heinemann.

Jaques, E. (1976) *A General Theory of Bureaucracy*, London: Heinemann.

Jaques, E. (ed.) (1978) *Health Services*, London: Heinemann.

Jaques, E. with Gibson, R.O. and Isaac, D.J. (1978) *Levels of Abstraction in Logic and Human Action*, London: Heinemann.

Johnson, N. (1975) Editorial in *Public Administration*, Autumn.

Jones, G.W. (1973) 'The functions and organisation of councillors', *Public Administration*, Summer, 51.

Jones, G.W. (1977) *Responsibility and Government*, London School of Economics.

Jones, Julie (1979) *The Relationship Between Research and Policy-Making in the Social Services*, MA. Thesis, Government Department, Brunel University.

Jones, K. *et al.* (1978) *Issues in Social Policy*, London: Routledge and Kegan Paul.

Kanovsky, E. (1966) *The Economy of the Israeli Kibbutz*, Boston: Harvard University Press.

Kelly, J. (1968) *Is Scientific Management Possible?* London: Faber and Faber.

King's Fund Working Party (1979) *The Organisation of Hospital Clinic Work*, Project Paper No.22, November, King's Fund Centre.

Klein, R. (1980) 'The social policy man: priest or pragmatist', *Times Higher Educational Supplement*, 15 November.

Kogan, M. (1973) 'Social policy and public organisational values', *Journal of Social Policy*, 3, 2.

Kogan, M. and Henkel, M. (1983) *Government and Research: A Rothschild experiment in a government department*, London: Heinemann.

Kogan, M. and Terry, J. (1971) *The Organisation of a Social Service Department: A Blueprint*, London: Bookstall Publications.

Kramer, Ralph (1981) *Voluntary Agencies in the Welfare State*, Berkeley: University of California Press.

Kuhn, T. (1970a) 'Reflections on my critics', in Imre Lakatos and A. Musgrave (eds.) *Criticism and The Growth of Knowledge*, London: Cambridge University Press.

Kuhn, T.S. (1970b) *The Structure of Scientific Revolution*, 2nd edn., University of Chicago.

Laffin, M. (1980) 'Professionalism in central local relations' in G.W. Jones, (1980) *New Approaches to the Study of Central Local Relationships*, London: Gower Press.

Lakatos, I. and Musgrave, A. (eds.) (1974, first published 1970) *Critcism and the Growth of Knowledge*, Cambridge University Press.

Leach, Edmund (1976) *Culture and Communication*, Cambridge University Press.

Leach, Edmund (1981) 'British social anthropology and Levi-Straussian structuralism' in P.M. Blau, and R.K. Merton, (eds.) *Continuity in Structural Inquiry*, London/Beverly Hills: Sage Publications.

Leissner, A., Powley, T. and Evans, D. (1977) *Intermediate Treatment*, National Childrens Bureau.

Leonard, P. (1975) 'Exploration and education in social work', *British Journal of Social Work*, 5, 3.

Lessnoff, M. (1974) *The Structure of Social Science*, London: Allen and Unwin.

Lewin, K. (1963) *Field Theory in Social Science*, London: Tavistock Publications.

Lonsdale, S., Webb, A. and Briggs, T.L. (eds.) (1980) *Teamwork in The Personal Social Services and Health Care*, London: Croom Helm and Syracuse University School of Social Work.

Lukes, S. (1979) 'Power and Authority', in T. Bottomore and R. Nisbet (eds.) (1979) *A History of Sociological Analysis*, London: Heinemann.

Lorenz, K. (1977) *Behind the Mirror*, London: Methuen.

Lupton, T. (1971) *Management and the Social Sciences*, 2nd edn., Harmondsworth: Penguin.

Macdonald, J.S. (1981) 'Mitterrand's new France, Reagan's new America', Inaugural Lecture, 10 December, Chelsea College, University of London.

Maslow, A. (1970) 'A theory of human motivation' in V.H. Vroom, and E.L. Deci, *Management and Motivation*, Harmondsworth: Penguin.

Merton, R.K. (1967) *On Theoretical Sociology*, New York: Free Press.

Merton, R.K. *et al.* (eds.) (1952) *Reader in Bureaucracy*, New York: Free Press.

Miliband, R. (1970) 'Capitalist state – reply to N. Poulantzas' *New Left Review*, 59.

Miringoff, Marc L. (1980) *Management in Human Service Organisations*, New York: Macmillan.

Mishra, Ramesh (1977) *Society and Social Policy*, London and Basingstoke: Macmillan.

Mitchell, Ann (1977) Report published by Scottish Council of Social Services, Edinburgh, January.

Mouzelis, N.P. (1967) *Organisation and Bureaucracy*, London: Routledge and Kegan Paul.

Myrdal, G. (1972) 'The place of values in social policy', *Journal of Social Policy*, 1, 1, January.

National Development Group for the Mentally Handicapped (1977) *Day Services for the Mentally Handicapped Adults*, Pamphlet No. 5, July.

National Institute for Social Work (1982) *Social Workers: Their Role and Tasks (The Barclay Report)*. London: Bedford Square Press.

Nevitt, D.A. (1977) 'Demand and need' in H. Heisler (1977) *Foundations of Social Administration*, London: Macmillan Press.

Newman, E. and Turem, G. (1974) 'The crisis of accountability', *Social Work*, 19, 1.

Norman, P. (1975) *Housing Allocation Procedures in Slum Clearance Areas – A Comparison of Departmental Styles*, Discussion Paper in Social Research, University of Glasgow.

Oxfordshire County Council (1979) *Social Services in Oxfordshire — An Outline*, June, mimeo.

Oxfordshire County Council (1980) *Delegation of Powers to Chief Officers*, September, mimeo.

Paley, J. and Thorpe, D. (1974) *Children: Handle With Care*, National Youth Bureau.

Parker, R. (1981) 'Tending and Social Policy' in E.M. Goldberg and S. Hatch (1981) *A New Look at the Social Services*, Policy Studies Institute, Discussion Paper No.4, Feburary.

Parsloe, P. (1981) *Social Services Area Teams*, London: Allen and Unwin.

Parsons, Talcott (1960) *Structure and Process in Modern Societies*, New York: The Free Press.

Personal Social Services Council (1977) *A Future of Intermediate Treatment*.

Piaget, J. (1971) *Structuralism*, London: Routledge and Kegan Paul.

Pinker, R. (1971) *Social Theory and Social Policy*, London: Heinemann.

Pinker, R. (1979a) *The Idea of Welfare*, London: Heinemann.

Pinker, R. (1979b) 'Slimline social work', *New Society*, 13 December.

Piper, D.W. (1980) 'The application of theory in higher education', mimeo, University of London.

Polanyi, M. (1969) *Knowing and Being*, London: Routledge and Kegan Paul.

Popper, Karl, R. (1972) *The Logic of Scientific Discovery*, London, Hutchinson.

Popper, Karl, R. (1974a) *Conjectures and Refutations: The Growth of Scientific Knowledge*, 5th edn., London: Routledge and Kegan Paul.

Popper, Karl, R. (rep.) (1974b) *Objective Knowledge*, London/Oxford University Press.

Popper, Karl, R. (1976) *Unended Quest*, London: Fontana/Collins.

PORTVAC Document V.34 (1979a) mimeo, BIOSS, Brunel University.

PORTVAC Document LHT/32 (1979b) mimeo, BIOSS, Brunel University.

Rapoport, R.N. (1970) 'Three dilemmas in action-research – with special reference to the Tavistock experience', *Human Relations*, 23, 6.

Ravetz, J. R. (1971) *Scientific Knowledge and Its Social Problems*, Harmondsworth: Penguin.

Reddin, M. (1970) 'Universality versus selectivity' in W.A. Robson and B. Crick (eds.) *The Future of the Social Services*, Harmondsworth: Penguin.

Regan, D.E. (1978) 'The pathology of British land use planning', *Local Government Studies*, April.

Regan, D.E. (1980) *A Headless State: The Unaccountable Executive in British Local Government*, Inaugural Lecture, University of Nottingham, 2 May.

Report of the Committee of Enquiry into Mental Handicap, Nursing and Care (The Jay Report) (1974), London: HMSO.

Residential Care Association (1982) *Middle Management in Residential Care (The Ollerton Report)*. London: RCA Publications.

Rex, J. (1970) *Key Problems of Sociological Theory*, London: Routledge and Kegan Paul.

Richardson, A. and Goodman, M. (1983) *Self-Help and Social Care: Mutual Aid Organisations in Practice*, London: Policy Studies Institute.

Robinson, M. (1978) *Schools and Social Work*, London: Routledge and Kegan Paul.

Rose, Gordon (1976) 'Approaches to the analysis of social service organisation', *Journal of Social Policy*, 5, 3, July.

Rowbottom, R.W. (1973) 'Organizing social services, hierarchy or . . . ?', *Public Administration*, 51.

Rowbottom, R.W. (1977) *Social Analysis*, London: Heinemann.

Rowbottom, R.W. *et al.* (1973) *Hospital Organization*, London: Heinemann.

Rowbottom, R.W and Billis, D. (1977) 'Stratification of work and organisational design', *Human Relations*, 30, 1.

Rowbottom, R.W. and Bromley, G. (1978) 'The future of child guidance – a study in multi-disciplinary teamwork' in Jaques (ed.) *Health Services*, London: Heinemann.

Rowbottom, R.W. and Hey, A. (1973) 'Organizing social services – a second chance', *Local Government Chronicle*, 5526.

Royal Institute of Public Administration and Policy Studies Institute (1980) *Party Politics in Local Government: Officers and Members*, A Symposium Report.

Russell, B. (1970) *Authority and The Individual*, London: Unwin Books.

Salzedo, S. (1981) 'A brake on the road to delinquency', *Social Work Today*, 2 June, 12, 37.

Schon, D. (1973) *Beyond the Stable State*, Harmondsworth: Penguin.

Schumacher, E.F. (1974) *Small is Beautiful*, London: Abacus.

Schumpeter, J.A. (1947) 'The creative response in industry', *Journal of Economic History*, 7 November; quoted in A.D. Chandler Jr. (1963) *Strategy and Structure*, Cambridge, Mass.: M.I.T. Press.

Scott, W.R. (1965) 'Reactions to supervision in a heteronomous professional organisation', *Administrative Science Quarterly*

Self, P. (1971) 'Elected representatives and management in local government: an alternative analysis', *Public Adminsitration*, 49.

Self, P. (1976) 'Rational decentralization' in J.A.G. Griffiths (ed.) *From Policy to Administration*, London: Allen and Unwin.

Shatil, J.E. (1968) *Criteria for Socio-Economic Efficiency of the Kibbutz*, mimeo, Israel: Kibbutz Artzi.

Shaw, Bernard (1944) *Everybody's Political What's What*, London: Constable.

Shipman, M. (1981) *The Limitations of Social Research*, London: Longmans.

Sinfield, Adrian (1978) 'Analyses on the social division of welfare', *Journal of Social Policy*, 7, 2, April.

Slack, K. (1966) *Social Administration and the Citizen*, London: Michael Joseph.

Smith, G. (1979) *Social Work and the Sociology of Organizations*, revised edn. London: Routledge and Kegan Paul.

Smith, G. (1980) *Social Need: Policy, Practice and Research*, London: Routledge and Kegan Paul.

Smith, G. and Ames, J. (1976) 'Area teams in social work practice: a programme for research', *British Journal of Social Work*, 6, 1.

Smith, J.H. (1979) 'The human factor in social administration', *Journal of Social Policy*, 8, 4, October.

Sofer, C. (1973) *Organization in Theory and Practice*, London: Heinemann.

Specht, H. and Vickery, A. (eds.) (1978, first published 1977) *Integrating Social Work Methods*, London: Allen and Unwin.

Steven, L. (1979) 'Power and authority', in T. Bottomore and R. Nisbet (eds.) *A History of Sociological Analysis*, London: Heinemann.

Stevenson, O. and Parsloe, P. (1978) *Social Service Teams: The Practitioners' View*, London: HMSO.

Suchman, E.A. (1967) *Evaluative Research: Principles and Practice in Public and Social Action Programs*, New York: Russell Sage Publications.

Sumner, W.G. (1907) *Folkways*, Boston.

Szasz, T. (1974) *Ideology and Insanity*, Harmondsworth: Penguin.

Tannenbaum, A.S., Kavcic, B., Rosner, M. Vianello, M. and Wieser, G. (1974) *Hierarchy in Organizations*, San Francisco: Jossey Bass.

Taylor-Gooby, P. (1981a) 'The politics of caring', *Times Higher Education Supplement*, 25 December.

Taylor-Gooby, P. (1981b) 'The state, class ideology and social policy', *Journal of Social Policy*, 10, 4.

Taylor-Gooby, P. and Dale, J. (1981) *Social Theory and Social Welfare*, London: Edward Arnold.

Thomas, D., Kat, B. and McPherson, F. (1980) 'An independent profession', *Health and Social Service Journal*, 23 May.

Thomason, G.F. (1977) 'The organisation of professional work in the social services' in H. Heisler (1977) *Foundations of Social Administration*, London: Macmillan Press.

Thursz, D. and Vigilante, J.L. (eds.) (1975) *Meeting Human Needs*, Volume 1 London/Beverly Hills: Sage Publications.

Town, Steven W. (1978) 'Action research and social policy: some recent British experience', in M. Bulmer (ed.) *Social Policy Research*, London: Macmillan.

Titmuss, R.M. (1958) *Essays on the Welfare State*, London: Allen and Unwin.

Titmuss, R.M. (1974) *Social Policy*, London: Allen and Unwin.

Titmuss, R.M. (1976) *Commitment to Welfare*, London: Allen and Unwin.

Townsend, D. (1983) 'Chronicle', *Social Work Today*, Vol. 15, No. 12, 22 November.

van der Eyken, W. (1982) *Home Start*, Home-Start Consultancy, Leicester.

Van Doorn, Jaques (1979) 'Organisation and the social order: a pluralist approach' in C.J. Lammers and D.J. Hickson, (eds.) *Organizations, Alike and Unlike*, London: Routledge and Kegan Paul.

Van Meter and Van Hom (1975) 'The policy implementation process: a conceptual framework', *Administration and Society*, 6, 4, Feb.

Van Sell, M., Brief, A.P. and Schuler, R.S. (1981) 'Role conflict and role ambiguity: integration of the literature and directions for future research', *Human Relations*, 34, 1.

Vincent, J. (1980) *Planning Resources for Community-based Treatment of Juvenile Offenders*, Social Policy Research Ltd.

Viteles, H. (1967) *A History of the Co-operative Movement in Israel, Book II, The Evolution of the Kibbutz Movement*, London: Valentine Mitchell & Co.

Walker, A. (1981) 'Social policy, social administration, and the social construction of welfare', *Sociology*, 15, May.

Watkins, B. (1975) *Documents on Health and Social Services*, London: Methuen.

Webb, A. (1977) 'The governance of the personal social services in England', Workshop Paper, UN Social Welfare Centre, Baden.

Webb, A. (1981) *Collective Action and Welfare Pluralism*, Association of Researchers in Voluntary Action and Community Involvement.

Webb, A., Day, L. and Weller, J. (1976) *Volunteer Social Service Manpower Resources*, Personal Social Services Council, September.

Webb, A.C. and Hobdell, M. (1980) 'Co-ordination and teamwork in the health and personal social services', in S. Lonsdale, A. Webb and T.L. Briggs (eds.) *Teamwork in the Personal Social Services and Health Care*, London: Croom Helm and Syracuse University School of Social Work.

Weber, M. (1947) *The Theory of Social and Economic Organization*, New York: The Free Press/Collier Macmillan.

Whittington, C. and Bellaby, P. (1979) 'The reason for hierarchy in social services departments: a critique of Elliott Jaques and his associates', *Sociological Review*, 27, 3.

Wilensky, H.L. and Lebeaux, C.N. (1965) *Industrial Society and Social Welfare*, New York: The Free Press.

Winnicot, C. (1970) *Child Care and Social Work*, Hitchin: Codicote Press.

Wolfenden Committee (1978) *The Future of Voluntary Organisations*, London: Croom Helm.

Wolin, Sheldon, S. (1968) 'Paradigms and political theories' in Preston King (ed.) *Politics and Experience*, London: Cambridge University Press.

Wright Mills, C. (1971) *The Sociological Imagination*, London: Penguin.

Young, K. (1981) 'Discretion as an implementation problem: framework for interpretation' in M. Adler and S. Asquith, *Discretion and Welfare*, London: Heinemann.

Index

Abrams, P. 11
action research 24
administrative capacity *see* capacity 60
Adult Training Centre (ATC) 181–2
advisers 177–88
Alaszewski, A. 46
Alexander, A. 48
Amir, Y. 160
Anderson, D.C. 235
area team 97–8, 136–8, 175
Argyris, C. 29, 32
Aston University 60
authority: a case study 199–207; and
    accountability 136, 138–44, 150–51, 228;
    and assistance 147–52, 227; and
    control 147–52, 227; definition of 60;
    delegated *see* delegation; pluralistic 132–5;
    role types 133–5, 205–6

Bains Report 46
Baker, J. 51, 80, 97
Baker, R.J.S. 47
Barclay Report 5, 78, 80
Barnes, J. and Connelly, N. 67
Bartlett, H.M. 87
basic services 170
basic social work 170
Beaver Committee 21
Bebbington, A.C. and Davies, B. 79
Becker, H.S. 10
Bell, C. and Newby, H. 107
Bennis, W.G. 14
Berger, P.L. and Luckman, T. 13, 45
Berlin, I. 44
Billis, D. 5, 42, 48, 59, 60, 73, 95, 97, 98, 106,
    119, 124, 127, 131, 138, 145, 159, 199, 207,
    208, 209, 212, 220, 226, 236
Billis *et al.* 159, 164
Birch, A.H. 153
Blau, P.M. 53
Blau, P.M. and Scott, W.R. 19, 81
Borger, R. and Cioffi, F. 42
Bottomore, T.H. 35
Bottomore, T.H. and Nisbet, R. 61
Boudon, R. 12
Bradshaw, J. 80
Brent (London Borough of) 189–91
British Association of Social Workers
    (BASW) 50
British Nationality Laws 16
Brown, A. and Heller, F. 42
Brown, R.G.S. 57
Brown, W. 38, 42, 87, 95, 141, 172

Brown, W. and Jaques, E. 27, 35, 172
Bruce, I. and Darville, G. 80
Brunel Institute of Organisation and Social
    Studies (BIOSS) 1, 41, 79, 95, 119, 130,
    152, 169, 170, 176, 198
Bulmer, M. 41
bureaucracy: and definitions 2, 11, 224; and
    delegation 46; and growth 23, 145–6; and
    the political process 46–9, 151, 229–33;
    and professional discretion 49–51; and
    quality of service 55–7; direct appointee
    model 140–41; directorial model 140–46,
    228; nascent 110; practitioner–king
    model 142–4
bureauphobic tendency (in social
    administration) 4, 230
Burgess, R.G. and Bulmer, M. 41
Burns, T. and Stalker, G.M. 130

capacity: a case study of 208–21; and level of
    work 155–8 and patch systems 159;
    definitions 60, 155, 214–15
Carrier, J. and Kendall, I. 57
case accountability 171, 191
categorization: and SSDs 63–80, 169–70, 225;
    case studies of 177–88, 204, 207;
    definition of 59, 231
Central Council for Education and Training
    (CCETSW) 170, 171, 177, 196
Central Housing Advisory Committee 113
Central–local government relationships 159–60
Cherns, A. 38, 41
Child, J. 19
Children's Regional Planning Committee 199
Clark, P. 33
Clean Air Act (1956) 20
clients 229–30
Cloward, R.A. and Piven, F.F. 130
Cohen, J.L. 41
Cohen, S. 55, 73
Colwell, Maria 144
community administration 52–5
consultants 142–3
Cooper, D. 159, 176
Cooper, J. 199
Culler, J. 95
Curran, J. and Stanworth, J. 95
Curtis Report 106–7, 142
Curzon, L.B. 144
Cypher, J.R. 88
Cyprus 11, 119–20

Dahrendorf, R. 61

Darville, G. 91–4
day care 98, 177–88
Dean, Sir Maurice 150
decentralization 159, 190, 227, 237
Degania, Alef 14–15
delegation 140, 142–52, 227
deputies 138–9, 145, 147, 159
de Saussure, F. 95
development 98, 159
DHSS 12, 70, 78, 98, 144, 159, 199, 200, 207
Diamond, S. 210
directors 104, 117, 119, 138–9, 145, 147
Donnison, D.V. 16, 23, 52, 55, 56
Donnison, D.V. and Chapman V. 21, 22, 23, 57, 95
Durkheim, E. 45
Durkheim, E. and Mauss, M. 44
duty officers 91–4

Education Departments 100, 127, 161–3
Education Welfare Service 127, 161–3
Eisenstadt, S.N. 212
Etzioni, A. 23, 34, 42, 212
Evans, J.S. 174

Follett, Mary Parker 145, 146, 152
Ford, P. 10, 97
Fox, A. 29
French, W.L. and Bell, C.H. 41
Friedrich, C.J. 2, 61

Gemeinschaft 101
Gerard, D. 2
Gerth, H. and Wright Mills, C. 61, 97, 109
Giddens, A. 36
Glacier Project 27, 35, 89, 172
Gladstone, F.J. 80
Glaser, B.G. and Strauss, A.L. 23, 25, 41
Glennerster, H. 23, 228–9
Goldsmith, M. 231, 232
Goodlove, C., Richard, R. and Rodwell, G. 80
Gouldner, A. 35
Grades 174, 179
Greenwood, R. *et al.* 46, 47

Hadley, R. and Hatch, S. 53, 54, 80
Hadley, R. and McGrath, M. 101, 159
Hadley, R., Webb, A. and Farrell, C. 69–70
Hall, A.S. 89–91, 94, 95
Hall, Phoebe 70
Hall, P. *et al.* 17, 20, 21
Hall, R.H. 53
Hampton, W.A. 231
Hanson, A.H. 17
Haraway 41
Harris, M. 152
Hatch, S. 80
Hayek, F.A. 9, 39, 40, 42, 133
Hayton, C.R. 176
Health Service 100
Herbst, P.G. 14, 15
Hesse, M. 39, 40, 42

Hey, A.M. 123, 164, 171
Higgins, J. 234
Hill, M.J. 47, 57
Holland 11
Holman, R. 54, 234
Holme, A. and Maizels, J. 80, 82, 95
Home Help Service 148, 150
Home Office 70, 145
Home Office Advisory Council 199
Home Start 11
Housing Associations 113, 163–4
Housing Departments 100, 112–13
Hume, S. 200

Illich, I. 72–3
independent social institutions 104–5
industrial achievement model 233–4
informal sector 6
INLOGOV 47
Institute of Economic Affairs 235
Institute of Housing Managers 113
institutional redistributive model 233–41
intermediate treatment 73, 98, 199–207

Jacques, E. 23, 27, 31, 35, 41, 61, 97, 132, 135, 139, 140, 155, 166, 174, 182, 220
Jaques, E., Gibson, R.O. and Isaac, D.J. 175
Jay Report 76
Jenkins, Roy 16
Johnson, N. 32
Jones, G.W. 48, 49
Jones, Julie 99
Jones, K. *et al.* 79, 97

Kanovsky, E. 212
Kelly, J. 36
kibbutz 14–15, 55, 159, 160–61, 208–21
King's Fund 143, 176
Klein, R. 44
Kogan, M. 237
Kogan, M. and Terry, J. 48
Kogan, M. and Henkel, M. 229
Kramer, R. 53, 76, 80
Kramer, R. and Specht, H. 130
Kuhn, T.S. 23, 40, 42, 57
Kvutza *see* kibbutz

Laffin, M. 49
Lakatos, I. 40
Lakatos, I. and Musgrave, A. 23, 42
Leach, E. 45
Leissner, A., Powley, T. and Evans, D. 207
Leonard, P. 34
Lessnoff, M. 42
levels of work: basic expected work (BEW) 87–95, 117, 128–9, 142–4, 162–5, 183, 227–8, 232–6; change 126–7; client impact *see* BEW; definitions 59, 82–9, 96–105, 202; developmental bureaucracies 109–14; highest expected work (HEW) 105–7, 116, 227, 234–6; history of theory 169–76, 189–98; hybrid responses 128–9; patch

systems 101, 227; planning 127; political
systems 102, 112, 113, 122; prescribed-
output bureaucracies 109–14;
recruitment 161–4; situational-response
bureaucracies 114–21; social
territories 99–101, 113; societal impact *see*
HEW; specialist practitioner 106;
typology of responses 108–23
Lewin, K. 45
Local Government Studies 46
Lonsdale, S., Webb, A. and Briggs, T.L. 55
Lorenz, K. 59
Lukes, S. 61
Lupton, T. 60

MacDonald, J.S. 23
managerial role 86, 95, 110, 134–40, 150, 172–
5, 205, 210
Maslow, A. 67–8, 74, 79
Maud Report 46
medicine and medical practitioners 88
Mental Health Department 115
Merton, R.K. *et al.* 61
Miliband, R. 154
Miringoff, M.L. 5
Mishra, R. 234
Mitchell, A. 80
Mouzelis, N.P. 12
Myrdal, G. 34

National Development Group for the Mentally
Handicapped 63
National Institute for Social Work 50, 80, 101,
107
National Smoke Abatement Society 21
National Youth Bureau 207
need 63–79, 99–104, 227–36
New Society 201
Norman, P. 232
Nuffield Foundation 221
nurses and nursing 88

occupational therapist (OT) 182
organization: and behaviour 18–19; and
methods 18–19; and structure 11–12, 18–
19, 154; design and change 19;
development 24; expected work 82–3;
explanations 14–17, 23;
grades 174, 179; hierarchy and non-
hierarchy 13–15, 81, 127, 212–20;
informal 19, 224; maintenance 17;
manifest, assumed, extant and
requisite 37–8, 89, 173–4; problems 12–
13; role types 133–5, 155, 172–4; span of
control 113–14
Owen, David 16
Oxfordshire County Council 131, 145

Paley, J. and Thorpe, D. 207
Parker, R. 17, 23, 44
Parsloe, P. 82
Parsons Talcott 61, 233

Personal Social Services 75, 207
Piaget, J. 12
Pinker, R. 4, 44, 45, 57, 234
Piper, D.W. 176
planning 231
Polanyi, M. 45
policy 97, 99, 203–4
Policy Studies Institute (PSI) 48
Popper, Karl, R. 23, 40, 41, 42, 66; and
problem solving 12–13, 22, 31, 37, 169;
falsifiability 38; tentative theory 25–7,
67, 166, 171; Three Worlds 18–19, 28
prevention 64–74, 77–8, 187–8, 204, 225–6
privatization 226
professionals 121–2
Programme of Research and Training into
Voluntary Action (PORTVAC) 130, 140,
164
public administration 46, 230–33

Rapoport, R.N. 41
Ravetz, J.R. 42
reception and duty systems in SSDs 89–95
receptionists 89–91, 93–4
recruitment 160
Reddin, M. 237
Regan, D.E. 48, 151, 231, 232, 233
Report of the Committee of Enquiry into Mental
Handicap, Nursing and Care (Jay
Report) 63, 80
research 98–9
residential care 98, 123–5, 170–71, 189–98, 226
Residential Care Association 98
residential welfare model 233–4
Rex, J. 34
Richardson, A. and Goodman, M. 11
Robinson, M. 59, 63
Rose, G. 49, 54
Rowbottom, R.W. 3, 33, 38, 41, 138, 172, 176,
198
Rowbottom, R.W. and Billis, D. 130, 172, 220
Rowbottom, R.W. and Bromley, G. 59
Rowbottom, R.W. and Hey, A. 190
Royal Institute of Public Administration
(RIPA) 48
Russell, B. 154

Salzedo, S. 200
Scarman, Sir Leslie 32
Schon, D. 45
Schumacher, E.F. 1
Schumpeter, J.A. 106
Scott, W.R. 53
Seebohm Report 5, 46, 54, 55, 64–5, 71–2, 97,
98, 105–7, 119, 126, 173, 198
selectivity 234–6
Self, P. 47, 55
Shatil, J.E. 212
Shaw, Bernard 49
Shipman, M. 24
Sinfield, A. 235
Slack, K. 57

Smith, Gilbert 49, 79
Smith, G. and Ames, J. 55, 97
Smith, J.H. 49, 56
social administration 5, 49, 225, 227, 233–6
social analysis *see* usable theory
social breakdown 64–70, 226, 234–6
social conscience thesis 51–2, 54, 234, 236
social discomfort 64, 67–70, 77–8, 102, 226, 234–6
social policy: and administrative capacity 158–60, 228; and planning 10, 23; and usable theory 233–7; and the middle ground 2, 10, 223–37; definitional clarity in 44–6; 63–4, 77–8; levels of work 97, 99, 112; priorities 19–22
social problems 9–12
Social Services Department (SSD) 12, 48, 49, 50, 59, 63–80, 81, 97, 105, 111, 124, 129, 138, 144, 159, 161, 169–71, 187, 225, 230
Social Services Organisation Research Unit (SSORU) 123, 130
social work assistants 82, 85, 87–8, 147
Social Work Departments 80
Social Work Today 201
social workers 87–95, 117, 137–81, 147, 171
Sofer, C. 12
Specht, H. 50
Specht, H. and Vickery, A. 50
specialisation 88
Stevenson, O. and Parsloe, P. 82, 89, 91–2, 95, 138, 151
strata, work *see* levels of work
Suchman, E.A. 41
Sumner, W.G. 19
supplementary services 170
supporting roles 64
Szasz, T. 63

Tannenbaum, A.S. *et al.* 81–2, 208, 220
Task Force 69, 73
Tavistock Institute of Human Relations 35
Taylor-Gooby, P. 57, 237
Taylor-Gooby, P. and Dale, J. 79
Thomas, D., Kat, B. and McPherson, F. 176
Thomason, G.F. 49
Thursz, D. and Vigilante, J.L.
Times, The 16, 88, 151
Titmuss, R.M. 52, 57, 233–5
Town, S.W. 28
Townsend, D. 227
training 164–5, 211–12

United Nations Social Welfare Centre 131
universality 234–6
usable theory 1, 3; and better theory 26, 223; and concept utilisation 31, 37; and explication 32, 180, 188, 224; and grounded theory 25, 41; and insiders and outsiders 28, 155–8, 180, 186; and the middle range 25; and prediction and evaluation 39–40; and research 24, 27, 38; and situational analysis 31–3, 37–9, 180; and social adminstration 233–7; and social analysis 24, 27; and social science 39; strategy and access 28–31, 37, 155–8, 180, 188, 224; and tentative theory 25–7, 154, 199; and values 33–5

Van der Eyken, W. 11
Van Doorn, J. 12
Van Meter and Van Hom 20
Van Sell, M., Brief, A.P. and Schuler, R.S. 155
Vigotsky 45
Vincent, H. 207
Viteles, H. 15
voluntary sector 5, 53, 79, 94, 102, 109–10, 117, 140–41, 163–4, 208–21, 226, 236
Volunteer Centre 80

Walker, A. 57
Webb, A. 80, 160
Webb, A., Day, L. and Weller, J. 75
Webb, A. and Hobdell, M. 55
Weber, M. 61, 97, 109
welfare bureaucracies: and the kibbutz society 208–21; and social administration 52–5; choice and change in 103, 126–7, 184–7, 224, 227; definition 3; high level responses in 102–5, 114; Model A and Model B 190–7; recruitment 161–4; training 164–5
Whittington, C. and Bellaby, P. 36
Wilensky, H.L. and Lebeaux, C.N. 75, 233, 234
Williams, Shirley 16
Winnicot, C. 191
Wolfenden Committee 76
Wolfenden Report 5
Wolin, S. 39
work strata *see* levels of work
Wright-Mills, C. 35, 233

Young, K. 2